# 自然遗产与文博研究

## （第七卷　Vol. 7）

莫运明　主编

**NATURAL HERITAGE
AND MUSEUM STUDIES**

广西科学技术出版社
·南宁·

图书在版编目（CIP）数据

自然遗产与文博研究 . 第七卷 / 莫运明主编 . -- 南宁：
广西科学技术出版社，2024.7. --ISBN 978-7-5551-2262-3

Ⅰ.K872.67-53；G269.276.7-53

中国国家版本馆 CIP 数据核字第 2024EJ5611 号

ZIRAN YICHAN YU WENBO YANJIU（DI-QI JUAN）

# 自然遗产与文博研究（第七卷）

莫运明　主编

责任编辑：陈剑平　　　　　　　　　　　责任校对：吴书丽
责任印制：陆　弟　　　　　　　　　　　装帧设计：韦娇林

出 版 人：岑　刚
出版发行：广西科学技术出版社
社　　址：广西南宁市东葛路 66 号　　　邮政编码：530023
网　　址：http://www.gxkjs.com

印　　刷：广西民族印刷包装集团有限公司

开　　本：787mm×1092mm　1/16　　　字　　数：240 千字
印　　张：12
版　　次：2024 年 7 月第 1 版
印　　次：2024 年 7 月第 1 次印刷
书　　号：ISBN 978-7-5551-2262-3
定　　价：48.00 元

# 《自然遗产与文博研究》编委会

主 办 单 位：广西自然博物馆

编辑部地址：广西南宁市人民东路 1-1 号广西自然博物馆

邮 政 编 码：530012

电话 / 传真：0771-2820904

投 稿 信 箱：gxzrbwg@nhmgx.cn

# 目　录

1

# 2018 年广西猫儿山国家级自然保护区
# 两栖动物观测报告

廖晓雯，莫运明

广西自然博物馆，南宁　530012，中国

【摘要】在 2018 年广西猫儿山开展的两栖动物观测工作中，通过样线法共记录到两栖动物 20 种，隶属 2 目 8 科。其中，属于国家一级重点保护野生动物的有猫儿山小鲵 *Hynobius maoershanensis* 1 种，属于广西重点保护野生动物的有中华蟾蜍 *Bufo gargarizans*、猫儿山林蛙 *Rana maoershanensis*、沼蛙 *Boulengerana guentheri*、泽陆蛙 *Fejervarya multistriata*、棘侧蛙 *Quasipaa shini*、棘胸蛙 *Quasipaa spinosa*、斑腿泛树蛙 *Polypedates megacephalus* 和侏树蛙 *Rhacophorus minimus* 共 8 种。通过观测，掌握广西猫儿山观测点两栖动物现状与动态，调查观测点两栖动物面临的威胁，评估观测点两栖动物保护成效，提出适应性管理对策。

【关键词】两栖动物；猫儿山；动物观测

## 0　引言

猫儿山位于中亚热带向南亚热带交界的区域，属中亚热带季风气候区，其气候属于中亚热带季风湿润气候类型。在植被区划上，猫儿山属于亚热带常绿阔叶林区、东部湿润阔叶林亚区、中亚热带常绿阔叶林南部亚地带的三江流域山地栲类木荷林石灰岩植被区和南岭山地栲类蕈树林区的过渡地带，地带性原生植被为常绿阔叶林。猫儿山是广西主要的水源林区之一，森林覆盖率高，涵养水源丰富，地表水系十分发育。它是长江水系和珠江水系的分水岭之一，也是桂林的母亲河——漓江的源头。猫儿山

蕴藏着丰富的生物资源，已发现有大型菌类 264 种，蕨类植物 132 种，裸子植物 14 种，被子植物 1574 种；昆虫 566 种，淡水鱼类 53 种，两栖动物 51 种，爬行动物 22 种，鸟类动物 271 种，哺乳动物 73 种（黄金玲等，2002；粟通萍等，2012；谭伟福，2014；汪国海等，2016；侯绍兵等，2017）。

根据《中国两栖动物观测项目 2018 年度实施方案》，2018 年对广西猫儿山两栖动物开展观测工作，目的是掌握广西猫儿山国家级自然保护区两栖动物种群现状与动态和受到威胁的原因，科学评估保护区的保护管理成效，并提出适应性管理对策。

# 1　调查地点和方法

## 1.1　调查位置、范围

广西猫儿山国家级自然保护区位于桂林北部，地理坐标为东经 $110°20'\sim 110°35'$，北纬 $25°48'\sim 25°58'$。区域面积 170.09 平方千米。在行政区划上地跨桂林市兴安、资源、龙胜 3 县。

## 1.2　调查时间

在广西猫儿山国家级自然保护区内共设置 10 条固定观测样线，野外工作分别于 2018 年 4 月 27—29 日、6 月 27—29 日、8 月 24—28 日分 3 期进行，每条样带在每月观测时连续进行 3 次重复调查统计。根据两栖动物的生活习性，所有观测工作均在 19：00—22：00 进行（表 1）。

## 1.3　调查方法

样线法：在林区内设置固定长度为 150～300 米的观测样线，根据两栖动物对生境选择的特殊性，样线多选择靠近水源或潮湿的生境，且尽可能包含保护区的实验区、缓冲区和核心区，以及林区内的典型植被类型。限时步行调查并记录样线单侧 2 米内发现的物种名称、数量、生境、干扰类型及地理坐标等信息（Sutherland，1999；Bibby et al.，2000）。

物种优势度统计：利用样线法记录的物种数量估算该物种的种群优势度（$P_i$），即

$P_i = \dfrac{N_i}{N_k}$（$N_i$：物种 $i$ 的个数；$N_k$：所有物种个数的总和）。

表 1　广西猫儿山国家级自然保护区两栖动物观测项目样线信息

| 样线编号 | 地点 | 长度/米 | 样线海拔/米 | 植被类型 | 栖息地现状 | 主要干扰因素 |
|---|---|---|---|---|---|---|
| 4500241001 | 九牛塘 | 155 | 1170～1137 | 人工林 | 人为干扰 | 旅游开发 |
| 4500241002 | 庵塘坪 | 198 | 1545～1531 | 常绿、落叶阔叶混交林 | 人为干扰 | 捕猎 |
| 4500241003 | 庵塘坪 | 203 | 1555～1626 | 常绿、落叶阔叶混交林 | 人为干扰 | 捕猎 |
| 4500241004 | 状元桥 | 200 | 1993～1995 | 常绿阔叶林 | 人为干扰 | 旅游开发 |
| 4500241005 | 猫儿山山顶 | 144 | 2001～1981 | 常绿阔叶林 | 人为干扰 | 旅游开发 |
| 4500241006 | 九牛塘 | 200 | 1135～1110 | 常绿、落叶阔叶混交林 | 人为干扰 | 捕猎 |
| 4500241007 | 洪家 | 270 | 848～888 | 常绿、落叶阔叶混交林 | 人为干扰 | 砍伐、采集 |
| 4500241008 | 同仁村 | 200 | 330～324 | 农田 | 人为干扰 | 耕种、施肥 |
| 4500241009 | 同仁村 | 250 | 330～340 | 农田 | 人为干扰 | 耕种、施肥 |
| 4500241010 | 同仁村 | 250 | 538～573 | 常绿、落叶阔叶混交林 | 人为干扰 | 旅游开发 |

## 2　调查结果

### 2.1　种类组成

经统计，在广西猫儿山国家级自然保护区及其周边林区共观测到 20 种两栖动物，隶属 2 目 8 科（表 2）。其中，小鲵科、蝾螈科、蟾蜍科、姬蛙科各 1 种，分别占观测物种总数的 5%；树蛙科 2 种，占观测物种总数的 10%；角蟾科、叉舌蛙科各 3 种，分别占观测物种总数的 15%；蛙科 8 种，占观测物种总数的 40%。属于国家一级重点保护野生动物的有猫儿山小鲵 *Hynobius maoershanensis* 1 种，属于广西重点保护野生动物的有中华蟾蜍 *Bufo gargarizans*、猫儿山林蛙 *Rana maoershanensis*、沼蛙 *Boulengerana guentheri*、泽陆蛙 *Fejervarya multistriata*、棘侧蛙 *Quasipaa shini*、棘胸蛙 *Quasipaa spinosa*、斑腿泛树蛙 *Polypedates megacephalus* 和侏树蛙 *Rhacophorus minimus* 共 8 种。

猫儿山小鲵、猫儿山林蛙和猫儿山掌突蟾 3 个物种为广西特有物种，瑶山肥螈、崇安
髭蟾、寒露林蛙、阔褶水蛙和棘侧蛙 5 个物种为中国特有物种（费梁等，2009；周放等，
2011）。

表 2　广西猫儿山国家级自然保护区及其周边林区两栖动物名录

| 目名 | 科名 | 属名 | 种名 |
|---|---|---|---|
| 有尾目<br>URODELA | 小鲵科<br>HYNOBIIDAE | 小鲵属<br>*Hynobius* | 猫儿山小鲵 *Hynobius maoershanensis* |
| | 蝾螈科<br>SALAMANDRIDAE | 肥螈属<br>*Pachytriton* | 瑶山肥螈 *Pachytriton inexpectatus* |
| 无尾目<br>ANURA | 角蟾科<br>MEGOPHRYIDAE | 髭蟾属<br>*Vibrissaphora* | 崇安髭蟾 *Vibrissaphora liui yaoshanensis* |
| | | 掌突蟾属<br>*Paramegophrys* | 猫儿山掌突蟾 *Paramegophrys maoershanensis* |
| | | 布角蟾属<br>*Boulenophrys* | 小角蟾 *Boulenophrys minor* |
| | 蟾蜍科<br>BUFONIDAE | 蟾蜍属<br>*Bufo* | 中华蟾蜍 *Bufo gargarizans* |
| | 蛙科<br>RANAIDAE | 林蛙属<br>*Rana* | 寒露林蛙 *Rana hanluica*<br>猫儿山林蛙 *Rana maoershanensis* |
| | | 琴蛙属<br>*Nidirana* | 弹琴蛙 *Nidirana adenopleura* |
| | | 沼蛙属<br>*Boulengerana* | 沼蛙 *Boulengerana guentheri* |
| | | 肱腺蛙属<br>*Sylvirana* | 阔褶水蛙 *Sylvirana latouchii* |
| | | 臭蛙属<br>*Odorrana* | 大绿臭蛙 *Odorrana graminea*<br>花臭蛙 *Odorrana schmackeri* |
| | | 湍蛙属<br>*Amolops* | 华南湍蛙 *Amolops ricketti* |
| | 叉舌蛙科<br>DICROGLOSSIDAE | 陆蛙属<br>*Fejervarya* | 泽陆蛙 *Fejervarya multistriata* |
| | | 棘胸蛙属<br>*Quasipaa* | 棘侧蛙 *Quasipaa shini*<br>棘胸蛙 *Quasipaa spinosa* |
| | 树蛙科<br>RHACOPHORIDAE | 泛树蛙属<br>*Polypedates* | 斑腿泛树蛙 *Polypedates megacephalus* |
| | | 树蛙属<br>*Rhacophorus* | 侏树蛙 *Rhacophorus minimus* |
| | 姬蛙科<br>MICROHYLIDAE | 姬蛙属<br>*Microhyla* | 小弧斑姬蛙 *Microhyla heymonsi* |

## 2.2 物种种群数量统计

各样线观测记录的两栖动物种类、数量（取连续 3 天观测的最大值）以及月际变化情况详见表 3。2018 年共观测到 20 种 376 只次个体。其中，4 月 10 条样线共观测到 17 种 107 只次个体，6 月共观测到 12 种 154 只次个体，8 月共观测到 10 种 115 只次个体。

表 3   2018 年广西猫儿山国家级自然保护区各样线两栖动物情况及月际变化表

| 样线编号 | 种类 / 种 | | | | 数量 / 只次 | | | |
|---|---|---|---|---|---|---|---|---|
| | 4 月 | 6 月 | 8 月 | 总计 | 4 月 | 6 月 | 8 月 | 总计 |
| 4500241001 | 3 | 3 | 4 | 6 | 3 | 8 | 5 | 16 |
| 4500241002 | 5 | 4 | 4 | 6 | 13 | 29 | 20 | 62 |
| 4500241003 | 5 | 4 | 4 | 5 | 13 | 24 | 18 | 55 |
| 4500241004 | 1 | 1 | 0 | 2 | 4 | 8 | 0 | 12 |
| 4500241005 | 2 | 3 | 2 | 4 | 8 | 7 | 4 | 19 |
| 4500241006 | 4 | 4 | 3 | 4 | 8 | 18 | 18 | 44 |
| 4500241007 | 4 | 3 | 2 | 4 | 14 | 20 | 14 | 48 |
| 4500241008 | 3 | 1 | 1 | 3 | 18 | 13 | 13 | 44 |
| 4500241009 | 3 | 2 | 2 | 4 | 15 | 9 | 7 | 31 |
| 4500241010 | 5 | 3 | 2 | 5 | 11 | 18 | 16 | 45 |
| 总计 | 17 | 12 | 10 | 20 | 107 | 154 | 115 | 376 |

## 2.3 物种种群数量的月际变化

2018 年全年遇到频次最多的是华南湍蛙，共观测到 88 只次，次之为泽陆蛙共 67 只次，而猫儿山掌突蟾、寒露林蛙、沼蛙和小弧斑姬蛙各只观测到 1 只次。4 月遇到频次最多的是华南湍蛙，共 29 只次，次之为泽陆蛙，共 28 只次；6 月遇到频次最多的是华南湍蛙，共 30 只次，次之为花臭蛙，共 28 只次；8 月遇到频次最多的是华南湍蛙，共 29 只次，次之为花臭蛙，共 28 只次。两栖动物观测物种种群数量及每月只次数如表 4 所示。

表 4   2018 年广西猫儿山国家级自然保护区两栖动物观测物种种群数量月际变化表

| 序号 | 种名 | 4 月数量 / 只次 | 4 月占比 | 6 月数量 / 只次 | 6 月占比 | 8 月数量 / 只次 | 8 月占比 |
|---|---|---|---|---|---|---|---|
| 1 | 猫儿山小鲵 | 6 | 5.61% | 13 | 8.44% | 0 | 0 |
| 2 | 瑶山肥螈 | 2 | 1.87% | 13 | 8.44% | 16 | 13.91% |
| 3 | 崇安髭蟾 | 1 | 0.93% | 1 | 0.65% | 0 | 0 |
| 4 | 猫儿山掌突蟾 | 1 | 0.93% | 0 | 0 | 0 | 0 |

续表

| 序号 | 种名 | 4 月数量 / 只次 | 4 月占比 | 6 月数量 / 只次 | 6 月占比 | 8 月数量 / 只次 | 8 月占比 |
|---|---|---|---|---|---|---|---|
| 5 | 小角蟾 | 4 | 3.74% | 22 | 14.29% | 2 | 1.74% |
| 6 | 中华蟾蜍 | 4 | 3.74% | 0 | 0 | 0 | 0 |
| 7 | 寒露林蛙 | 0 | 0 | 0 | 0 | 1 | 0.87% |
| 8 | 猫儿山林蛙 | 0 | 0 | 1 | 0.65% | 3 | 2.61% |
| 9 | 弹琴蛙 | 0 | 0 | 2 | 1.30% | 1 | 0.87% |
| 10 | 沼蛙 | 1 | 0.93% | 0 | 0 | 0 | 0 |
| 11 | 阔褶水蛙 | 2 | 1.87% | 1 | 0.65% | 2 | 1.74% |
| 12 | 大绿臭蛙 | 2 | 1.87% | 1 | 0.65% | 0 | 0 |
| 13 | 花臭蛙 | 7 | 6.54% | 28 | 18.18% | 28 | 24.35% |
| 14 | 华南湍蛙 | 29 | 27.10% | 30 | 19.48% | 29 | 25.22% |
| 15 | 泽陆蛙 | 28 | 26.17% | 21 | 13.64% | 18 | 15.65% |
| 16 | 棘侧蛙 | 2 | 1.87% | 0 | 0 | 0 | 0 |
| 17 | 棘胸蛙 | 8 | 7.48% | 21 | 13.64% | 15 | 13.04% |
| 18 | 斑腿泛树蛙 | 3 | 2.80% | 0 | 0 | 0 | 0 |
| 19 | 侏树蛙 | 6 | 5.61% | 0 | 0 | 0 | 0 |
| 20 | 小弧斑姬蛙 | 1 | 0.93% | 0 | 0 | 0 | 0 |
| | 总计 | 107 | 100% | 154 | 100% | 115 | 100% |

## 2.4　物种优势度

2018 年，广西猫儿山国家级自然保护区共观测到两栖动物 376 只次，根据 3 次观察期间物种的总观察只次数据得到观测地区内的物种优势度组成，如表 5 所示。从表 5 可知，华南湍蛙、泽陆蛙和花臭蛙在调查期间调查地区内的优势度较高；猫儿山掌突蟾、寒露林蛙、沼蛙和小弧斑姬蛙在该年度观测调查中各只记录到 1 只次，这 4 种蛙类的物种优势度较低。此外，2017 年观测工作中记录到的福建掌突蟾、大树蛙和饰纹姬蛙 3 个物种在 2018 年度未被记录，而寒露林蛙、棘侧蛙和小弧斑姬蛙是 2017 年度未记录的物种。

表 5　2018 年广西猫儿山国家级自然保护区样区两栖动物物种优势度

| 序号 | 物种名 | 数量 / 只次 | 物种优势度 $P_i$ |
|---|---|---|---|
| 1 | 猫儿山小鲵 | 19 | 0.0505 |
| 2 | 瑶山肥螈 | 31 | 0.0824 |
| 3 | 崇安髭蟾 | 2 | 0.0053 |

**续表**

| 序号 | 物种名 | 数量 / 只次 | 物种优势度 $P_i$ |
|------|--------|-----------|-----------------|
| 4 | 猫儿山掌突蟾 | 1 | 0.0027 |
| 5 | 小角蟾 | 28 | 0.0745 |
| 6 | 中华蟾蜍 | 4 | 0.0106 |
| 7 | 寒露林蛙 | 1 | 0.0027 |
| 8 | 猫儿山林蛙 | 4 | 0.0106 |
| 9 | 弹琴蛙 | 3 | 0.0080 |
| 10 | 沼蛙 | 1 | 0.0027 |
| 11 | 阔褶水蛙 | 5 | 0.0133 |
| 12 | 大绿臭蛙 | 3 | 0.0080 |
| 13 | 花臭蛙 | 63 | 0.1676 |
| 14 | 华南湍蛙 | 88 | 0.2340 |
| 15 | 泽陆蛙 | 67 | 0.1782 |
| 16 | 棘侧蛙 | 2 | 0.0053 |
| 17 | 棘胸蛙 | 44 | 0.1170 |
| 18 | 斑腿泛树蛙 | 3 | 0.0080 |
| 19 | 侏树蛙 | 6 | 0.0160 |
| 20 | 小弧斑姬蛙 | 1 | 0.0027 |

## 3　讨论与建议

在生态系统中，两栖动物是重要的中间类群，是环境健康的重要指示类群，对于维持生态系统的完整性和健康具有重要的作用。两栖动物素有"生态晴雨表"之称，被视为观测环境变化的关键的"早期预警系统"。近几十年来，全球的两栖动物面临着多种威胁，两栖动物种群数量变化被认为与环境变化密切相关。全球气候变化、栖息地被破坏、物种入侵和人为过度捕捉等是两栖动物受威胁的主要原因。

与 2017 年相比，2018 年在广西猫儿山国家级自然保护区所观测到的 20 个物种大部分在 2017 年也观测到，记录到的个体数 376 只次较 2017 年的 275 只次有所增加。从全年观测结果看，2012—2014 年观测到的物种数为 14～16 种，相对稳定，2015 年观测到 21 个物种，2016 年观测到 24 个物种，2017 年观测到 19 个物种，各年度观测记录的物种数略有波动。瑶山肥螈、小角蟾、华南湍蛙、泽陆蛙和棘胸蛙 5 个物种在各年度观测中均被记录到，其中华南湍蛙和泽陆蛙在各年度观测记录中的物种优势度均较高，是广西猫儿山国家级自然保护区的常见优势物种。根据历年观测结果可知，该保护区两栖动物物种及种群数量较为稳定，中国特有及广西特有的两栖动物种类较为丰富。

两栖动物物种种群资源主要取决于不同的地理环境，野外活动的种群数量受到各种环境因子，如温度、湿度、水的酸碱度、降水量、天气情况以及人为活动等的影响。2018 年，在广西猫儿山国家级自然保护区设置的 10 条观测样线中共有 9 条样线在 4 月、6 月、8 月均观测到两栖动物，只有样线 4 仅在 4 月和 6 月各观测到 1 个物种。2017 年样线 4 仅在 4 月观测到 1 个物种，其余样线的物种数量记录与 2018 年的统计数相似；2017 年 4 月记录的个体数量较为稳定，6 月和 8 月记录的个体数量略少于 2018 年的记录数量，说明广西猫儿山国家级自然保护区生态环境处于相对稳定的状态。样线 4 为保护区的旅游小路，受人类活动的影响较为严重，连续多年的观测中记录的物种和数量均较少，由此可见，人为活动的干扰是广西猫儿山国家级自然保护区两栖动物所面临的主要威胁因素。

对比 2018 年与 2017 年观测到物种数量的变化可知，全年遇见率最高的均为华南湍蛙。将各月份的遇见率记录进行对比，华南湍蛙、泽陆蛙和花臭蛙为各观测月份遇见率较高的物种，2017 年的记录结果与 2018 年的相似，说明这 3 个物种为广西猫儿山国家级自然保护区的优势物种。在 2018 年观测中猫儿山掌突蟾、寒露林蛙、沼蛙和小弧斑姬蛙仅分别记录到 1 只次，遇见率较低，且寒露林蛙和小弧斑姬蛙在 2017 年的观测中未被记录；2017 年观测中遇见率较低的弹琴蛙和沼蛙在 2018 年观测到的个体数量也较少，表明这几个物种的种群数量在广西猫儿山国家级自然保护区较少，种群优势度较低。

连续多年的观测结果表明，广西猫儿山国家级自然保护区的自然生态环境较为稳定，两栖动物种群数量受环境变化影响较小，在部分样线的调查范围内受旅游开发等人类活动影响，适合两栖动物活动的生境部分遭到破坏，记录到的两栖动物数量波动较大，说明人类活动的干扰是影响广西猫儿山国家级自然保护区内两栖动物种群数量的主要因素。

广西猫儿山国家级自然保护区生态环境的特殊性使其一旦遭受破坏便较难恢复，周边地区的经济发展也对猫儿山的生态环境造成一定的威胁。为了更好地保护两栖动物及其栖息环境，现提出以下保护建议。一是加强保护区及其外围地区的巡查管理，保护好现有的生态植被，积极恢复被破坏的生态环境。二是加强宣传教育，普及有关科学知识，提高周边居民的环境保护意识，让居民自觉加入保护环境的行动中。三是随着保护区周边区域旅游经济的升级发展，人类活动更加频繁，应加强普及有关的法律法规和科学知识，在新修道路路口、旅游景点等地点增设环境保护标识牌，规范游客的活动和行为，增强游客保护环境的意识，自觉维护猫儿山景区的生态环境。四是持续开展两栖动物观测工作，为生态资源保护管理和科学研究工作提供有效的基础资料。

# 参考文献

［1］黄金玲，蒋德斌.广西猫儿山自然保护区综合科学考察［M］.长沙：湖南科学技术出版社，2002.

［2］粟通萍，王绍能，蒋爱伍.广西猫儿山地区鸟类组成及垂直分布格局［J］.动物学杂志，2012，47（6）：54–65.

［3］谭伟福.广西自然保护区［M］.北京：中国环境出版社，2014.

［4］汪国海，李生强，施泽攀，等.广西猫儿山自然保护区的兽类和鸟类多样性初步调查：基于红外相机监测数据［J］.兽类学报，2016，36（3）：338–347.

［5］侯绍兵，袁智勇，车静，等.广西猫儿山两栖动物物种多样性垂直分布格局研究［D］.桂林：广西师范大学，2017.

［6］SUTHERLAND W J.生态学调查方法手册［M］.张金屯，译.北京：科学技术文献出版社，1999.

［7］BIBBY C J，BURGESS N D，HILL D A，et al. Bird Census Techniques［M］. 2nd ed. London：Academic Press，2000.

［8］费梁，胡淑琴，叶昌媛，等.中国动物志　两栖纲（下卷）无尾目［M］.北京：科学出版社，2009.

［9］费梁，胡淑琴，叶昌媛，等.中国动物志　两栖纲（中卷）无尾目［M］.北京：科学出版社，2009.

［10］周放，等.广西陆生脊椎动物分布名录［M］.北京：中国林业出版社，2011.

# 广西自然博物馆藏品收藏现状与分析

刘付永清

广西自然博物馆，南宁　530012，中国

【摘要】本文以广西自然博物馆已登记入藏的藏品数据为基础，对广西自然博物馆的藏品现状进行统计分析。结果显示，该馆藏品以第四纪哺乳动物化石最多，其后依次为现生动物标本、石器标本和现生植物标本。在珍贵藏品方面，共收藏模式标本 59 种 232 件，其中以现生动物标本最多；现有定级藏品 2646 件，其中国家级文物 309 件，馆藏定级标本 2337 件，各类定级标本数量差距大，种类还有待补充。各时期藏品收藏差距大，藏品来源相对单一，多数标本来源于野外采集和发掘。本文针对该馆藏品收藏现状存在的问题进行分析，并相应地提出建议，以期为博物馆的藏品收藏工作提供参考。

【关键词】藏品；收藏；征集；鉴定；信息提取

## 0　引言

收藏、科学研究和科普教育是自然类博物馆的三项基本功能。藏品是自然类博物馆的物质基础，没有标本收藏作为基础，自然类博物馆其他工作的开展将成为无本之木、无源之水（杨松年，2010）。随着自然类博物馆收藏理念的变化，藏品的收藏不再是个别藏品的简单叠加，也不能简单停留在采集、征集、购买等方式上，而应具有系统性（杨松年，2010）。通过对自然类博物馆现有藏品的类型进行研究，可以全面了解本馆藏品在时间和类型上的优势与劣势、藏品体系的缺失和薄弱环节、藏品的重复率等（姜雨风，2018），有利于自然类博物馆有目的、有针对性地不断补充各类藏品，完善和充实自身藏品收藏体系，同时为自然类博物馆开展研究、展览和科普教育等工作

提供参考。

广西自然博物馆是国家二级博物馆，历来重视馆藏文物标本的收藏工作。现已收藏各种自然标本和第四纪哺乳动物及古人类文物 6 万余件。关于藏品收藏现状与分析，仅植物类（许东先，2013）和化石类（蒋珊，2016）藏品已有调查报道。随着博物馆事业的发展，特别是第一次可移动文物普查工作的开展，广西自然博物馆不仅新增加了大量藏品，而且越来越多的藏品得到了鉴定和入库。随着藏品数据库建设的基本完成，藏品信息逐渐完善，为全面掌握藏品收藏现状打下坚实的基础。

# 1 方法

本文以截至 2021 年 6 月 30 日广西自然博物馆所有入馆和入库的标本为研究对象，以藏品数据库录入数据为基础，对部分藏品缺乏的类别、级别、科名、时代、来源情况等信息，通过查阅原始凭证、翻阅文献、咨询经手人等方式进行补充完善。根据最新修订的《广西自然博物馆藏品定级标准》对前人统计的《广西自然博物馆定级标本目录》进行修订、补充和完善，最后应用 Excel 对藏品信息进行统计分析。

# 2 结果

## 2.1 藏品及类别组成

广西自然博物馆共收藏有现生动植物、岩石、矿物、古生物等自然类藏品和古人类、古哺乳动物、石器等文物类藏品 6 万余件，其中已登记的藏品 47653 件。从已登记的各类藏品组成来看（表 1），馆藏标本以第四纪哺乳动物化石最多，共有 18053 件，占藏品总量的 37.88%；现生动物标本、石器标本和现生植物标本次之，分别占藏品总量的 16.23%、15.30% 和 14.20%；岩矿标本和古人类化石相对较少。文物类藏品中，第四纪哺乳动物化石和石器标本相对丰富，古人类化石在数量和种类上相对较少。自然类藏品中，古鱼类标本种类相对单一，古两栖动物标本和古鸟类标本非常稀缺，仅分别为 2 件和 6 件，古植物标本有 350 件，以宁明盆地采集的标本为主；现生无脊椎动物标本有 3798 件，包含 1286 件昆虫标本，现生脊椎动物标本以鱼类和两栖动物为主，哺乳动物相对较少；现生植物标本以被子植物为主，苔藓植物和低等植物比较稀缺；岩矿标本以矿物为主。

表1　广西自然博物馆馆藏各类标本组成情况调查表

| 藏品类别 | | 数量/件（套） | 合计/件（套） | 占比 |
|---|---|---|---|---|
| 文物类藏品 | 石器 | 7293 | 7293 | 15.30% |
| | 第四纪哺乳动物 | 18053 | 18053 | 37.88% |
| | 古人类 | 65 | 65 | 0.14% |
| 自然类藏品 | 古生物 古无脊椎动物 | 3201 | | |
| | 古鱼类 | 509 | | |
| | 古两栖动物 | 2 | | |
| | 古鸟类 | 6 | 5308 | 11.14% |
| | 古爬行动物 | 1188 | | |
| | 古植物 | 350 | | |
| | 其他 | 52 | | |
| | 现生动物 无脊椎动物 | 3798 | | |
| | 鱼类 | 1314 | | |
| | 两栖动物 | 1075 | | |
| | 爬行动物 | 648 | 7732 | 16.23% |
| | 鸟类 | 557 | | |
| | 哺乳动物 | 340 | | |
| | 现生植物 地衣植物 | 2 | | |
| | 苔藓植物 | 10 | | |
| | 蕨类植物 | 458 | | |
| | 裸子植物 | 204 | 6767 | 14.20% |
| | 被子植物 | 5789 | | |
| | 木材 | 304 | | |
| | 岩矿 岩石 | 450 | | |
| | 矿物 | 1664 | 2429 | 5.10% |
| | 陨石 | 295 | | |
| | 观赏石 | 20 | | |
| | 其他（分类不详） | 6 | 6 | 0.01% |
| 合计 | | 47653 | 47653 | 100% |

## 2.2 珍贵标本组成

### 2.2.1 馆藏模式标本

广西自然博物馆共收藏有模式标本 59 种 232 件，具体见表 2。

表 2  广西自然博物馆模式标本统计表

| 类别 | 种类 / 种 | 数量 / 件 |
|---|---|---|
| 古鱼类 | 4 | 15 |
| 古爬行动物 | 8 | 9 |
| 古哺乳动物 | 8 | 8 |
| 古人类 | 1 | 13 |
| 古植物 | 21 | 77 |
| 现生动物 | 12 | 102 |
| 现生植物 | 5 | 8 |
| 合计 | 59 | 232 |

### 2.2.2 定级藏品

广西自然博物馆现有定级藏品 2646 件。其中，国家级文物 309 件，馆藏定级标本 2337 件（表 3）。总体上，定级标本以现生植物（26.98%）、石器（23.36%）、现生动物（23.28%）和古动物（12.77%）为主，矿物、古植物和古人类标本较少。国家级文物均为石器类，其中国家二级文物 5 件，国家三级文物 304 件。馆藏定级标本中，馆藏一级标本 240 件，绝大部分为模式标本（232 件）；馆藏二级标本 382 件，以现生动物（146 件）和现生植物（131 件）为主；馆藏三级标本 1715 件，以现生植物（575 件）、现生动物（367 件）和石器（301 件）为主。

表 3  广西自然博物馆定级藏品

单位：件

| 类别 | 国家二级 | 国家三级 | 馆藏一级 | 馆藏二级 | 馆藏三级 | 合计 |
|---|---|---|---|---|---|---|
| 石器 | 5 | 304 | | 8 | 301 | 618 |
| 古人类 | | | 13 | 3 | 12 | 28 |
| 第四纪哺乳动物 | | | | 4 | 153 | 157 |
| 古动物 | | | 39 | 44 | 255 | 338 |
| 古植物 | | | 77 | 44 | 52 | 173 |
| 矿物 | | | | 2 | | 2 |
| 现生动物 | | | 103 | 146 | 367 | 616 |
| 现生植物 | | | 8 | 131 | 575 | 714 |
| 合计 | 5 | 304 | 240 | 382 | 1715 | 2646 |

  为了解馆藏定级标本的收藏水平，本文以馆藏定级标本的现生动植物为例，对国家级重点保护野生动植物标本的种类和数量进行分类统计。广西自然博物馆收藏了国家重点保护野生动植物标本共 265 种 1219 件（表 4）。其中，动物标本有国家一级重点保护野生动物标本 48 种 146 件，国家二级重点保护野生动物标本 95 种 367 件；植物标本有国家一级重点保护野生植物标本 20 种 131 件，国家二级重点保护野生植物标本 102 种 575 件。珍稀动物标本的收藏以哺乳动物和鸟类为主，珍稀植物标本的收藏以被子植物为主。对照国家重点保护野生动植物名录，广西自然博物馆在国家重点保护野生动植物标本方面的收藏还比较少，国家一级重点保护野生动植物标本均未达到名录的 20%，国家二级重点保护野生动植物标本也比较少（野生动物占比 7.56%，野生植物占比 10.67%）（图 1）。

表 4   广西自然博物馆国家重点保护野生动植物标本统计表

| 类别 | | 国家一级 | | 国家二级 | |
|---|---|---|---|---|---|
| | | 种类 / 种 | 数量 / 件 | 种类 / 种 | 数量 / 件 |
| 野生动物 | 无脊椎动物 | 1 | 15 | 4 | 40 |
| | 鱼类 | 1 | 2 | 1 | 42 |
| | 两栖类 | 2 | 9 | 5 | 57 |
| | 爬行类 | 9 | 21 | 20 | 68 |
| | 鸟类 | 14 | 30 | 49 | 114 |
| | 哺乳类 | 21 | 69 | 16 | 46 |
| | 小计 | 48 | 146 | 95 | 367 |
| 野生植物 | 蕨类植物 | 0 | 0 | 11 | 68 |
| | 裸子植物 | 9 | 67 | 11 | 78 |
| | 被子植物 | 11 | 64 | 80 | 429 |
| | 小计 | 20 | 131 | 102 | 575 |
| 合计 | | 68 | 277 | 197 | 942 |

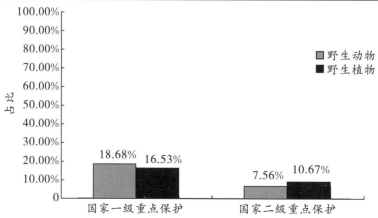

图 1   国家重点保护野生动植物名录中广西自然博物馆珍稀动植物标本占比

## 2.3 馆藏藏品的来源情况

广西自然博物馆的馆藏标本来源相对单一，多数标本来源于各个科研项目的野外采集和发掘（35222 件，占馆藏标本的 73.91%），这些标本基本产于广西各地，产于区外的标本较少；另有 8639 件标本（占馆藏标本的 18.13%）通过购买获得；通过捐赠、移交、调拨、交换等方式获得的标本较少（表 5）。

表 5 广西自然博物馆藏品来源情况调查表

| 来源方式 | 数量 / 件 | 占比 |
| --- | --- | --- |
| 采集和发掘 | 35222 | 73.91% |
| 购买 | 8639 | 18.13% |
| 捐赠 | 1144 | 2.40% |
| 移交 | 703 | 1.48% |
| 调拨 | 54 | 0.11% |
| 交换 | 3 | 0.01% |
| 旧藏 | 241 | 0.51% |
| 来源不明 | 1647 | 3.46% |
| 合计 | 47653 | 100% |

## 2.4 馆藏藏品征集时间统计

广西自然博物馆的首份标本采集于 1950 年 4 月。在该馆成立（1988 年）以前，各个时期获得的标本较少，从 1950 年至 1989 年，共征集标本 6092 件，仅占当前馆藏标本的 12.78%。广西自然博物馆成立后，馆藏标本数量大幅度增加，特别是在 2000—2009 年，该馆的藏品收藏迎来快速增长时期，共征集了 20096 件标本，占馆藏标本的 42.17%（图 2）。这一时期通过科研项目研究采集和发掘了大量文物和自然标本，特别是石器、第四纪哺乳动物化石。相比 2000—2009 年，2010—2021 年该馆藏品收藏数量有所减少。值得注意的是，在统计的标本中，有相当一部分标本（8233 件，占馆藏标本的 17.28%）缺少采集时间。

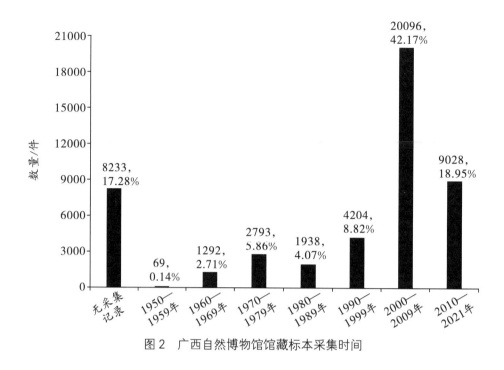

图 2　广西自然博物馆馆藏标本采集时间

## 3　讨论与建议

### 3.1　从藏品的组成来看，藏品收藏种类不均衡

广西自然博物馆历经 30 多年的积累，藏品种类多样。现收藏有丰富的广西各地质时期的古生物标本、旧石器时期的石器标本和产于广西各地的现生动植物、岩石和矿物标本，具有明显的广西地方特色。

受馆藏面积小、经费有限以及科研队伍不足等因素的影响，该馆标本收藏基础薄弱，藏品种类不均衡，藏品体系不够完善，标本量、物种数和代表性藏品都需要不断完善。许多类别的自然标本仍存在空白，如现生植物中的各类低等植物和苔藓植物、现生动物中的昆虫类、古生物中的古两栖动物和古鸟类标本等。标本收藏与国内同类博物馆相比存在较大差距，尤其在动植物标本的收藏方面，截至 2021 年 6 月底所入藏的标本还不足 5 万件（其中动植物标本各约 6000 件），而天津自然博物馆收藏的标本超过 36 万件（其中动物标本 25 万余件、植物标本约 8.3 万件），北京自然博物馆收藏的标本达 32 万件（其中动物标本 22.5 万件、植物标本 6 万件），上海自然博物馆收藏的标本 29 万件（其中动物标本约 12 万件、植物标本 15 万件）（刘付永清等，2022）。广西自然博物馆所收藏的标本主要来源于广西本地，产自全国其他地方的标本较少，不能反映我国丰富的自然遗产与资源。

藏品是自然博物馆赖以生存和发展的重要物质基础和根本保障（龙秀华，2016）。在藏品征集工作中，一方面该馆需要通过加强馆藏标本全面性、系统性的收藏，以满足观众对不同地区不同类型的自然藏品鉴赏及蕴含的自然科学知识的需求；另一方面需要继续加强广西地方特色藏品的收藏，如桂西南喀斯特地区及北部湾沿海地区的各类现生动植物标本，广西各个地质时期的古生物、古人类标本等，打造地方特色博物馆，避免"千馆一面"。

### 3.2 从藏品的珍贵程度来看，各类珍贵藏品种类、数量差距大

经过 30 多年的积累，广西自然博物馆收藏了较多的模式标本。但从模式标本的组成来看，各类模式标本的种类和数量有较大的差距，这与该馆专业人员的研究领域有很大关系。该馆在爬行动物、古植物、恐龙、古鱼类、第四纪哺乳动物化石等方面的研究具有很高的学术水平。多年来，该馆申请获批了大量的科研基金，通过科研项目采集和发掘了大量标本，其中不乏模式标本。但 2000—2015 年，该馆的植物学专业人员不断流动，导致现生植物的研究工作相对薄弱，通过研究获得的模式标本十分有限。

从定级标本的统计来看，广西自然博物馆收藏的定级标本以馆藏定级标本为主，国家级标本较少。各类定级标本数量差距大，种类还有待补充和完善。由于我国尚未出台关于自然类标本的国家定级标准，因此该馆许多珍贵的自然类标本和古人类、第四纪哺乳动物化石无法像其他文物标本一样鉴定为国家级标本。野外采集和发掘是自然类博物馆获得标本的重要来源，但随着一系列保护自然资源法律法规的颁布实施，不被认为是科研部门的自然博物馆缺乏标本采集权，自然类博物馆通过野外采集、发掘的方式获得的珍贵标本十分有限（刘付永清等，2022）。虽然一些珍贵标本可以通过购买方式获得，但是这类标本往往售价高，很难在短时间内大量征集。

模式标本和其他珍贵标本是自然类博物馆开展科学研究、展览和教育等活动不可或缺的标本。因此，为做好珍贵藏品的征集工作，广西自然博物馆一要及时补充急需缺口人才，通过发挥"以老带新"的传帮带作用，积极培养新生科研人才，通过科研力量推进对珍贵藏品的征集；二要积极与林业部门、动物园等建立长期联系，争取获得有关部门管理的自然死亡的珍稀动物标本。

### 3.3　从藏品来源来看，馆藏标本来源相对单一

广西自然博物馆馆藏标本来源相对单一，多数标本来源于野外采集和发掘，通过购买、捐赠、移交、调拨、交换等方式获得的标本较少。标本征集经费不足是影响该馆藏品多样性的重要因素。特别是新冠疫情以来，随着国家下拨给博物馆财政经费的逐年压缩，该馆每年通过购买获得的标本十分有限。

因此，在藏品征集工作中，广西自然博物馆要充分发挥有限的人力、物力和财力来拓宽藏品征集渠道。一是加强专业队伍的建设和新进专业技术人才的培养，继续发挥专业特长，通过以科研项目带动标本采集的方式加强各类藏品的收集工作；二是制订长期的标本征集计划，系统地推进各类藏品的征集工作；三是加强与外单位和外部人员的联系，多方争取海关、林业部门、动物园、科研院所、高校、企业、收藏家等的标本资源。

### 3.4　从征集时间来看，各时期收藏的藏品数量差距大

从藏品征集时间来看，各时期收藏的藏品数量差距大。2000—2009 年，该馆增加了大量标本，而近年来，动物学、植物学和古生物学等专业技术人员的频繁流动使得藏品征集数量有所减少。特别是 2014 年后，该馆缺少古人类、石器和第四纪哺乳动物化石研究人员，客观上影响了馆藏标本的征集工作。此外，该馆还有相当一部分近十年来获得的藏品尚未整理入库，这在一定程度上影响了藏品数据的精确度。

今后，该馆需要加强对考古专业人才的引进和培养，补足人才短板。此外，还要不断完善藏品的管理制度，进一步加强对现有未入藏标本的整理、登记和办理入库。

### 3.5　从藏品信息来看，藏品信息有待完善

本次调查发现，广西自然博物馆有许多藏品缺少来源、年代、地层及采集等重要信息，还有一些标本缺少鉴定信息，或仅是鉴定到某一大类。自然类藏品是人类及其环境的见证物，能从不同的领域和侧面真实地反映事物的本来面貌，是人们认识人类社会和自然界的原始信息资料（王方平，2003）。藏品所携带的信息是藏品的灵魂，是体现藏品价值的关键。全面翔实的藏品信息对于博物馆科研、展览、科普教育工作至关重要。由于藏品信息提取不完整、藏品鉴定不到位，这类标本往往只能止步于博物

馆库房，成为沉睡在库房中的"无用"标本，不能有效地为科学研究、展览教育、科普活动等工作服务。

在标本征集经费有限、藏品征集工作日益面临困境的情况下，广西自然博物馆更要利用好每份来之不易的标本。针对以上问题，广西自然博物馆可以通过完善藏品入藏管理制度、制定藏品信息提取细则、回访采集人员等方式加强藏品信息的提取和完善，通过加强专业人员的培训和聘请专家协助鉴定等方式对未鉴定或鉴定不完整的标本进行补充鉴定。

# 参考文献

[1] 杨松年. 自然博物馆的三个收藏实例 [J]. 上海科技馆，2010，2（3）：15–19.

[2] 姜雨风. 浅谈藏品研究对博物馆发展的重要性 [J]. 黑河学刊，2018，239（5）：160–161.

[3] 许东先. 广西自然博物馆馆藏植物标本数据统计分析 [C] // 陈运发. 自然遗产与文博研究：第二卷. 南宁：广西人民出版社，2013.

[4] 蒋珊. 广西自然博物馆馆藏古生物化石标本数据分析 [C] // 陈运发. 自然遗产与文博研究：第四卷. 南宁：广西人民出版社，2016.

[5] 龙秀华. 浅谈如何做好博物馆藏品的保管工作 [J]. 科研，2016（12）：87.

[6] 刘付永清，梁馨，罗怡，等. 我国自然博物馆藏品收藏现状与分析 [J]. 自然科学博物馆研究，2022，7（6）：5–14.

[7] 王方平. 浙江省博物馆藏品建设论析 [J]. 东方博物，2003（1）：87–96.

# 广西自然博物馆古生物化石标本保存现状调查分析与修复保护对策

谢耀樟，莫进尤，刘付永清

*广西自然博物馆，南宁 530012，中国*

**【摘要】**本文通过对广西自然博物馆入藏古生物化石标本保存现状进行调查分析，充分了解化石标本受损程度和受损类型，分析其受损原因，并针对性提出可行的修复保护对策及预防措施。调查结果显示，广西自然博物馆现有古生物化石标本23426件，其中受损标本354件（包括古脊椎动物化石标本309件、古无脊椎动物化石标本4件、古植物化石标本41件，分别占87.0%、1.0%和12.0%）。这些数据可使博物馆清晰地了解入藏古生物化石标本的受损情况，为下一步制订科学、合理的修复保护方案提供技术支撑与信息资料。

**【关键词】**藏品；古生物化石；受损；调查分析；修复保护对策

## 0　引言

古生物化石是自然类博物馆收藏的重要组成部分，是地质历史时期形成并赋存于地层中的动物和植物的实体化石或遗迹化石，是经过多种地质作用形成的、不可再生的地质遗产，是一种珍贵的自然资源，在科学研究和展览教育等方面具有重要意义。

广西自然博物馆的前身为1934年成立的广西省立博物馆自然科学部，1988年从广西壮族自治区博物馆独立分出。经过30多年的发展，广西自然博物馆现收藏有各类丰富的自然类标本5万余件，包括现生动植物化石标本、岩石矿物化石标本和古生物（含古人类）化石标本，其中古生物化石标本约占50.0%，种类包括古植物、古无脊椎动物、古鱼类、古爬行类、古鸟类、古两栖类、古哺乳类等。受化石本身及保存环境诸多因素的影响，部分古生物化石出现了不同程度的损坏。本文通过对馆藏古生物化石标本保存现状和受损程度进行调查分析，初步掌握古生物化石标本的具体保存情况，分析化石受损的原因，为下一步制订科学、合理的保护修复方案提供详细的信息资料。

## 1  调查方法

截至 2021 年 9 月，广西自然博物馆已登记入藏的古生物化石标本共 23426 件，包括古脊椎动物（含古人类）化石标本 19875 件、古无脊椎动物化石标本 3201 件以及古植物化石标本 350 件。

通过详细调查已登记入藏的古生物化石标本，对损坏的古生物化石标本进行登记和图像采集，并将每件受损的古生物化石标本信息录入系统，然后进行统计分析。

## 2  古生物化石标本的受损情况

受化石质地、保存环境、管理诸多因素影响，部分古生物化石标本存在不同程度的损坏。调查统计显示，受损的古生物化石标本共 354 件，其中古脊椎动物化石标本 309 件、古无脊椎动物化石标本 4 件、古植物化石标本 41 件，分别占 87.0%、1.0% 和 12.0%（图 1）。

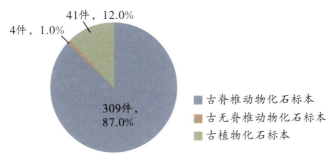

图 1 古生物化石标本受损调查结果

### 2.1  古脊椎动物化石标本

古脊椎动物化石标本受损 309 件。其中，古爬行类 154 件，占 49.8%；古哺乳类 146 件，占 47.2%；古鱼类 4 件，占 1.3%；古鸟类 4 件，占 1.3%；古两栖类 1 件，占 0.3%（图2）。

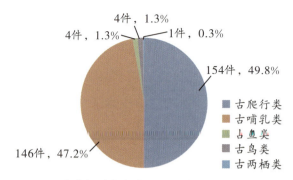

图 2  古脊椎动物各类化石标本受损调查结果

## 2.2  古无脊椎动物化石标本

古无脊椎动物化石标本受损 4 件，包括三叶虫类、昆虫类和甲壳类。其中，三叶虫类 2 件，占 50.0%；昆虫类 1 件，占 25.0%；甲壳类 1 件，占 25.0%（图 3）。

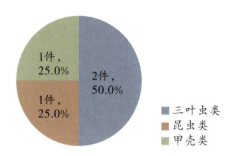

图 3  古无脊椎动物各类化石标本受损调查结果

## 2.3  古植物化石标本

古植物化石标本受损 41 件，包括被子植物类、裸子植物类和未能鉴定门类。其中，被子植物类 25 件，占 61.0%；裸子植物类 6 件，占 14.6%；未能鉴定门类 10 件，占 24.4%（图 4）。

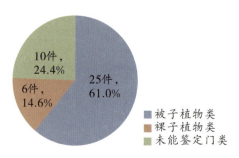

图 4  古植物各类化石标本受损调查结果

## 3 古生物化石标本受损等级

古生物化石标本受损共 354 件，按化石标本受损程度等级划分为轻度、中度和重度 3 个等级。调查评估统计结果表明，古生物化石标本轻度受损 299 件，占 84.4%；中度受损 53 件，占 15.0%；重度受损 2 件，占 0.6%（图 5）。

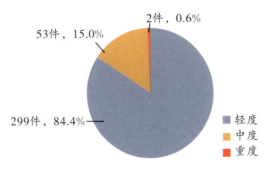

图 5　古生物化石标本受损等级调查结果

### 3.1 古脊椎动物化石受损等级分析

古脊椎动物化石标本受损 309 件。其中，古爬行类 154 件，轻度受损 151 件，占 48.9%；中度受损 3 件，占 1.0%；无重度受损。古哺乳类 146 件，轻度受损 110 件，占 35.6%；中度受损 37 件，占 12.0%；无重度受损。古鱼类 4 件，均为轻度受损，占 1.3%。古鸟类 4 件，轻度受损 3 件，占 1.0%；中度受损 1 件，占 0.3%。古两栖类 1 件，为轻度受损，占 0.3%（图 6）。

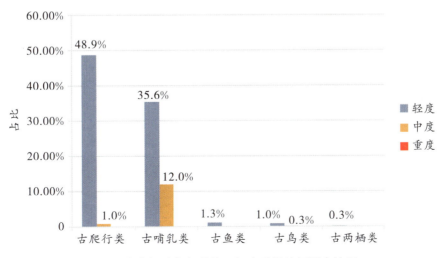

图 6　古脊椎动物各类化石标本受损等级调查结果

## 3.2　古无脊椎动物化石标本受损等级分析

古无脊椎动物化石标本受损 4 件。其中，三叶虫类 2 件，均为轻度受损，占 50.0%；无中度、重度受损。昆虫类 1 件，为中度受损，占 25.0%。甲壳类 1 件，为轻度受损，占 25.0%（图 7）。

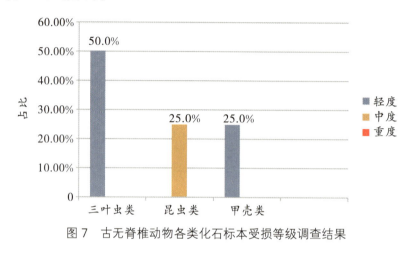

图 7　古无脊椎动物各类化石标本受损等级调查结果

## 3.3　古植物化石标本受损等级分析

古植物化石标本受损 41 件。其中，被子植物类 25 件，轻度受损 17 件，占 41.5%；中度受损 8 件，占 19.5%；无重度受损。裸子植物类 6 件，均为轻度受损，占 14.6%；无中度、重度受损。未能鉴定门类 10 件，轻度受损 5 件，占 12.2%；中度受损 3 件，占 7.3%；重度受损 2 件，占 4.9%（图 8）。

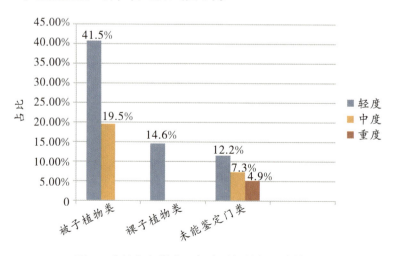

图 8　古植物各类化石标本受损等级调查结果

## 4 古生物化石标本损坏类型

### 4.1 化石围岩开裂

化石保存在不同地质时期的围岩里，当采集入库的化石标本受保存自然环境中的相对温湿度变化影响时，随着表面水分的蒸发、流失，化石标本表面、侧面岩体的性质发生改变，标本内部应力分布不均，最终导致化石标本发生岩性开裂，以保存在三叠纪和第三纪的板状页岩化石标本居多，如贵州龙化石、茂名龟类化石、鱼化石等（图9）。

贵州龙化石：a—正面视，a1—左侧面视，a2—右侧面视；翼龙化石：b—正面视，b1—左侧面视，b2—右侧面视；龟类化石：c—正面视，c1—背面视。

图9 爬行类化石标本

### 4.2 骨骼化石开裂

骨骼化石本身含有一些细微的孔隙和各类矿物质成分，在饱水状态下，容易发生水化作用，由此造成的化石膨胀、开裂、疏松等加快标本的损坏。化石在埋藏过程中的压力、温度和湿度长期保持均衡，采集收藏后其所处的自然环境发生了变化，造成化石表面与内部应力分布不均衡，引起实体化石风化开裂、疏松，有些化石甚至出现酥脆掉渣的现象，如哺乳动物类骨骼和牙齿化石（图10）。

a、b—亚洲象白齿；c、d—象门齿。

图 10　哺乳动物类化石标本

### 4.3　古植物叶片和翅果化石风化

古植物叶片和翅果化石在埋藏过程中长期处于饱水状态，容易发生水化作用，采挖时化石标本由于未得到及时的保护处理，随着表面水分的蒸发、流失，易造成叶片化石干裂、剥离或膨胀酥粉等，如古植物叶片和黄杞类翅果化石等（图 11）。

a、b—古植物叶片；c、d、e—黄杞类翅果。

图 11　古植物叶片和黄杞类翅果化石标本

# 5 古生物化石标本损坏原因分析

## 5.1 库房面积狭小

广西自然博物馆经过 30 多年的发展，博物馆事业不断发展扩大，藏品数量不断增加。但是，博物馆现有库房还是 20 世纪五六十年代建筑的红砖瓦房，面积仅有约 200 平方米。狭小的库房已经无法满足藏品的储存需求，导致一部分化石标本无地存放，只能临时存放在外面长期租赁的场地。临时库房场地和环境的不确定性，给藏品带来诸多潜在的安全隐患（刘付永清，2021）。小件化石标本存放在移动柜架和固定式标本储存柜里，大件化石标本存放在铁架上，部分标本未配置辅助保管材料。部分藏品储存柜陈旧，移动柜架不够密闭、防尘一般，又不防震，已不能满足现代文物收藏保护要求。有些化石标本还未进行整理分类，直接堆放在简易的木框里或摆放在铁架顶上，容易造成化石标本的物理损伤，不利于藏品的管理和保护。

## 5.2 藏品保存环境和保护设备相对落后

古生物化石是在不同地质时期的地层中形成的，馆藏化石标本的自然损坏与保存环境的条件因素变化有关，与自身材质的风化变质也有一定关系。因此，保护馆藏化石标本实质就是保护其本身及其所依附的材质。造成馆藏化石标本损坏的原因很多，有温度的影响，也有湿度的影响，而室内环境相对湿度无疑是最重要的指标（徐方圆等，2012）。相对湿度的变化会引起物理的变化，从而造成材质扭曲变形、开裂错位、断裂分离等。这是吸湿材质在相对湿度高时膨胀、在相对湿度低时收缩的反复机械作用产生的结果。相对湿度变化对材质体积胀缩的影响远远大于温度变化的影响。例如，吸湿性盐在吸湿、潮解、结晶过程中产生的压力，会使象牙、石刻、壁画、泥塑、玻璃等质地的馆藏文物材料开裂、剥落、崩裂（戴子佳，2014）。

《博物馆建筑设计规范》（JGJ 66—2015）中规定藏品的库房温度冬季不应低于 5℃，夏季不应高于 30℃，相对湿度在 40%～50% 之间（华东建筑设计研究院有限公司，2015）。广西自然博物馆标本库房属于老旧建筑，标本库房没有恒温、恒湿控制设备，功能和设施建设相对薄弱，不能对库房内温度、湿度、空气质量、光照等自然因素进行有效控制，化石标本尚处于自然保存状态，受环境的温度、湿度变化影响较大。目前的库房保存环境与设施还处于化石标本保管的初级阶段，远远达不到藏品的保存标准需求，且广西南宁空气温度、湿度变化较大，更加不利于藏品的保存。

# 6 修复保护应对措施

## 6.1 修复保护的方法

修复是对已经发生损坏的化石标本采取科学的方法进行复原保护，一般可分修复前期调研、制订修复方案、修复保护实施 3 个阶段。修复前期调研主要是对化石标本损坏的初步判断以及文字、影像资料记录，确认损坏机理及形成过程。制订完善的修复方案，包括修复方案的可行性、修复预算和修复期限等。修复方案可以根据化石标本损坏程度和损坏类型进行分类制订，如需要粘接的化石标本分为一类，需要加固保护的化石标本分为另一类等。化石标本修复的基本流程为粘接—加固—修补。在修复过程中，也可以根据化石标本的受损情况调换流程顺序。

### 6.1.1 粘接材料和方法

粘接、加固断裂化石标本的目的是使断裂部分重新黏合在一起，恢复其本质结构的完整性和原有的外观。由于馆藏化石标本长时间受到各种自然因素的影响而发生不同程度的断裂、开裂等，需要对这些化石标本进行粘接修复保护。例如化石标本断为数块，或断块较多、较碎，首先进行仔细拼接，找出每块断块的相对应位置，按排序标记。然后进行断面清理，之后再进行调胶、拼接、固定。胶黏剂是由各种树脂组成的材料，包括氰基丙烯酸乙酯（502 胶水）、云石胶、环氧树脂、聚酯树脂等，根据化石标本损坏情况选用不同的胶黏剂。

### 6.1.2 加固材料和方法

由于受自身因素和保存环境的影响，有些化石标本会发生不同程度的风化、膨胀、开裂、疏松等，特别是河床采集的哺乳类牙齿和植物翅果化石风化更严重。对于这一类化石标本可以通过加固保护提高其稳定性，增强其抗风化能力，从而延长其寿命。加固材料有硝基清漆、丙酮、氰基丙烯酸乙酯和丙烯酸树脂等。目前，对风化、开裂、疏松的围岩或化石标本进行加固基本上都采用丙烯酸树脂 Paraloid B-72（颗粒胶）。这种加固材料无色透明，性能稳定，具有良好的可逆性和耐老化性。可用丙酮稀释配比

5.0%、10.0% 和 15.0% 几种不同浓度的丙烯酸树脂溶液进行加固保护（付华林，2012；缪克佳等，2019）。丙烯酸树脂 Paraloid B-72 是在青铜器、铁器、石器等文物修复加固保护中应用最广泛的一种加固材料（栗荣贺，2014）。加固方法有滴灌法和涂刷法。不同程度的风化、开裂、松散的围岩或化石标本，加固时应注意加固剂量、浓度及次数的把握，一般加固到加固剂不能再渗透为止，这样才能使加固达到最佳效果。

### 6.1.3 修补材料和方法

修补是对化石标本局部损坏缺失或裂隙部位进行修复，一般只针对化石标本结构性或局部缺失部位进行修复。在修补过程中要根据化石标本不同部位的实际损坏情况，选用不同的材料，包括石膏粉、聚酯树脂、云石胶、环氧树脂等。此外，也可以根据需要，用颜料对修补部位进行着色，使其与化石整体颜色一致。

### 6.1.4 做托加固保护材料和方法

馆藏化石标本修复保护除上述方法外，还可以做托加固保护。有些化石标本保存在不同地质时期且围岩较薄的板状页岩里，如宁明鱼类化石、贵州龙化石等。由于化石标本受本质因素和保存环境因素的影响，其岩性发生不同程度的开裂、膨胀、脱落等。为了防止这类标本进一步开裂、剥落、损坏，应用相对较好的材料制作框托来加固保护。加固方法是先采用硝基清漆或丙烯酸树脂 Paraloid B-72 溶液进行反复多次加固保护，然后用高强度石膏粉制作一定厚度的石膏底托和边框增强加固保护作用，最后用稀胶对石膏底托和边框加固封护。

## 6.2 改善藏品保存环境

博物馆库房藏品保存环境的改善和有效监控，是防止各种环境因素对化石标本损坏的有效保护路径。广西自然博物馆由于无法对现有库房藏品保存环境、技术设备等进行较大的改善，因此应在现有的自然条件下积极探索化石标本的预防保护工作。一是在没有恒温、恒湿设备的条件下，购置一些除湿机、空调等设备对库房环境进行调控。二是做好化石标本入库前的加固保护处理，这是藏品预防保护的关键。三是提高工作人员的藏品防护意识，避免藏品遭受人为无意识损坏。四是定期监测化石标本状态的变化，并做好记录，及时清除表面沉积的尘土，尤其是在回南天气更需要加强对化石标本的管理。

## 7 结语

通过对广西自然博物馆馆藏古生物化石标本保存现状调查情况进行分析，发现该馆化石标本受损的主要类型是古哺乳动物类和古爬行类，其次是古植物类叶片和翅果化石。化石标本损坏现象包括化石风化和开裂、标本围岩开裂、化石从围岩中膨胀和脱落。影响馆藏古生物化石标本损坏的因素很多，室内温度和湿度变化较大无疑是最主要的原因。藏品库房是 20 世纪五六十年代建筑的红砖瓦房，库房面积狭小，储存柜陈旧，无法满足现代文物标本收藏保护要求。因此，当务之急是在环境条件不佳的情况下积极探索化石标本的预防性保护措施，如购置一些除湿机、空调等设备对库房环境进行调控，定期对化石标本进行日常检查和维护，着手编写、制订馆藏化石标本抢救修复保护方案，使损坏的化石标本能够早日得到有效保护。

## 参考文献

［1］刘付永清.地方博物馆自然类藏品管理难题及策略［C］//莫运明.自然遗产与文博研究：第六卷.南宁：广西科学技术出版社，2021.

［2］徐方圆，吴来明，解玉林，等.文物保存环境中温湿度评估方法研究［J］.文物保护与考古科学，2012，24（增刊1）：6–12.

［3］戴子佳.甘肃博物馆馆藏文物保存环境现状调查与保护技术的应用研究［D］.兰州：西北师范大学，2014：23.

［4］华东建筑设计研究院有限公司.博物馆建筑设计规范：JGJ 66—2015［M］.北京：中国建筑工业出版社，2015.

［5］付华林.化石修理中常见的问题及其解决方法：下［J］.化石，2012（3）：38–41.

［6］缪克佳，单鹛，沈志欣.基于博物馆展示环境的化石加固剂比较研究：以大型脊椎动物为例［J］.科学教育与博物馆，2019（1）：23–27.

［7］栗荣贺.简述文物保护用丙烯酸树脂 Paraloid B-72［M］.辽宁省博物馆馆刊，沈阳：辽海出版社，2014.

# 浅谈广西鱼类化石的发现、采集与修复

雷学强

广西自然博物馆，南宁　530012，中国

【摘要】化石是了解地质历史时期生命的直接证据，是科普展览和科学研究的物质基础。化石标本来源于野外采集，通常需要精心修复才能完美地展现，因此标本的采集与处理是自然类博物馆一项基础而重要的工作。本文根据作者长期的工作实践和观察，以广西鱼类化石标本为例，谈谈鱼类化石的发现、采集与修复工作。

【关键词】鱼类化石；采集；修复

鱼类是脊椎动物中重要的一个类群，其种数几乎占脊椎动物全部种数的一半（NELSON，1994），广泛栖居于河流、湖泊、海洋中。鱼类有着漫长的演化历史，产自云南寒武系的海口鱼和昆明鱼是目前已知最早的鱼类化石（舒德干、陈苓，2000）。从海口鱼到人类的出现，时间跨度长达5亿年。通过对鱼类化石研究可以了解过去的鱼类，它不仅能帮助我们认识古老鱼类的形态特征、分布特点和演化规律，还能帮助我们了解5亿年来海陆的变迁、河流水系的变化以及确定地层的时代等。鱼类化石的研究很有意义，也很有必要。鱼类化石的发现、采集和修复是展现和研究鱼类化石的基础。

## 1　如何发现鱼类化石

据统计，广西已发现的鱼类化石有甲胄鱼纲、盾皮鱼纲、软骨鱼纲、棘鱼纲和硬骨鱼纲，共计24目44科72属76种，分别产自南宁等地泥盆系、田东等地三叠系、扶绥白垩系、宁明等地古近系以及邕江流域全新统（罗怡、梁馨，2021）。这些化石都只发现于沉积岩中，如泥岩、页岩、粉砂岩、砂岩结核、碳酸岩、煤矸石等。南宁早

泥盆世的鱼类化石产自紫红色或灰绿色砂岩中（盖志琨等，2021），田东等地三叠纪的鱼类化石发现于灰岩中（王念忠等，2001），扶绥白垩纪的鱼类化石发现于河流沉积中，宁明等地古近纪的鱼类化石发现于湖泊相沉积岩中，在泥质岩中的鱼类化石比在泥质砂岩中的丰富，保存相对较好。此外，在泥质砂岩结核中也常保存有化石；百色盆地古近纪的鱼类化石多发现在暗红色或灰黄色泥岩和黑灰色煤矸石中；在南宁市郊古近纪的东北部和东部河流或三角洲相沉积岩中也发现鱼类化石，但通常比较破碎。由于火山作用和变质作用，岩浆岩（如花岗岩）和变质岩（如板岩、大理岩、石英岩等）中不可能含有鱼类化石，因此必须在沉积岩中寻找鱼类化石。

在一个区域寻找鱼类化石，首先要了解该区域的地层分布情况，确定踏勘路线，多走、多看，若在偏僻的地方要和同行伙伴做好联动，规避风险意外。在建筑施工工地深挖层出土的岩块、山体新开挖剖面、煤矿区出矿的伴生煤矸石中都有可能发现鱼类化石。例如，在广西寻找新生代的鱼类化石，首先要查找地质资料，通过文献资料我们知道广西新生代地层主要出露于南宁、宁明和百色，然后根据掌握的线索和判断踏勘（踏勘时要随身携带地质锤、罗盘或定位系统仪器、放大镜等地质三大件，以便随时观察采集到的标本）。发现鱼类化石后要分析其所在位置是原生层还是搬运而来的，若为原生层应做好化石点的定位，并沿着原生层的位置展开寻找，有可能发现一片丰富的鱼类化石掩埋层。

## 2　如何采集鱼类化石

### 2.1　采集前的准备

采集鱼类化石应准备以下工具：用于去除化石层上的浮土和覆盖层的工具，如锄头、铲子等；用于将化石从围岩中取出的工具，如地质锤和粗细不同的多种錾子、劈子，在潮湿的泥页岩（如新出露的宁明古近系泥页岩）中采集标本时，油灰刀是很好的工具，可以单独或与地质锤合用将围岩劈开；用于加固化石围岩或化石的胶黏剂，如502胶水、高透稀胶等；用于保护化石的包装用品，如绵纸或卫生纸、标本袋、胶带等；用于野外记录地层和标写信息的用品，如标本笔、铅笔、笔记本等。

## 2.2　采集过程

在了解鱼类化石大致分布地点和层位后即可开始采集。首先去掉岩层上的浮土，然后选用平头地质锤和劈子逐层剖开岩石，查看是否有鱼类化石。注意岩石断面是否有化石，如有化石，应追踪邻接岩块。在野外不要急于剖开含有化石的岩块，应留到室内慢慢修理，这样才能修出更完美的标本，最大限度地保留生物特征信息。每层化石都要做好标号和记录，不可混淆。对于分开正副两面的鱼类化石，或者断成数块的鱼类化石应做好标记。当遇到断裂面时应及时采用 502 胶水或高透稀胶小范围临时定位加固化石、围岩，同时收集和标注每块关联的化石块。新生代的鱼类化石一般不够坚固，采集标本后不能用刷子反复清扫化石表面，以免化石的牙齿或骨片脱落。采集到完整的鱼类化石固然理想，但不要忽略完整的头部骨片、构造特殊的鳍刺等骨片和牙齿，它们也是研究人员理想的研究材料。近 20 年来，城市建设快速发展，施工开辟出的山体临时剖面、堆积的岩块为寻找化石提供了方便，但是施工也破坏了宝贵的自然资源。

在广西野外少见需要打"皮劳克"（石膏包装）采集的大块鱼类化石。如果围岩比较松散，风化后成泥土样，在采集肉眼易见的鱼类化石后，应用放大镜查看其是否有细小的鱼牙、耳石等具有鉴定意义的化石，如有，可用筛洗法筛选出来。我们采用筛洗法在南宁盆地渐新统地层取得了较好的效果，如采集到伍氏南宁鲤的咽喉骨和咽喉齿以及南宁鳅的眼下刺化石。筛洗法的基本步骤是先用布袋盛装采集的土样，然后将其放置于水中浸泡、软化附着在化石上的泥岩和杂物，一般浸泡 1 小时以上，以取一捧土样在水里晃动能看见整体散开为准，若没有散开则应继续浸泡。待土样充分泡软疏散后，使用小目数（小于目标化石）的筛网托底，将大目数的筛网套在上面，放置适量土样，在湍急的水流中反复晃动冲刷，去除附着的泥沙、杂物。筛网的目数根据目标化石的大小来决定，一般选用 3 ～ 20 目的筛网。当筛选后丢弃上层大目数筛网内的杂物时，应反复检查是否有遗漏的化石，待小目数筛网的样品晾干后再查找化石。这类化石大小不一，大的清晰可见，小的需要在显微镜下用剔针或小毛笔挑出来，并放在适当的标本盒中保存。标本盒上须写上明确的采集信息，如时间、地点、采集人、采集号等。

### 2.3　化石打包

化石运输返回后的打包、叠放、记录十分讲究。打包化石时首先选用柔韧的纸张、棉花覆盖在化石面上，然后用粗糙的报纸、卷纸等缠绕并固定化石，将化石放入标本袋（盒），最后装箱。装箱时要注意叠放次序，应先大后小、平缛铺开（厚重的化石不要压在酥脆小块的化石上），也可按大小、重量、岩性硬度分类装箱，同一个采集点的化石尽量放在同一批箱子里，层叠间放置绵软缓冲物（软纸团、珍珠棉）调平，并填充过大的间隙，以免化石晃动，互相碰撞损伤化石面。信息记录要做到对号对组，确保单块化石信息完整，整箱化石采集点信息明确，避免后期分类的信息混乱。

## 3　如何修复鱼类化石

### 3.1　修复思路

目前发现的鱼类化石骨骼多且细小，空间分布叠加复杂，可鉴定细节部位多有缺失，在修复中应保留化石的真实形态特征，这是展现和研究鱼类化石的基础。如何达到理想的修复效果？在修复前应了解鱼类的一般构造、研究方向，同时观察、判断围岩的胶结程度，以便选用合适的工具，顺着化石延伸的方向去除包裹化石表面的围岩，从而达成修复的目标。

### 3.2　工具的选择

鱼类化石的修复一般采用机械修理方法，即借助工具进行物理修理。经常使用的修理工具有小锤子、各种细长凿子、粗细不同的剔针、斜面的刮针、气吹、手持式小型雕刻打磨机、化石修复气动笔等。在实际操作中，细小的剔针尖易钝化、磨损，需要经常研磨，以保持剔针细长、尖锐。当遇到高硬度围岩包裹酥脆的化石时，可用雕刻打磨机或化石修复气动笔在体视显微镜下去除邻近化石面表层的围岩。化石修复气动笔稳定性较高的是德国 HW 系列和美国 paleoTools ME9100 系列，稳定性不高的化石修复气动笔在使用一段时间后会经常出现卡针或跳针的现象。石化程度高的古生代和中生代鱼类化石应使用化石喷砂机修复，其修复效果较好。修复常使用的材料有 502 胶水、丙烯酸树脂 Paraloid B-72、丙酮、醋酸、云石胶、石膏等。

### 3.3 修复细节

#### 3.3.1 化石面的处理

首先把采集到的鱼类化石放在缓冲垫上定位，然后根据化石的酥脆程度及围岩硬度采用小锤子和钝角、锐角两种高硬度含铬的细长凿子来敲除厚实的覆盖层，或用雕刻打磨机或化石修复气动笔来处理；同时需要不断用气吹和毛刷去除散落在化石覆盖层上的破碎围岩，确认敲击的效果。要耐心、逐层、浅薄地向下敲除覆盖层，直至接近化石面（化石修复气动笔自带吹气功能，需要根据化石胶结程度来使用）。在修复到化石面后，一般选用 15 倍带灯源的台式放大镜或体视显微镜来处理后续修复工作。在放大原生的化石面与围岩后较容易分辨化石面，需要注意的是，在涂抹过清水或高透稀胶后，化石面分层色差明显，但水分挥发后化石面会越来越模糊，莹润的分层表象将不存在，非必要尽量避免此操作。当手持修复工具时，双手应握稳工具，在没有看见化石面时应靠触感和包裹化石的围岩色泽变化来判定是否为化石面。当使用剔针时应采用 90° 或约 45° 的角度落针，针尖力度以可挑动围岩又不伤及化石面为准，以月弧形将一小块一小块的围岩刮分剥离即可。在化石石化程度和围岩硬度较高、化石分布平顺的情况下，可考虑使用手持式小型雕刻打磨机、化石修复气动笔、化石喷砂机来快速剔除化石面的覆盖层。如果遇到较细小、叠加复杂、酥脆的化石，为避免化石修复气动笔吹出的气流过大而吹走化石，应采用手工修复。油滑的油泥岩的处理方式与泥质砂岩的基本一致，在微处理上要使用斜口刮针来刮除化石表面的油泥，再用细毛笔轻轻地平复绵软的油泥岩留在化石面上的划痕。

当遇到化石围岩为碳酸岩时，可先采用醋酸浸泡的方法来溶解化石表面的部分围岩，然后再用机械修理。需要注意的是，需提前选择局部化石来验证醋酸的浓度比例，以不伤及化石为标准来调试醋酸浓度。

#### 3.3.2 边沿的处理

除了化石整体形态特征展露部分，具体开挖的深度需要与研究员确认，原则上应按俯视图观察面来展现鱼类化石在一个平面上的形态特征，非必要不建议深挖内侧孔径。在板状的鱼类化石上，化石的叠加高低不一，整体是一个相对平面，有落差时应在化石轮廓边处留下一圈适当宽度的分断平面来区分化石和围岩。从研究方面来看，这一圈分断平面在处理上应保持平整，而在科普展出时留下适当的针槽痕迹亦有别致的美感。

### 3.3.3 断裂面的处理

在鱼类化石的采集过程中，难免会出现断裂的情况，关联明确的尽量拼接成一个整体，缺失部分非必要不作同色填补。拼接断面在显微镜下定位可准确对接，在可调节夹紧物件的工作台上也能很好地确保对接断面不移位，没有工作台的也可在做好化石面保护的情况下使用橡皮筋夹紧木板来固定。遵循由内到外、从轻到重的原则依照编号顺序在对接面滴上（抹上）相应黏结剂来定位加固，部分无法整块平面对接的多边形化石，在胶水凝固过程中可能因自身重量下沉走位，必要时可做一个底托支撑固定化石后再对化石断面进行对接黏合，这样效果更好。

在野外临时使用 502 胶水黏结的化石，出现叠加错位的可用丙酮（有剧毒，使用时要做好呼吸过滤保护）洗去胶水后再重新处理即可，非必要少用非可逆性的黏结胶水。

## 3.4 修复后的处理

鱼类化石围岩多为页岩、泥岩，其在温度、湿度多变的情况下易风化脆裂，附着的化石也会随之崩裂，因此很有必要给修复后的整块化石覆上封膜保护胶，以尽量延长鱼类化石完整的存世时间。早期常使用硝基清漆兑二甲苯调制的稀胶（浓度 15% 左右）来多次刷化石，使化石表面整体色泽暗淡失真，修复效果一般；如使用 502 瞬干胶，易使化石发脆变色，耐候性一般。经多次试验摸索，得知采用丙烯酸树脂 Paraloid B-72 兑丙酮调试的稀胶具有可逆性、稳定性及耐老化性，无色透明，适中的柔韧性及很好的黏结附着力等优点，因此其又作为首选的黏结胶水。使用黏结胶水来封膜和渗透化石整体，可以锁住化石与围岩内部松散的空隙，预防开裂（一般采用 5% ～ 15% 浓度的黏结胶水来渗透化石表面缝隙和封膜，用 40% ～ 50% 浓度的对断面、脱离层进行黏结）。目前，鱼类化石的存放条件很难做到恒温、恒湿，建议为所有定级的鱼类化石都定制专用囊匣来存放，减少温、湿度变化给鱼类化石带来的影响。日常持续性地酌情维持封膜的完整，对延长鱼类化石的完整性具有很好的保护作用。当鱼类化石出现崩裂迹象、上胶固化效果不佳时，应考虑为整块鱼类化石做围托，调整重心的平衡，减小内应力的剪切。

在多次验证后有 3 种方法效果较显著。一是用云石胶做围边底托，能达到用量少、强度够、多变环境中物理性能稳定的效果，但缺陷是在调制过程中异味挥发广、气味呛鼻，毒性高；二是用水晶树脂做围边托底，其成品晶莹美观，像艺术品且异味不浓，但缺陷是调制过程复杂（必要时还要做定位模具），接触面过于光滑，与包裹化石的围岩黏结不好；三是用石膏做围托（可考虑用超硬度牙科石膏，牙科石膏在吸水度、固化时间、硬度方面比普通石膏提升 50% 左右的性能），其成型外观石质感自然，与围岩同呼吸，性价比高（成品也要刷涂稀胶），但缺陷是调制过程复杂，含有大量水分，轻薄化石吸水后可能整体翘曲变形，同时水汽挥发、固化时间久。

# 参考文献

［1］NELSON J S. 世界鱼类［M］. 李思忠，陈星玉，陈小平，译. 台湾：水产出版社，1994.

［2］舒德干，陈苓. 最早期脊椎动物的镶嵌演化［J］. 现代地质，2000（3）：315-322.

［3］罗怡，梁馨. 广西鱼类化石统计分析［C］//莫运明. 自然遗产与文博研究：第六卷. 南宁：广西科学技术出版社，2021.

［4］盖志琨，曾广春，陈耿娇，等. 广西南宁下泥盆统盔甲鱼类新发现及其生物地层学意义［C］//2020年中国地球科学联合学术年会论文集（二十五）：专题七十三：古脊动物学最新进展、专题七十四：污染物地球化学过程与循环、专题七十五：超大陆演化及其生物环境效应，2020.

［5］王念忠，杨守仁，金帆，等. 中国海相早三叠世弓鲛鱼类（软骨鱼类）的首次报道：华南二叠系—三叠系界线上下鱼类序列研究之一［J］. 古脊椎动物学报，2001，39（4）：237-250.

# 自然类博物馆提升社会影响力的几点实践与思考

付琼耀

*广西自然博物馆，南宁　530012，中国*

【摘要】自然类博物馆是集收藏、研究和展示自然及其环境物证以及自然文化遗产的博物馆，承载着传播自然生态文明理念的重大使命，具有收藏研究、展览教育、休闲旅游等多项社会功能。本文阐述自然类博物馆可以从馆际合作、馆校合作、人才培养、博物馆建设、社会教育、文创产品开发等方面着手，提升和扩大自身社会影响力，真正体现自然类博物馆的公益性与服务性，为新时代博物馆事业发展添砖加瓦。

【关键词】自然类博物馆；社会影响力；博物馆建设

## 0　引言

著名古生物学家杨钟键院士曾说过："我每到一个城市，最想看的不是庄严的宫殿、秀丽的公园、整肃的教堂，而是伟大的陈列馆。"的确，博物馆在体现一个地方的经济文化水平方面有着不可替代的作用，是一个地区社会文明发展的标志。而自然类博物馆是集收藏、研究和展示自然及其环境物证以及自然文化遗产的博物馆（孟庆金，2013），承载着传播自然生态文明理念的重大使命。近年来，随着人民生活水平的不断提高以及科学普及活动的深入，自然类博物馆越来越受到大众特别是青少年群体（敬向红，2010）的喜爱。基于这种广泛的喜爱，自然类博物馆的影响力在潜移默化中形成并逐步提升。

相比于过去仅有收藏藏品、展示藏品的功能，现在的自然类博物馆集收藏研究、展览教育、休闲旅游于一身。特别是在文化和旅游深度融合的大背景下（钱兆悦，2018），自然类博物馆如何发挥自身功能属性，以更好地服务于经济社会发展大局就显得尤为重要。本文通过以下几个方面，阐述自然类博物馆主体功能的发挥及其对经济社会发展的作用。

## 1　馆际合作

馆际合作是博物馆之间开展日常工作、扩大影响力的普遍做法。自然类博物馆之间需要加强沟通和交流，了解彼此的优势，互通有无，实现双赢。我国几个比较大的自然类博物馆的优势在于藏品比较全面、体量比较大，但可能还未涉及一些带有地方特色的藏品；而各地区特别是生物物种比较丰富的地区的自然类博物馆，优势在于收藏有一些特色物种。比如广西独有的白头叶猴资源，上海自然博物馆就非常希望白头叶猴展能到上海展出。大馆需要特色的东西吸引大众的眼球，扩大自身的影响力；而小馆则可以通过临时展出一些在大馆比较成功的展览来提升自身的综合实力。其实，这种馆际间的合作在我国一级大型综合博物馆之间已经比较频繁，如浙江自然博物院在西藏开设了"吉祥彩光——院藏珊瑚精品展"，给高原内陆的人们带去了一道有关海洋生物多样性的知识大餐，同时西藏牦牛博物馆也将"牦牛走进浙江——高原牦牛文化展"带给了沿海地区的观众。据了解，浙江自然博物院的临展档期经常提前一两年就已排满，馆际间的交流活跃程度可见一斑。广西自然博物馆和北京自然博物馆建立了多年的合作关系。这几年，两馆之间进行了一些交换展览的活动，北京自然博物馆将一些比较成熟的展览，包括"小昆虫大世界""恐龙时代的小精灵——昆虫化石展""恐龙木乃伊——浓缩的生命"等，搬到南宁供广西人民参观，而广西自然博物馆制作的具有本地特色的展览又放到北京供当地观众欣赏。这是一种良性循环，可以更好地发挥展览的宣传教育作用，扩大展览的覆盖面。

## 2　馆校合作

馆校合作现在越来越受到博物馆人的重视，因为它是实现博物馆社会教育功能的重要途径，而学校对博物馆这个第二课堂的兴趣也愈发浓厚。在此背景下，加强馆校合作理所当然地成为博物馆人做好宣传教育的重点。国家文物局、教育部《关于加强文教结合、完善博物馆青少年教育功能的指导意见》文件提出："实现博物馆青少年教育资源与学校教育的有效衔接……把博物馆资源与中小学课堂教学、综合实践活动的实施有机结合，增强博物馆青少年教育的针对性……以构建中小学生利用博物馆学习的长效机制，使利用博物馆学习成为中小学校日常教学的有机组成部分。"上有政策支持，下有现实需求，馆校合作模式势在必行。在我国，上海自然博物馆很早就开始了这方面的尝试，已经开发出一套"菜单式"的校本课程，将自然博物馆资源与学校课程有机结合，开设课程 60 多门，涉及生物、地理、地质、化学等多门学科，覆盖了从小学到高中的课程，通过探究学习的方式让学生对自然科学从认知到了解，再到产生兴趣，从而达到教育的终极目的。这种"菜单式"教育课程让上海自然博物馆每年接待学校约 60 所，来馆参加学习的学生人数超过 2000 人，而且还有逐年上升的趋势。重庆自然博物馆结合校本课程编写教材 8 本，设计教育课程 22 个，基本覆盖了从幼儿园到初中学段的学生群体（李小英，2016）。广西自然博物馆这几年也在探索加大与学校合作力度、扩大教育覆盖范围的办法，每年有 15 所中小学校到馆参观，但受场地空间、人员以及展品丰富程度等条件的限制，学生以参观为主，在展品前停留时间较短，并没有深入的课程开发、探究学习等过程，与我国一级自然类博物馆还存在很大差距；开发的一些实践类活动，比如小小讲解员、环球自然日演讲比赛等，虽深受学生欢迎，但毕竟受益人数少，教育覆盖面有限。除了学生到馆参观，广西自然博物馆每年也会开展 7～8 次"科普大篷车""流动的博物馆"等活动，到各个设区市的中小学校做科普宣传。

通过双向的馆校合作交流，各地自然类博物馆提高了对藏品、场馆的利用率，让学生群体获得更真实、更亲近自然的社会教育，同时也为自然类博物馆在今后开展教育活动提供了经验和人气，所以馆校合作模式已成为自然类博物馆扩大社会影响力、传播自然科学知识的重要抓手。如果能深挖两者间的共有资源，去做课程创新、课程图书创新等一系列工作，相信应该能获得更高的教育成效。

## 3　人才培养

作为自然类博物馆，收藏研究是为展览教育做支撑的基础工作。科研是自然类博物馆的核心竞争力（孟庆金，2013），科研做得好不好，直接关系到展览教育的质量。而科研对人才的依赖性很强，特别是专业技术人才。上海自然博物馆、广西自然博物馆具有硕士、博士学位的人数占比都达45%，浙江自然博物院具有高级职称的人数比例达到在编总人数的50%以上。近年来，随着高校扩招，人才的竞争愈发激烈，人才引进不算难，难就难在对人才的培养，毕竟博物馆工作对人才要求较高，既要讲专业又要懂科普。在国外，这类综合性人才叫作策展人，深厚的专业学术背景往往能让他们把展览教育做得更深入人心。这类人才可遇不可求，但可以从以下三个方面做好人才培养工作。一是对教育专业人才的培养，包括策展人员和教育工作者。每年给他们提供到专业机构培训或外出学习的机会，比如派人员到北京、上海等大城市的自然博物馆参与展览教育全过程的业务培训，学习时间可以是一年或半年。学习结束后，要根据本馆条件摸索出一套符合实际的展览教育活动，并承担培训本馆专业人员的责任，最大化发挥其学习成果。二是对科研人才的培养。对科研人员来说，了解行业最新动态至关重要，出国和参加学术会议是促进知识更新的有效途径。像浙江自然博物院，新冠疫情发生之前馆内人员每年有3次出国学习的机会，出国经费大约100万元。三是对科研项目加大支持。做科研项目最能锻炼一个人各方面的能力素质，不论项目大小，从申请到课题实施再到结题，每一步实践都可以有收获和提高。人才培养也应注重因材施教，以人为本，最大限度地激发他们的潜能，以人才驱动博物馆事业健康向上发展（王丽娟，2017）。

## 4   博物馆建设

随着改革开放的深入实施，我国经济迅速增长，这些年各地博物馆如雨后春笋般建立起来。根据数据统计，1979年全国各类博物馆仅有300多家，截至2022年，登记注册博物馆已达6565家。但问题也随之而来，博物馆数量多但质量堪忧，综合类博物馆多而特色博物馆少，导致场馆常出现节假日爆满而平时空空荡荡的现象。原浙江自然博物馆馆长康熙民曾一针见血地指出："一些地方打着'文化促经济'旗号，把博物馆的建筑外观当作当地科学文化建设的重要标志，甚至把博物馆当成地方政绩工程来建，不惜投入巨额资金，至于建成后的标志性建筑能在当地科学文化教育中发挥出多少作用和什么样的作用，一般考虑不多，反正是先建起来再说。"的确，盲目建设不仅浪费国家资源，还会消耗人们对博物馆的美好期望。近年来，自然类博物馆呈现越建越多的趋势。据统计，从 1991 年至 2020 年的近 30 年里，2011—2020 年这 10 年我国建设的综合性自然类博物馆数量占近 30 年来国内综合性自然类博物馆总量的 55%，发展速度之快令不少科学家表示担忧，因为场馆的新建以及对标本需求的增加，势必会造成动物遭大量捕杀、珍稀植物遭盗挖、化石资源遭破坏等严重后果，所以对于一些没有多年馆藏积累和建馆经验的地区，建设自然类博物馆还需仔细斟酌，权衡利弊。

博物馆数字化建设也是提升博物馆软实力的重要举措，包括博物馆收藏、研究、展教、管理、利用等工作的方方面面（纪远新，2010）。藏品数字化建设是博物馆数字化的基础性工作。自然类博物馆收藏的都是矿物标本、动植物标本、古生物标本以及古人类标本等，将这些数量庞大的标本建成数字化资源库后，将给政府决策、机构评估、学术交流等提供重要的参考资料，也能给普通民众日常检索和博物馆内部查询带来极大的便利；办公自动化网络方便博物馆日常管理，能使博物馆运营"活"起来；展教服务平台是日常开展展览教育活动的宣传互动窗口，是方便观众第一时间获取博物馆资讯的网络化平台。然而，由于这些平台数据库的建设及维护成本较高，大多数博物馆并未实现真正的数字化，这严重制约着博物馆的发展。随着科技水平的提高，更廉价、更简易的数字化平台已经普及起来，比如微信公众号、微博、抖音、快手等平台已经能承担一些宣传互动功能。未来随着云计算、大数据、区块链、物联网等数字技术的发展，博物馆事业发展将开辟更广阔的空间（沈业成，2022）。

## 5　社会教育

博物馆教育作为学校教育的有力补充，是学校教育向外扩展延伸的第二课堂（宋奇，2007）。博物馆教育能不能取得较好的成效，受诸多因素的影响。比如教育人才的数量和层次、教育体制和奖励激励机制、场馆条件和配套设施等，其中教育体制是否健全至关重要。博物馆教育一方面要能吸引人去做教育，另一方面要能吸引人来接受教育。

博物馆教育主要有展览教育和课程教育。展览教育是针对博物馆展览内容设计的教育活动（蔡黎明，2018），往往受益人数多，知识面广，具有实物性、实践性以及时代性特征。课程教育则是针对某一方面或某个知识点进行的针对性教育，往往受益人数有限，年龄层次也有限制，知识面相对较窄。自然类博物馆在开发课程教育上相较于学校有先天的优势，因为自然科学有丰富的内容素材供选择（刘雅竹等，2017）。新冠疫情之前，浙江自然博物院每年可开展700多场教育活动，分8大类50多个项目，与6所学校合作做课程研发。丰富的社会教育内容离不开人才队伍的支持，其馆内专职教育人员24人（其中编内4人、编外20人），每年都派人员出国做交流，一些科普教育活动适当收取费用用于奖励付出，积极进行教育成效的问卷调查（包括展览教育及课程教育）。上海自然博物馆紧紧围绕"教育是终极目的，展示是传播载体，研究是学术支撑，收藏是物质基础"的总体思路来做工作，近年来利用"网络自媒体＋专家教授授课"的方式，吸引了大量受众关注和参与，取得了很好的教育成效。

研究性学习（研学）活动是近年来比较流行的教育活动方式，简单来说是指个体以研究的方式学习知识。研学的实施根本上就是学生、知识、研究三个要素在具体时空中的操作性整合过程（刘庆昌，2008）。青少年对自然的好奇使得自然类博物馆开展研学活动具有先天的优势。针对不同年龄层次的青少年开展有针对性的探究性学习教育实践活动将成为未来博物馆社会教育的新趋势，也必将成为自然类博物馆实现社会教育功能的新手段。

## 6　文创产品开发

自然类博物馆作为文博单位，依托自身丰富的馆藏资源，在文创产品开发中具有天然的优势。但受到体制政策、思想观念等因素的影响，自然类博物馆的文创产品开发在"大众创业、万众创新"新时代下显得不温不火，很多做自主开发的博物馆工作者都失去了积极性，甚至选择了放弃，这无疑是对博物馆资源的一种浪费。从文创产品本身的特点来看，它能在一定程度上满足民众日益增长的文化需求，拉近博物馆与民众间的距离，扩大博物馆的影响力，实现"将博物馆带回家"的愿望。博物馆文创产品是博物馆宣传自身理念的重要渠道，可以帮助博物馆增加经济收入，激发博物馆内生活力。正是因为文创产品能产生种种益处，所以各家博物馆都跃跃欲试，通过授权外包、贴牌、转让版权等方式，将自身资源转化为产品出售，获取效益（熊雯，2016）。相信随着博物馆改革的深入和一些限制的放开，博物馆文创产品开发将重新焕发生机，真正做到让博物馆提质增效，让文物"火"起来。

## 7　结语

综合以上几个方面，自然类博物馆需要依托自身资源优势，把握自身定位，结合本馆实际，在收藏研究、展览教育、旅游休闲等方面发挥博物馆主体功能。做好同行间的强强联合，扩大自身社会影响力；紧紧拥抱学校师生，做宣传大自然的使者；加强人才培养，让博物馆保持源源不断的活力；完善博物馆建设，使博物馆软硬实力紧跟时代步伐；扎根教育，筑牢我国生态文明建设的土壤；积极尝试制作文创产品，为我国文化产业创造"百花齐放，百家争鸣"的良好业态。俗话说"打铁还需自身硬""实践里头出真知"，在改革开放浪潮的引领下，在党和政府的领导下，自然类博物馆只有不断吸取过往的经验教训，才能在我国经济社会发展中发挥展示自然文化遗产、宣传生态环境保护方面的作用。

# 参考文献

［1］孟庆金.科研是自然类博物馆的核心竞争力［J］.中国博物馆，2013（4）：14–21.

［2］敬向红.利用自然博物馆资源开展青少年科普教育的思考与实践［C］//三十年科普理论研究回顾与展望：2010《全民科学素质行动计划纲要》论坛暨第十七届全国科普理论研讨会，2010.

［3］钱兆悦.文旅融合下的博物馆公众服务：新理念、新方法［J］.东南文化，2018（3）：90–94.

［4］李小英.探究重庆自然博物馆开展科普教育的新途径［J］.中国科技投资，2016（25）：341.

［5］王丽娟.博物馆人才培养存在的问题及对策［J］.河北职业教育，2017，1（4）：98–100.

［6］纪远新.博物馆数字化建设［J］.科技传播，2010（21）：15–16，9.

［7］沈业成.关于博物馆数字化转型的思考［J］.中国博物馆，2022（2）：19–24.

［8］宋奇.试论新形势下博物馆教育如何面向学校教育［J］.中国教育导刊，2007（7）：19–20.

［9］蔡黎明.场馆非正式学习中的科普教育活动：以上海自然博物馆为例［J］.科协论

坛，2018（4）：34–35.

［10］刘雅竹，顾洁燕.博物馆展览资源与学校基础课程内容相结合［J］.自然科学博物馆
　　　研究，2017（3）：23–32.

［11］刘庆昌.研究性学习的三个序列［J］.教育学术月刊，2008（5）：9–12.

［12］熊雯.博物馆文创产品开发的几点思考［J］.科学咨询（科技·管理），2016
　　　（32）：73–74.

# 博物馆夜间自然科普研学初探索

## ——以蛙类为例

廖晓雯，莫运明

广西自然博物馆，南宁 530012，中国

【摘要】近年来，国家出台了一系列的政策，让博物馆成为社会教育的重要力量，以自然科学为主题的研学实践活动越来越受到重视。随着研学实践活动的兴起，探索夜间经济创新模式的自然科普研学活动，开发主题鲜明、内容丰富，具有知识性、趣味性和可玩性的研学线路，成为时下博物馆践行生态文明建设的迫切需求。因此，打造具有地方特色、满足不同年龄段和不同消费阶层的夜间自然科普研学活动，具有十分重要的意义。

【关键词】自然科普；研学旅游；夜间经济

## 1　夜间研学活动主题的选择

我国从 21 世纪开始对夜间旅游进行研究。随着社会经济发展和博物馆行业的进步，夜间开放作为博物馆公共文化服务新模式，能够通过其社会影响力，积极融入城市的晚间休闲和消费体系之中（常莉，2022）。因此，利用自然类博物馆的科普教育职能和地方自然资源优势，打造具有地方特色、能够满足不同年龄段和不同消费阶层需求的夜间自然科普研学活动，具有十分重要的意义。

近年来，广西自然博物馆依托现有的标本馆藏和研究成果，将两栖动物作为科普教育项目研发的重要内容之一，在两栖动物科普教育方面开展了从知识普及到互动体验的系列科普活动，为今后持续开展两栖动物自然科普和夜间研学活动积累了丰富的

活动组织策划经验。

两栖动物分布广泛、种类繁多，在生态系统中扮演着重要角色，也是研究生物进化和生态学的重要对象。蛙类作为两栖动物中的一大类群，是十分常见的动物之一。大部分蛙类的体色使它们能很好地隐藏在自然环境中。它们大多昼伏夜出，在黄昏至黎明时活动。因此，蛙类可以作为夜间自然科普活动的观察对象。和其他许多动物一样，随着城市的发展，蛙类越来越少被人们见到，然而人与自然的联系从未断开。广西自然条件优越，为蛙类的栖息繁殖提供了良好的环境，通过自然科普活动，可以让参与者重新找回人与自然的联系。

## 2　户外夜间研学场地选择

广西的自然资源十分丰富，城市中的公园及城市附近的乡村和旅游景区就有十分适合开展自然探索活动的自然环境。南宁地处亚热带，夏季白天天气炎热，夜间凉爽宜人，夜间出行人的体感温度更为舒适，因此南宁居民一直都有在夜间进行休闲活动的习惯，这也为夜间旅游的发展提供了良好的基础（周志超等，2021）。

城市绿地是"向公众开放，以游憩为主要功能，兼具生态、景观、文教和应急避险等功能，有一定游憩和服务设施的绿地"（王洁宁等，2019）。城市公园绿地拥有便利的交通，是居民日常休闲的重要场所，也是城市居民最接近大自然的地方（程馨玫等，2022），因此城市公园是开展自然科普活动的最佳场所之一。2021年4—9月及2022年4—9月，笔者以南宁市绕城高速、那安快速路、庆玉快速路为边界围合的中心城区为调查范围，根据公园的规模、绿化、分布地点等情况，选取了16处城市公园及邕江两岸休闲绿地作为调查区域，对蛙类种群资源及夜间科普活动可行性进行实地调查，为开展夜间户外科普活动提供了科学依据。

### 2.1　调查时间、地点及方法

调查时间一般选择在天黑之后，沿预先选取的样线行走，记录沿线观察到的蛙类种类及其个体数量，并填写相关信息。

调查地点包括广西药用植物园、五象岭森林公园、那考河湿地公园、人民公园、南湖公园、金花茶公园、石门森林公园、狮山公园、新秀公园、凤岭儿童公园、花卉公园、相思湖公园、五象湖公园、邕江南岸（江南区江滨休闲公园段及良庆区南宁市博物馆段）和邕江北岸（民生广场段）。

### 2.2　南宁城市公园蛙类调查结果

在南宁市 16 处城市公园的调查中记录到蛙类 13 种（表 1），属于国家二级保护野生动物的有虎纹蛙 1 种，属于广西重点保护野生动物的有黑眶蟾蜍、沼蛙、泽陆蛙和斑腿泛树蛙和花姬蛙 5 种，保护物种占记录种类的 46.2%。广西药用植物园记录到的蛙类物种最多，共 11 种；花卉公园记录到的蛙类物种最少，仅 2 种。分布最广的蛙类为黑眶蟾蜍，在 16 个调查点均有记录；而棘胸蛙和花细狭口蛙仅在广西药用植物园观测到，背条螳臂树蛙仅在五象岭森林公园观测到。

表 1　南宁城市公园蛙类物种统计

| 地点 | 物种名称 | | | | | | | | | | | | | 蛙类种类合计/种 |
| --- | --- | --- | --- | --- | --- | --- | --- | --- | --- | --- | --- | --- | --- | --- |
| | 黑眶蟾蜍 | 沼蛙 | 泽陆蛙 | 虎纹蛙 | 棘胸蛙 | 背条螳臂树蛙 | 斑腿泛树蛙 | 粗皮姬蛙 | 小弧斑姬蛙 | 饰纹姬蛙 | 花姬蛙 | 花狭口蛙 | 花细狭口蛙 | |
| 广西药用植物园 | +++ | ++ | ++ | + | + | | +++ | ++ | ++ | +++ | + | | ++ | 11 |
| 五象岭森林公园 | + | + | + | | | ++ | ++ | + | + | + | + | | | 9 |
| 那考河湿地公园 | ++ | +++ | + | | | | | | + | ++ | | | | 5 |
| 五象湖公园 | ++ | | + | | | | + | | | | | | | 3 |
| 狮山公园 | +++ | + | + | + | | | + | | | + | | ++ | | 7 |
| 花卉公园 | +++ | | | | | | | | | + | | | | 2 |
| 金花茶公园 | +++ | + | + | | | | ++ | | | | | | | 4 |
| 相思湖公园 | + | | | | | | + | | | + | | + | | 4 |
| 新秀公园 | + | + | | | | | + | | | | | | | 3 |
| 凤岭儿童公园 | ++ | + | | | | | + | | | + | | | | 4 |
| 石门森林公园 | +++ | | | | | | ++ | | | + | | | | 3 |
| 南湖公园 | + | + | | | | | + | | | + | | + | | 5 |
| 人民公园 | +++ | + | + | | | | ++ | | | + | | | | 5 |
| 邕江南岸（南宁市博物馆段） | +++ | | + | | | | | | | ++ | | | | 3 |
| 邕江南岸（江滨休闲公园段） | + | | ++ | | | | + | | | | | | | 3 |
| 邕江北岸（民生广场段） | + | | + | | | | + | | | | | | | 3 |
| 公园合计/个 | 16 | 9 | 10 | 2 | 1 | 1 | 13 | 2 | 3 | 11 | 2 | 3 | 1 | |

注：遇见频次 1～5：+；6～15：++；＞15：+++。

以 2021 年开展南宁城市公园蛙类调查的资料为基础，2022 年 4—9 月对 16 个调查点进行补充调查，选取 6 月集中样线调查的记录数据进行统计，得到南宁城市公园蛙类的物种优势度（$P_i$：物种只次 / 总只次）组成。由表 2 可知，在南宁城市公园中蛙类物种优势度最高的为黑眶蟾蜍（0.532138），次之为斑腿泛树蛙（0.152466）、饰纹姬蛙（0.106129）和沼蛙（0.068759），说明这 4 种蛙类对城市环境的适应性较好，在南宁城市公园中分布较广，种群数量较多。此外，虎纹蛙、棘胸蛙、花姬蛙和花狭口蛙的物种优势度不到 0.0100，说明这 4 种蛙类在南宁城市公园的种群数量较少。从蛙类物种优势度可知，黑眶蟾蜍、斑腿泛树蛙、饰纹姬蛙和沼蛙在南宁城市公园中分布广泛，易于观察，是南宁城市公园中较为常见的蛙类物种，可作为开展蛙类的形态特征、生活习性和繁殖生态等自然科普观测的优先选择对象。

表 2　南宁城市公园蛙类物种优势度

| 序号 | 物种名 | 数量 / 只次 | 物种优势度 $P_i$ |
| --- | --- | --- | --- |
| 1 | 黑眶蟾蜍 | 356 | 0.532138 |
| 2 | 斑腿泛树蛙 | 102 | 0.152466 |
| 3 | 饰纹姬蛙 | 71 | 0.106129 |
| 4 | 沼蛙 | 46 | 0.068759 |
| 5 | 泽陆蛙 | 37 | 0.055306 |
| 6 | 小弧斑姬蛙 | 17 | 0.025411 |
| 7 | 花细狭口蛙 | 12 | 0.017937 |
| 8 | 粗皮姬蛙 | 9 | 0.013453 |
| 9 | 背条螳臂树蛙 | 7 | 0.010463 |
| 10 | 花狭口蛙 | 6 | 0.008969 |
| 11 | 花姬蛙 | 3 | 0.004484 |
| 12 | 虎纹蛙 | 2 | 0.00299 |
| 13 | 棘胸蛙 | 1 | 0.001495 |

使用 IBM SPSS Statistics 19 软件系统聚类分析法对调查数据进行聚类分析，以蛙类物种数量为变量对城市公园进行分类。根据计算绘制得到的聚类结果树状图（图 1）可将南宁城市公园分为四类。第一类为石门森林公园，在此次调查中石门森林公园的黑眶蟾蜍物种数量明显高于其他城市公园的。该公园免费开放，位于交通十分便利的市区，绿地率达到 87.19%，园内有保存完好的原始次生林和丰富的水资源，适于开展

夜间休闲科普活动。第二类为广西药用植物园，在此次调查中在该公园记录到最丰富的蛙类物种数量。该公园是亚太地区规模最大、种植药用植物最多的专业性药用植物园。广西药用植物园共收集、保存活体药用植物 5600 多种，其中珍稀濒危药用植物100 多种，园内植被类型丰富，适于不同种类的蛙类生活繁殖。第三类为邕江南岸（南宁市博物馆段），相比其他公园，邕江沿岸城市绿地的开放性和共享性可以让居民更贴近自然。沿江公园绿地地势平坦，易于观察两栖动物的活动情况，为开展观察和实践操作类科普研学活动提供了便利的环境条件。第四类为其他 13 处城市公园。依据聚类分析结果，可综合这四类公园的特点制订不同的科普研学活动课程。

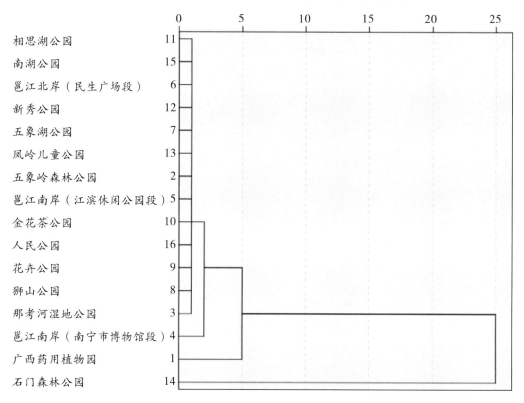

图 1　南宁城市公园 Ward 联结聚类结果树状图

## 3　夜间研学活动内容设计

随着博物馆免费开放政策的落实和"文旅融合"战略的实施，博物馆成为社会教育的重要力量。2021 年 5 月，中央宣传部等 9 个部门联合印发《关于推进博物馆改革发展的指导意见》，要求丰富博物馆教育课程体系，为大中小学生利用博物馆学习提供有力支撑，发挥博物馆作为公众教育场所的重要作用。2021 年，广西自然博物馆成为南宁市首批中小学生研学实践教育基地，以自然科学为主题的研学实践活动越来越受到重视。

2019 年以来，广西自然博物馆与南宁市的多所小学合作开展了多门科普教育进校园活动，科普课程"蛙蛙世界的奥秘"和各类两栖动物标本走进课堂。广西自然博物馆"小小博物学家"科普课堂开设了两栖动物科普课程：2021 年开设了"蛙崇拜与壮族文化"科普课程；2022 年暑假开设了"蛙鸣初识"科普课程。科普课程内容丰富，在广大小学生中引起了强烈反响，他们对自然科学表现出极大的好奇心和探索精神。此外，2021 年，广西自然博物馆成功举办了以两栖动物为主题的"热爱自然，发现城市生态之美""绿城蛙鸣"摄影比赛。比赛活动得到了许多动物摄影爱好者的积极参与和踊跃投稿，作品内容包括蛙类的捕食、鸣唱、繁衍、休息等生活瞬间，收到投稿 60 余份，网络投票共计 17304 票，社会反响热烈。

对参与过科普活动的观众的调查结果显示，71% 的观众期望参与户外研学活动，并期待博物馆能够结合科普课堂增加科普研学活动的频次和类型。在科普活动开展的方式上，大多数观众期望家长和孩子能够共同参与，活动不仅需要满足青少年儿童的科普教育需求，还需要满足家长群体提高自身科学知识水平的需求。基于城市公园调查结果和观众反馈，结合两栖动物科普课程教学及活动的内容，笔者从自然科普教育视角进行夜间科普研学课程设计（表 3），以期为今后开展夜间研学活动提供借鉴和参考。

表 3   城市公园夜间自然科普两栖动物研学内容设计

| 研学主题 | 主要内容 | 活动地点 |
|---|---|---|
| 主题一：丰富的外形特征 | 了解蛙类两个分类（蛙和蟾蜍）的不同外貌特点，如体形大小、皮肤颜色、头和四肢特征等，以及生物学上的动物分类方式。在专业人员指导下，在活动地点寻找蛙类，比较不同种类的形态特征，并以文字、图画、照片或视频等方式描述观察对象的外貌特征和不同种类的鉴别特点 | 广西药用植物园等 |
| 主题二：有趣的生活习性 | 了解蛙类，包括栖息环境、捕食方式、鸣叫特点、运动方式等，在活动地点由专业人员带领观察蛙类的生活习性，并以文字、图画、照片或视频等方式记录观察结果和研学体会 | 广西药用植物园、石门森林公园等 |
| 主题三：独特的繁殖方式 | 通过听专业讲解了解蛙类的繁殖方式，如求偶行为、抱对产卵、蝌蚪形态、变态发育的过程等，并在专业人员指导下开展分组观察，在活动地点寻找正在繁殖的蛙类，以文字、图画、照片或视频等方式记录并描述观察结果和研学体会 | 广西药用植物园、石门森林公园等 |

续表

| 研学主题 | 主要内容 | 活动地点 |
| --- | --- | --- |
| 主题四：动物生态摄影体验 | 认真听专业人员讲解，学习动物生态摄影的方法；个人或分组进行动手操作，在公园绿地寻找观察对象并进行拍摄体验 | 各城市公园、绿地 |

## 4　讨论

### 4.1　以蛙类作为夜间研学活动主题，受到季节限制

南宁市地处华南地区广西南部偏西，坐落在以邕江河谷为中心的长纺锤形盆地中，属亚热带季风气候地区，四季常青，夏长冬短。夏季炎热多雨，冬季霜少稍干，春秋两季气候温和。南宁市温暖潮湿的气候、丰富多样的植被生境，为蛙类的栖息繁衍提供了得天独厚的生活环境，同时也为开展以两栖动物为主题的科普研学活动提供了适宜的气候条件。

蛙类属于变温动物，它们自身没有调节体温的机制，体温随环境温度的变化而变化，对环境的依赖性大，因此形成了它们独特的生活方式。大多数蛙类在春夏两季活动更加活跃，繁殖期一般在 3—7 月；当秋季到来气温逐渐降低时，蛙类会藏到比外界温度高的地方（如地下、水下、洞穴等）开始冬眠，其间它们会停止大部分的活动。因此，以两栖动物为主题的科普研学活动更适合在春夏两季开展。

### 4.2　城市公园能够满足开展活动的必要条件

近年来，城市生态环境越来越受到重视，南宁市不断提高城市绿地质量。截至 2018 年底，南宁市建成区（不含武鸣区）绿地总面积 11300 公顷，公园绿地面积 4165.59 公顷，建成区（不含武鸣区）绿地率 37.93%、绿化覆盖率 43.78%（南宁市地方志编纂委员会，2019）。随着城市公园数量的增长和环境质量的提高，南宁城市公园已能够满足居民近距离参与户外研学活动的需求。

作为以开展自然观察和实践操作为主要形式的科普研学活动场所，城市公园与其他城市公共活动场所相比，具有更丰富的自然资源。在专业人员指导下参与者对自然

生物的直接观察与接触，可以激发参与者探索自然、学习自然科学知识的兴趣。而实践操作活动能够使参与者在观察和接触自然生物之后进一步感受自然，学习与动植物接触的安全距离和正确的相处方式，提高环境保护意识和对自然科学知识的理解，以减少对动植物和自然环境的影响。

随着人们对户外娱乐空间安全性的要求越来越高（杨梅等，2018），相较于其他类型的公园（如湿地公园、森林公园等），城市公园内的各类基础设施更为丰富，其管理服务、设施维护服务更为完善，安全性也得到很好的保障；其拥有更加便利的交通，与城市居民的日常生活联系更为密切（程馨玫等，2022）。因此，在自然环境中开展科普研学活动，距离最近、最安全、最适合的场所就是城市公园。

## 4.3 自然科普研学活动可以提高参与者的环境保护意识

利用夜间闲暇时间参加自然科普研学活动，参与者可以放松身心亲近自然，在亲自参与观察和动手中了解自然，逐步认识一些不同于日间的自然现象和生物类群，在游玩中增长知识，在实践中提高动手能力。同时，自然类博物馆各类科普课程及研学活动的开展，可以使参与者树立生态文明理念，增强全民节约意识、环保意识、生态意识，培养生态道德和行为习惯，加快形成绿色生活方式，让"天蓝地绿水清"深入人心，把建设美丽中国转化为全体人民的自觉行动。

党的二十大报告指出，中国式现代化是人与自然和谐共生的现代化。促进人与自然和谐共生，要强化生态文明体制建设，生态文明是以可持续发展为特征建立起人与自然、人与社会的良性运行和协调发展关系。随着研学实践活动的兴起，探索夜间经济创新模式的自然科普研学活动，开发主题鲜明、内容丰富，具有知识性、趣味性和可玩性的研学线路，成为时下博物馆践行生态文明建设的迫切需求。

## 4.4 自然科普研学活动能够充分发挥博物馆开展城市形象宣传的职能

2007 年，国际博物馆协会维也纳会议将博物馆定义为"一个为社会及发展服务的、非营利的常设机构，向公众开放，为教育、研究和欣赏之目的征集、保护、研究、传播、展示人类及人类环境的有形遗产和无形遗产"（陈建明，2012）。自然类博物馆作为自然科普教育资源的拥有者，应积极承担起社会宣传教育职能，通过科普研学活动展示城市风貌和生态文明建设成果，增强人们的城市认同感和自豪感，促进文化传播交流，提高城市影响力。

南宁古称"邕城"，简称"邕"，素有"绿城"的美誉，先后获评全国首批"国家生态园林城市"、全国首批海绵城市建设试点城市。绿城南宁自然风光秀美，保护物种资源丰富，处处呈现出人与自然和谐共处的生态之美。根据资料统计，南宁市有无尾目两栖动物27种（莫运明等，2014）。在城市公园调查中记录到蛙类13种，包括国家二级重点保护野生动物和广西重点保护野生动物。随着城市生态文明建设工作的积极开展，保护成果逐渐显现，一些常见于森林溪沟的两栖动物（如棘胸蛙等）也现身城市公园之中。通过科普研学活动宣传南宁市绿色发展理念，展示南宁城市生态建设成就，具有重要意义。

# 参考文献

［1］常莉.博物馆夜间开放研究与思考［J］.博物馆管理，2022（2）：83–94.

［2］周志超，吴欢欢，黎芷宏.南宁市发展夜间经济对策研究［J］.中共南宁市委党校学报，2021，23（3）：55–60.

［3］王洁宁，王浩.新版《城市绿地分类标准》探析［J］.中国园林，2019，35（4）：92–95.

［4］程馨玫，郭超.城市公园绿地自然教育内容与形式初探［J］.现代园艺，2022，45（15）：159–161，164.

［5］南宁市地方志编纂委员会.南宁年鉴2019［M］.北京：方志出版社，2019.

［6］杨梅，杨远东，古新仁.公园绿地中的不安全行为调查［J］.安徽农业科学，2018，46（31）：101–103.

［7］陈建明.从博物馆的定位看其类型研究与实践［J］.中国国家博物馆馆刊，2012（8）：35–36.

［8］莫运明，韦振逸，陈伟才.广西两栖动物彩色图鉴［M］.南宁：广西科学技术出版社，2014.

# 现生动植物标本藏品种类及利用现状分析

## ——以广西自然博物馆为例

黄忠

广西自然博物馆，南宁　530012，中国

【摘要】自然类博物馆要让大量沉睡在库房中的标本藏品"活起来"，就要发挥自身标本藏品的优势，充分挖掘标本藏品背后的自然科学知识，满足大众特别是中小学生的文化需求。广西自然博物馆现有各种标本 5 万多件，现生动植物标本 12874 件，标本类别涵盖了动物界和植物界主要的类群，其中植物藏品以腊叶标本为主，而动物藏品包括包埋标本、剥制标本、骨骼标本、浸制标本、干制标本等类型。据统计，现生动植物标本藏品综合利用率为 17.40%，其中，用于研究直接产生科研成果的占 4.40%，用于展览的占 11.60%，用于开展科普教育的占 1.30%。广西自然博物馆馆藏现生动植物标本藏品数量丰富，标本类群和类型较齐全，但标本藏品利用率不高。因此，应加强完善标本收藏设施，有针对性地征集精品标本，并充分发掘精品标本的全方位价值，逐步提高标本藏品在场景的利用率。

【关键词】现生动植物标本；藏品；种类；利用

## 0　引言

自党的十八大以来，习近平总书记对保护我国的文化遗产，弘扬传统文化作出了系列重要指示，进一步强调"要系统梳理传统文化资源，让收藏在禁宫里的文物、陈列在广阔大地上的遗产、书写在古籍里的文字都活起来"，这成为文博领域工作新的风向标。在国家持续推进博物馆改革、大力倡导中小学教育研学旅行活动的新时代背景下，深入挖掘博物馆藏品背后的文化内涵和科学知识，提高藏品的利用价值，对广大

博物馆而言意义重大。要让大量沉睡在库房中的藏品"活起来"，就要充分发挥藏品自身的优势，将藏品最大限度地转化成可为社会公众特别是中小学生共享的公共文化成果，满足人们对美好生活的追求。

自然类标本是认识和研究自然的宝贵科学资料，是自然类博物馆发挥社会功能和开展业务活动的物质基础和保障。自然类标本中以生物标本最具代表性，它们是自然界各种生物最真实、最直接的表现形式和实物记录，为科学研究提供多种多样的材料，向社会大众展示千姿百态的生命。自然类博物馆以大量的标本藏品为依托，开展形式多样的陈列展览、学术研究、科普教育活动，开发令人耳目一新的文创产品、数字产品，充分调动公众的积极性和求知欲，向大众特别是中小学生传播自然学科知识。

广西自然博物馆是一座集地质标本、古生物标本、动物标本、植物标本等收藏、研究、展示于一体的综合性自然历史博物馆，现有各种标本 5 万多件，包括古生物化石标本、有色金属矿物标本和珍稀动植物标本，其中现生动植物标本 12874 件。现生动植物标本作为生物科学知识的载体，连接起生物知识沟通和传播的桥梁，肩负起让博物馆藏品"活起来"的重任。本文以广西自然博物馆现生动植物标本为研究对象，对其种类和利用情况进行调查，为进一步挖掘现生动植物标本藏品价值提供参考依据。

# 1 方法

通过录入藏品数据库中的总账数据，以及对临时标本室及展厅中经过分类鉴定的标本进行统计，确定动植物藏品的总数量。通过查阅国内外网站及其他文献数据库，收集利用广西自然博物馆馆藏动植物标本发表的研究论文资料，统计用于研究并直接产生科研成果的藏品数量；通过查阅用于陈列展览和科普教育的藏品的出入库档案资料，统计用于陈列展览和科普教育的藏品数量。最后，应用 Excel 对藏品及利用信息进行统计分析。

## 2 结果

### 2.1 馆藏藏品

#### 2.1.1 藏品类别

截至 2022 年 10 月 31 日，广西自然博物馆馆藏现生动植物标本共有 12874 件，其中植物类标本 6499 件，动物类标本 6375 件（表 1）。在植物类标本中，以被子植物标本为主，共 5826 件，占动植物标本总数的 45.25%；裸子植物标本、蕨类植物标本、苔藓植物标本、地衣植物标本共有 673 件，仅占动植物标本总数的 5.23%。动物类标本包括哺乳动物、鸟类、爬行动物、两栖动物和无脊椎动物等类别标本，以两栖动物标本、无脊椎动物标本数量较多，分别占动植物标本总数的 16.61%、11.92%。

表 1　现生动植物标本藏品统计情况

| 主要类群 | | 数量 / 件 | 占比 |
|---|---|---|---|
| 现生植物标本 | 被子植物 | 5826 | 45.25% |
| | 裸子植物 | 203 | 1.58% |
| | 蕨类植物 | 458 | 3.56% |
| | 苔藓植物 | 10 | 0.08% |
| | 地衣植物 | 2 | 0.02% |
| | 小计 | 6499 | 50.48% |
| 现生动物标本 | 哺乳动物 | 333 | 2.59% |
| | 鸟类 | 565 | 4.39% |
| | 鱼类 | 1129 | 8.77% |
| | 爬行动物 | 676 | 5.25% |
| | 两栖动物 | 2138 | 16.61% |
| | 无脊椎动物 | 1534 | 11.92% |
| | 小计 | 6375 | 49.52% |
| 合计 | | 12874 | 100% |

#### 2.1.2 藏品类型

动植物标本藏品以各种标本形式得以保存，其中植物标本藏品以腊叶标本收藏为主，而动物标本藏品包括包埋标本、剥制标本、骨骼标本、浸制标本、干制标本、毛皮标本等类型。包埋标本主要是一些昆虫类小型标本；剥制标本通常也称为生态标本，是中大型兽类标本、鸟类标本、爬行动物标本和大型鱼类标本的主要保存方式；骨骼标本以兽类标本、鸟类标本、爬行动物标本为主；浸制标本是两栖动物标本和小型鱼类标本的主要保存方式；干制标本主要是蝴蝶等其他昆虫类标本，或仅供研究使用的鸟类标本的主要保存方式；毛皮标本是经过鞣制的兽类皮张标本。各类型标本数量及占比详见表 2。

表 2　不同类型标本藏品统计情况

| 主要类群 | 标本类型 | 数量 / 件 | 占比 |
|---|---|---|---|
| 现生植物标本 | 腊叶标本 | 6455 | 50.14% |
| | 包埋标本 | 16 | 0.12% |
| | 干制标本 | 28 | 0.22% |
| | 小计 | 6499 | 50.48% |
| 现生动物标本 | 包埋标本 | 207 | 1.61% |
| | 剥制标本 | 890 | 6.91% |
| | 骨骼标本 | 7 | 0.05% |
| | 浸制标本 | 3926 | 30.50% |
| | 干制标本 | 1341 | 10.42% |
| | 毛皮标本 | 4 | 0.03% |
| | 小计 | 6375 | 49.52% |
| 合计 | | 12874 | 100% |

### 2.1.3　来源与产地

馆藏标本主要通过采集、征集、捐赠、调拨及移交方式取得。其中，通过采集取得的标本数量占总标本数的 72.45%，主要为分布于广西各地区的植物、两栖动物、爬行动物、鱼类和鸟类，采集年份主要在 1986—1992 年、2001—2005 年、2008—2009 年和 2013—2016 年；通过征集取得的标本数量占总标本数的 26.61%，主要为分布于广西各地、海南及东部沿海地区的植物、鸟类、兽类、昆虫及贝类，征集年份主要在 1980—1982 年和 2013—2016 年；通过捐赠取得的标本数量占总标本数的 0.76%，主要为分布于广西西南部、云南、四川等地的兽类、鸟类及爬行动物，捐赠年份主要在 1986—1991 年；在 20 世纪五六十年代调拨和移交的标本数量占总标本数的 0.18%，主要为分布于广西、河北、北京、福建等地的兽类、鸟类及两栖动物（表 3）。

表3　标本藏品来源与产地统计情况

| 来源方式 | 数量/件 | 主要年份 | 主要产地 | 标本类型 | 占比 |
|---|---|---|---|---|---|
| 采集 | 9327 | 1964、1973、1986—1992、1998、2001—2005、2008—2009、2013—2016 | 广西 | 浸制标本<br>腊叶标本<br>毛皮标本<br>干制标本 | 72.45% |
| 征集 | 3426 | 1980—1982、1997、2009、2013—2016 | 广西南宁、北海、桂林、河池、百色、崇左、防城港，广东、海南、上海、江苏、福建，以及越南北部及非洲等地 | 剥制标本<br>包埋标本<br>骨骼标本<br>腊叶标本<br>干制标本 | 26.61% |
| 捐赠 | 98 | 1986—1991 | 广西南宁、北海、百色、崇左、防城港，湖北、四川、云南，以及越南等地 | 浸制标本<br>剥制标本 | 0.76% |
| 调拨 | 16 | 1950、1957、1968 | 广西龙胜、河北、福建福州等地 | 剥制标本 | 0.12% |
| 移交 | 7 | 1951 | 北京、河北 | 剥制标本 | 0.06% |
| 合计 | 12874 | | | | 100% |

## 2.2　藏品利用情况

### 2.2.1　研究利用

广西自然博物馆持续开展现生动植物学术研究，利用现有馆藏动植物标本发表论文33篇（表4），涉及两栖动物标本、爬行动物标本及被子植物标本567件，标本利用率为4.40%。其中，国外期刊论文17篇，涉及标本145件，占比1.13%；国内期刊论文16篇，涉及标本422件，占比3.27%。研究团队依靠自身科研优势及博物馆丰富的馆藏标本，先后发表了老山树蛙、广西拟髭蟾等17种蛙类新种和近30种两栖爬行动物新记录种（表5），这些新种的正模标本、副模标本和新记录种的分布标本均作为藏品收藏在馆中。

表4　现生动植物标本藏品在论文发表中的利用情况

| 期刊类别 | 发表论文数量/篇 | 涉及生物类群 | 数量/件 | 标本利用率 |
|---|---|---|---|---|
| SCI | 13 | 两栖动物 | 107 | 0.83% |
| 国外重点期刊 | 4 | 两栖动物 | 38 | 0.30% |
| 国内核心期刊 | 4 | 两栖动物、爬行动物 | 88 | 0.68% |
| 国内重点期刊 | 4 | 两栖动物 | 42 | 0.33% |
| 馆刊 | 8 | 两栖动物、被子植物 | 292 | 2.26% |
| 合计 | 33 | | 567 | 4.40% |

表5　利用现生动植物标本藏品发表新种、新记录种情况

| 新物种 | 新记录种 |
|---|---|
| 老山树蛙、广西拟髭蟾、荔浦臭蛙、十万山刘树蛙、弄岗纤树蛙、弄岗狭口蛙、上思掌突蟾、瑶琴蛙、广西琴蛙、十万大山琴蛙、十万大山掌突蟾、十万大山浮蛙、金秀肥螈、平龙树蛙、金秀刘树蛙、瑶山角蟾、田林纤树蛙等17种 | 三岛掌突蟾、茅索水蛙、隐耳蜓蜥、粗皮角蟾、黑带水蛙、罗默小树蛙、滇南臭蛙、八线游蛇等近30种 |

同时，广西自然博物馆基于近30年的调查研究成果及大量馆藏标本，出版了《广西两栖动物彩色图鉴》和《自然广西》两部专业性与科普性相结合的著作。其中，《广西两栖动物彩色图鉴》以两栖动物标本为基础，系统介绍了广西两栖动物的种群分布状况，具有较强的科学性、知识性、实用性，为我国两栖动物研究提供了重要的基础资料；《自然广西》收录了众多古生物化石、矿物及现生珍稀动植物特色标本，用于反映广西漫长的陆地历史、自然地理和生物资源。

### 2.2.2　展览利用

广西自然博物馆充分发挥作为全国青少年科普教育基地的优势和功能，采取立足本馆基本陈列并主动"走出去"的发展战略。目前，馆内陈列有基本展览2个，分别为"珍稀动物展"与"地球和生物历史展"；专题展览4个，分别为"生命之美——走进斑斓的蝴蝶世界展""自然广西""一树花开——中国传统树木文化展""北部湾贝类与贝文化展"。

基本陈列展览利用各种珍禽猛兽、大型鲸鱼、深海鱼类、鸟类等珍稀、濒危物种类别标本共491件，展示北部湾地区丰富的陆地与海洋动物资源，增强广大观众保护环境、爱护北部湾的意识（表6）。

专题展览用于参加其他自然博物馆、政府、协会组织的有关展览展示活动，共使用馆藏标本1008件，标本利用率为7.83%，包括蝶类、贝类、两栖类、鸟类、哺乳类及植物等类别标本（表7）。

表6　珍稀动物展利用标本类群情况

| 类群 | 标本类型 | 数量/件 | 标本利用率 | 备注 |
|---|---|---|---|---|
| 鸟类 | 剥制标本 | 86 | 0.67% | |
| 兽类 | 剥制标本 | 38 | 0.30% | |
| 鲸鲨豚 | 剥制标本、骨骼标本 | 12 | 0.09% | 骨骼标本1件 |
| 鱼类 | 剥制标本、浸制标本 | 27 | 0.21% | |

**续表**

| 类群 | 标本类型 | 数量／件 | 标本利用率 | 备注 |
|---|---|---|---|---|
| 爬行动物 | 剥制标本 | 6 | 0.05% | |
| 贝类 | 干制标本 | 168 | 1.30% | |
| 海螺 | 干制标本 | 122 | 0.95% | |
| 珊瑚 | 干制标本 | 32 | 0.25% | |
| 合计 | | 491 | 3.81% | |

表 7  专题展览利用标本藏品情况

| 专题展览 | 类群 | 标本类型 | 数量／件 | 标本利用率 |
|---|---|---|---|---|
| 生命之美——走进斑斓的蝴蝶世界展 | 蝶类 | 干制标本 | 88 | 0.68% |
| 北部湾贝类与贝文化展 | 贝类 | 干制标本 | 650 | 5.05% |
| 自然广西 | 贝类、两栖动物、哺乳类、鸟类、植物 | 剥制标本 干制标本 腊叶标本 | 60 | 0.47% |
| 一树花开——中国传统树木文化展 | 植物 | 腊叶标本 | 210 | 1.63% |
| 合计 | | | 1008 | 7.83% |

### 2.2.3  科普教育方面

广西自然博物馆面向社会特别是中小学生开展形式多样的科普教育活动，主要有科普进校园、进社区、进山区，研学旅行，寒暑假"小小博物学家"科普授课等。然而，目前博物馆可用于这些活动的现生动植物标本仅有 173 件，包括鸟类、哺乳动物、植物等 7 个常见生物类群，标本利用率为 1.34%。这种低利用率主要是由自然标本易损坏、易发霉、不好储存等不利因素所致。因此，在科普活动中能利用的标本数量较少、类型单一，在一定程度上影响了馆藏标本在科普方面的利用效果（表 8）。

表 8  现生动植物标本藏品在科普教育方面的利用情况

| 类群 | 标本类型 | 数量／件 | 标本利用率 |
|---|---|---|---|
| 鸟类 | 包埋标本 | 2 | 0.02% |
| 哺乳动物 | 包埋标本 | 5 | 0.04% |
| 鱼类 | 包埋标本 | 2 | 0.04% |
| 两栖动物 | 包埋标本 | 13 | 0.10% |
| 昆虫 | 包埋标本 | 128 | 1.00% |
| 贝螺类 | 包埋标本 | 7 | 0.05% |
| 植物 | 包埋标本 | 16 | 0.12% |
| 合计 | | 173 | 1.34% |

## 3　讨论及建议

广西自然博物馆馆藏现生动植物标本丰富，标本类群和类型较齐全，既具有生物从低级向高级发展进程中代表重要类群的标本，又有从浸制到干制的满足多样化需求的生物标本类型。该馆通过各种类群和类型的标本藏品向民众传播自然科学和生命演化知识，深入挖掘标本藏品背后的展示价值、科普价值及文创价值，架设起公众与自然科学的桥梁。然而，调查发现，广西自然博物馆缺少能展示某个物种生活史各阶段或生态习性的标本组合，同一类群的标本数量参差不齐，缺少多个标本类型。这些问题使得标本在不同场景和展览中的持续使用受到限制。许多馆藏的浸制标本和腊叶标本亟待进行更深层次的研究和探索，以充分展现其突出的生态要素或特性，从而提高标本的利用效率。

针对自然类博物馆标本藏品利用率不高的问题，为更好地利用标本藏品，首先应加强标本的收藏和保护，完善库房基础设施，做好藏品的科学分类和预防性保护。其次，应根据馆藏标本的利用情况，有针对性地征集精品标本。最后，充分发掘精品标本在研究、科普和展览中的一体化、全方位价值，利用互联网及数字化技术，通过线上和线下、馆内和馆外的互联共享途径，提升标本在各种场景的利用效率。

## 参考文献

［1］焦丽丹.如何让馆藏文物"活起来"［J］.中国博物馆，2015，33（3）：30–34.

［2］李宏龙.新时代下自然博物馆藏品的日常管理和统计分析工作［J］.博物馆研究，2019（1）：56–62.

［3］王宏均.中国博物馆学基础［M］.上海：上海古籍出版社，2001.

［4］楼锡祜.中国的自然博物馆［J］.科普研究，2009（2）：61–67.

［5］蔡敏.浅析博物馆文物藏品保护与利用策略［J］.科学大众（科学教育），2019（8）：191.

［6］雷鸣霞.自然类博物馆藏品使用的新思路探索［J］.博物馆研究，2016（2）：119–123.

［7］魏巍.我国博物馆文物藏品利用研究［D］.山东大学，2015.

［8］张思桐. 提升历史类博物馆文物藏品利用率的途径探析［J］. 自然与文化遗产研究，2019，4（8）：96-99.

［9］祁林林. 浅谈"互联网+"对馆藏文物保护与利用的认识［J］. 文物世界，2017（6）：54-55.

［10］吴幻波. 可移动文物普查：从数据管理到共享知识社区［J］. 博物馆研究，2016（4）：69-71.

# 广西靖西寒武纪晚期果乐生物群化石整理报告

胡敏航

广西自然博物馆，南宁　530012，中国

【摘要】果乐生物群是广西靖西市果乐乡寒武纪晚期地层中保存精美的无脊椎动物化石群。本文对采集于靖西市果乐乡的 573 件果乐生物群化石标本进行整理、鉴定和统计后发现，这些化石中的三叶虫化石标本数量处于绝对优势地位，占比达 78%，腕足动物和棘皮动物分别居第二位和第三位。三叶虫作为果乐生物群中的第一优势类群，共计 4 目 8 科 10 属 12 种，分异程度极高。果乐生物群中三叶虫动物的整体面貌为后续进行全球寒武纪晚期生物群对比研究提供了良好材料。

【关键词】三叶虫；果乐生物群；寒武纪晚期；靖西；广西

## 0　引言

三叶虫是寒武纪生物群中非常重要的生物类群，是一类已经灭绝的海生无脊椎动物，属于节肢动物门。而节肢动物门是所有现生动物种群中数量最大、种类最多且分异最突出的一类动物，从寒武纪时期出现发展延续至今，其起源是当今生物进化学的研究热点，也是生命发展起源的重要研究方向。

果乐生物群化石的发现地果乐乡位于广西边陲靖西市西北，距离靖西市区约 40 千米。1977 年，周天梅首次在《中南地区古生物图册》中描述了几个产自靖西市寒武纪芙蓉世的三叶虫（周天梅等，1977）。2000 年，韩乃仁在该地区实测了一条剖面，将其与邻区地层进行对比后，认为果乐剖面是较深水的陆棚相沉积，将该地区地层命名为果乐组。该地区地层以深灰色薄层状泥质条带灰岩为主，夹多层深灰色中厚层状白

云岩，属于上寒武统上部的地层，但并未达到寒武系顶部（韩乃仁等，2000）。此后，国内学者对该地区开展了大量的野外地质研究工作，取得了丰硕的科研成果（韩乃仁、陈桂英，2004，2008；朱学剑，2005；朱学剑等，2007；陈桂英、韩乃仁，2013，2014；熊铎等，2015）。2016 年，国内学者将这套寒武纪晚期地层中发现的丰富且保存精美的生物群化石，命名为果乐生物群（Zhu et al.，2016）。作为首个被报道的晚寒武世芙蓉统伯吉斯页岩型生物群，果乐生物群填补了伯吉斯页岩型生物群在中寒武世和早奥陶世之间的空白，对晚寒武世的古生物、古地理及古环境研究具有重要意义（Zhu et al.，2021）。

本文对采集于寒武纪晚期地层中的 573 件果乐生物群化石标本进行整理、鉴定和古生物类群统计，并详细统计了果乐生物群中三叶虫各属种的分异情况，进一步揭示了果乐生物群中三叶虫的整体面貌，为后续进行全球寒武纪晚期生物群对比研究提供了良好材料。

2016 年 5 月，广西自然博物馆的黄超林、熊铎等研究人员赴广西靖西市果乐乡开展古生物化石的野外发掘工作。本次化石标本采集点分布在果乐乡果乐街北部至西北部的山坡，地层为上寒武统下部黄色灰质泥岩和灰色泥灰岩，采集到的古生物化石标本共计 573 件，主要包含有三叶虫、腕足动物、棘皮动物等。

# 1　统计分析结果

## 1.1　古生物化石主要类群统计分析

在本次发掘的化石属种数量统计中，三叶虫化石标本数量多达 447 件，占比78.01%；腕足动物次之，占比 10.65%；棘皮动物居第三位，占比 9.42%；腔肠动物和双壳动物稀少，较为罕见（表 1）。

表 1　果乐生物群化石主要类群数量比例统计

| 化石类群 | 数量 / 件 | 占比 |
| --- | --- | --- |
| 三叶虫 | 447 | 78.01% |
| 腕足动物 | 61 | 10.65% |
| 棘皮动物 | 54 | 9.42% |

续表

| 化石类群 | 数量 / 件 | 占比 |
|---|---|---|
| 腔肠动物 | 6 | 1.05% |
| 双壳动物 | 5 | 0.87% |
| 合计 | 573 | 100% |

据研究报道，果乐乡已经发现有 8 个主要化石类型，包括节肢动物、腕足动物、棘皮动物、刺胞动物、笔石动物、软舌螺、古蠕虫类和藻类（韩乃仁等，2000；韩乃仁、陈贵英，2008；Zhan et al.，2010；Zhu et al.，2016）。其中以三叶虫为主的节肢动物，无论是数量还是属种多样化都居于首位。此外，该地区的腕足动物以 *B.guangxiensis*、*B.costata* 和 *Palaeostrophia jingxiensis* 的数量占据了绝对优势，因此该地区的腕足动物群被命名为 *Billingsella-Palaeostrophia* 群（Zhan et al.，2010）。该地区的棘皮动物也独具特色，已经正式发表的有海桩类的靖西叶果（*Phyllocystis jingxiensis*）（陈贵英、韩乃仁，2013）、始海百合类的果乐靖西始海百合（*Jingxieocrinus guoleensis*）等（陈贵英、韩乃仁，2014）。

本次发掘获得的古生物化石类群构成与前期研究果乐生物群的组成较为相似，均以三叶虫为主，且腕足动物和棘皮动物较为常见，部分果乐乡特有的属种在本批次中均有发现，如三叶虫类的大里中华索克虫（*Sinosaukia daliensis*）、无刺和温虫（*Hewenia anacantha*）（图 1），棘皮动物海桩类的靖西叶果，始海百合类的果乐靖西始海百合等，其余类群的化石则发现较少。

## 1.2 三叶虫化石主要属种统计分析

三叶虫种群数量庞大，种类繁多，根据 Treatise 中的分类方法将整个三叶虫纲细分为 10 个目，分别是球接子目（*Agnostida*）、莱得利基虫目（*Redlichiida*）、耸棒头虫目（*Corynexochida*）、裂肋虫目（*Lichida*）、栉虫目（*Asaphida*）、褶颊虫目（*Ptychopariida*）、齿肋虫目（*Odontopleurida*）、砑头虫目（*Proetida*）、镜眼虫目（*Phacopida*）、镰虫目（*Harpetida*）。

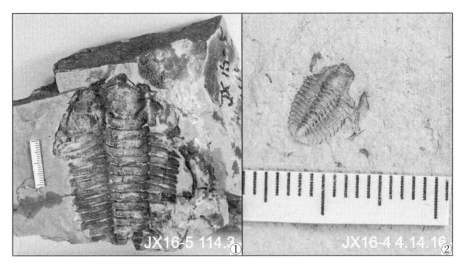

①大里中华索克虫（*Sinosaukia daliensis*）；②无刺和温虫（*Hewenia anacantha*）。

图 1　果乐乡特有三叶虫属种

　　根据统计数据，本次发掘的三叶虫化石标本共计 447 件，分属 4 目 8 科 10 属 12 种，种类繁多，分异程度较高。根据分类统计，三叶虫化石全部归属于以下 4 个目：栉虫目、耸棒头虫目、褶颊虫目、球接子目。其中，栉虫目占比高达 38.47%，耸棒头虫目、褶颊虫目占比分列第二、第三位，球接子目占比最低（表 2）。

表 2　三叶虫分类数量比例统计

| 目 | 科 | 属种 | 数量 / 件 | 占比 |
| --- | --- | --- | --- | --- |
| 栉虫目 | 索克虫科 | 大里中华索克虫 *Sinosaukia daliensis* | 23 | 5.14% |
| | | 特殊中华索克虫 *Sinosaukia distincta* | 98 | 21.92% |
| | 刺尾虫科 | 靖西塔姆德盾壳虫 *Tamdaspis jingxiensis* | 48 | 10.73% |
| | 无肩虫科 | 长形埴轮虫 *Haniwa longa* | 3 | 0.67% |
| | 小计 | | 172 | 38.47% |
| 耸棒头虫目 | 济南虫科 | 光滑谢尔高德虫 *Shergoldia laevigata* | 88 | 19.68% |
| | | 长刺小网形虫 *Dictyella longispina* | 17 | 3.80% |
| | 蒿里山虫科 | 广西后蒿里山虫 *Postikaolishania guangxiensis* | 45 | 10.06% |
| | 小计 | | 150 | 33.55% |

**续表**

| 目 | 科 | 属种 | 数量 / 件 | 占比 |
|---|---|---|---|---|
| 褶颊虫目 | 美丽饰边虫科 | 无刺和温虫<br>*Hewenia anacantha* | 101 | 22.59% |
| | | 标准和温虫<br>*Hewenia typica* | 14 | 3.13% |
| | 盾壳虫科 | 广西广西盾壳虫<br>*Guangxiaspis guangxiensis* | 3 | 0.67% |
| | 小计 | | 118 | 26.39% |
| 球接子目 | Agnostidea 科 | *Micragnostus chuishuensis* | 4 | 0.89% |
| | | *Rhaptagnostus* cf. *R clarki maximus* | 3 | 0.67% |
| | 小计 | | 7 | 1.56% |
| | 总计 | | 447 | 100% |

### 1.2.1 栉虫目

栉虫目三叶虫占比最高，达到38.47%，包含3科3属4种（图2）。其中，索克虫科为优势科，化石标本体形较大，多残缺破损。特殊中华索克虫（*Sinosaukia distincta*）为优势属种，占比高达21.92%，特征是壳面布满纹饰瘤点。大里中华索克虫（*Sinosaukia daliensis*）为果乐乡特有属种，该种壳表面无瘤点，前边缘较宽且呈较钝的三角形，使其易于和本属的其他种相区别（朱学剑，2005；朱学剑等，2011）。索克虫科分布较广，在辽宁、安徽等地均有发现，其中皖北地区寒武系芙蓉统炒米店组发现的索克虫科三叶虫，与果乐乡发现的索克虫在形态上存在一定的相似，同属于 *Prosaukia* 属（雷倩萍、彭善池，2022）。

刺尾虫科的靖西塔姆德盾壳虫（*Tamdaspis jingxiensis*）也较为常见，占比为10.73%，为果乐乡特有属种，其化石标本多有畸形残缺，研究表明其畸形是被捕食者咬伤所致（朱学剑等，2007）。属于无肩虫科的长形埴轮虫（*Haniwa longa*）较为罕见，个体较小，其标本保存较为完整。

### 1.2.2 耸棒头虫目

耸棒头虫目三叶虫占比为33.55%，包含2科3属3种（图3）。其中，济南虫科的光滑谢尔高德虫（*Shergoldia laevigata*）为优势属种，占比达19.68%，部分标本保存较完整，特征为胸节和尾部较为平滑，该属种具有山东济南发现的华北型 *Tsinania* 的相似特征。长刺小网形虫（*Dictyella longispina*）同样属于华北型 *Dictyella* 属，最早发现

①特殊中华索克虫（*Sinosaukia distincta*）；②靖西塔姆德盾壳虫（*Tamdaspis jingxiensis*）；③长形埴轮虫（*Haniwa longa*）。

图 2    果乐乡栉虫目三叶虫

于辽宁五湖嘴白家山上寒武统凤山组，但从未发现过完整的虫体（Kobayashi，1933）。果乐乡发现的长刺小网形虫完整虫体填补了这一空白，对其生物分类位置及与其他三叶虫的演化关系研究有重要意义（韩乃仁、陈贵英，2004）。

蒿里山虫科的广西后蒿里山虫（*Postikaolishania guangxiensis*）为果乐乡特有的常见属种，2005 年朱学剑建立了后蒿里山虫属 *Postikaolishania*，并以新种广西后蒿里山虫（*Postikaolishania guangxiensis*）作为模式种（朱学剑，2005），其特征是尾部长有 2 根大而长的侧刺。

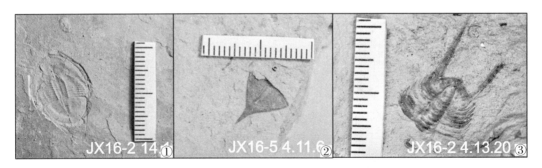

①光滑谢尔高德虫（*Shergoldia laevigata*）；②长刺小网形虫（*Dictyella longispina*）；③广西后蒿里山虫（*Postikaolishania guangxiensis*）。

图 3    果乐乡耸棒头虫目三叶虫

### 1.2.3 褶颊虫目

褶颊虫目三叶虫也较为常见，包含 2 科 3 属 3 种（图 4），尤其是美丽饰边虫科的无刺和温虫（*Hewenia anacantha*），占比高达 22.59%，为果乐乡优势属种，亦为果乐乡特有属种。和温虫属 *Hewenia* 最早由周天梅于 1977 年建立（周天梅等，1977），但往后鲜有报道，熊铎等人对陈贵英、韩乃仁等在 2009 年、2011 年采自广西靖西的无刺和温虫进行描述和统计分析，并将其与周天梅和朱学剑描述的同属标本进行了对比研究（熊铎等，2015）。标准和温虫（*Hewenia typica*）与无刺和温虫同属和温虫属，个体较小，发现的标本数量相对较少，保存相当完整。

广西广西盾壳虫（*Guangxiaspis guangxiensis*）为果乐乡发现的特有属种，但发现数量较少，本批次样品仅发现 3 块残缺虫体。

### 1.2.4 球接子目

球接子目三叶虫体形较小，只有两节胸节，其关节结构也十分独特，头部和尾部在大小和形状上都十分相似，因此较容易辨别（图 4）。本批次发现球接子目标本数量较少，仅占 1.56%，其中 *Micragnostus chuishuensis* 头部中轴明显，而 *Rhaptagnostus* cf.*R clarki maximus* 则无明显中轴。

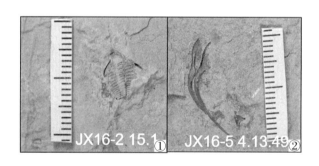

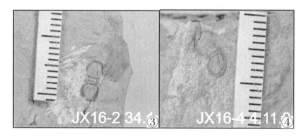

①标准和温虫（*Hewenia typica*）；②广西广西盾壳虫（*Guangxiaspis guangxiensis*）；③*Micragnostus chuishuensis*；④*Rhaptagnostus* cf. *R clarki maximus*。

图 4 果乐乡褶颊虫目和球接子目三叶虫

## 2 结语

根据上述统计分析，可以得出以下结论。一是本次发掘的果乐生物群化石以节肢动物三叶虫为优势属种，腕足动物和棘皮动物较为常见，其他类群物种发现较少。这与前期研究所展现的果乐生物群的生物类群构成较为相似。二是通过属种鉴定，447 件三叶虫化石标本被划分为 4 目 8 科 10 属 12 种，种类繁多，分异程度极高。三是经统计发现，三叶虫中的特殊中华索克虫、光滑谢尔高德虫以及无刺和温虫为优势种。四是采集的化石标本较多为残缺的虫体，尽管这在一定程度上干扰了三叶虫属种鉴定的准确性，但是仍然为进一步揭示果乐生物群中三叶虫的整体面貌，以及后续进行全球寒武纪晚期生物群对比研究提供了良好材料。

# 参考文献

[1] 湖北省地质科学研究所，等.中南地区古生物图册（一）：早古生代部分［M］.北京：地质出版社，1977.

[2] 韩乃仁，唐兰，韦仁山，等.广西靖西果乐晚寒武世地层［J］.桂林理工大学学报，2000（4）：350–355.

[3] 陈贵英，韩乃仁.广西靖西寒武纪海桩化石新材料［J］.古生物学报，2013，52（3）：288–293.

[4] 韩乃仁，陈贵英.广西寒武纪三叶虫 *Dictyella* 完整虫体的发现及其意义［J］.古生物学报，2004，43（3）：416–419.

[5] 韩乃仁，陈贵英.海桩纲化石在中国的发现：广西寒武系芙蓉统 *Phyllocystis* 一新种［J］.中国科学（D辑：地球科学），2008（1）：1–9.

[6] 朱学剑.广西寒武纪芙蓉世晚期三叶虫动物群：兼论三叶虫的畸形、性双形及眼脊的功能［D］.北京：中国科学院研究生院，2005.

[7] 朱学剑，彭善池，杜圣贤，等.广西靖西寒武纪三叶虫 *Tamdaspis jingxiensis* sp. nov. 的个体发育及畸形［J］.古生物学报，2007，46（2）：225–231.

[8] 熊铎，陈贵英，韩乃仁.广西靖西晚寒武世无刺和温虫（*Hewenia anacantha*）新材料［J］.古生物学报，2015，54（2）：240–249.

［9］ZHU XUEJIAN，PENG SHANCHI，ZAMORA S，et al. Furongian（upper Cambrian）Guole Konservat-Lagerstatte from South China［J］. 地质学报（英文版），2016，90（1）：30-37.

［10］ZHU XUEJIAN，RUDY L，JAVIER O. Furongian（Jiangshanian）occurrences of radiodonts in Poland and South China and the fossil record of the Hurdiidae［J］. PeerJ，2021，9：e11800.

［11］ZHAN RENBIN，JIN JISUO，RONG JIAYU，et al. Late Cambrian brachiopods from Jingxi，Guangxi Province，South China［J］. Alcheringa An Australasian Journal of Palaeontology，2010，34（2）：99-133.

［12］陈贵英，韩乃仁. 广西靖西寒武系芙蓉统始海百合一新属［J］. 古生物学报，2014，53（3）：290-301.

［13］朱学剑，胡有山，边荣春，等. 滇东南地区寒武纪中、晚期三叶虫研究［J］. 古生物学报，2011，50（1）：118-131.

［14］雷倩萍，彭善池. 皖北地区寒武系芙蓉统炒米店组中上部的索克虫类三叶虫［J］. 古生物学报，2022，61（4）：568-589.

［15］KOBAYASHI，T. Upper Cambrian of the Wuhutsui Basin，Liaotung，with special reference to the limit of the Chaumitien（or Upper Cambrian），of eastern Asia，and its subdivision［J］. Japanese Journal of Geology and Geography，1933a，11（1-2）：55-155.

# 关于边境地区文物保护工作的思考

## ——以防城港市为例

冯达添

防城港市博物馆，防城港　538001，中国

【摘要】边境地区文物保护工作是一项关系到边境地区和谐稳定、国家长治久安的重要工作。做好边境地区文物保护工作，有助于促进民族团结，铸牢中华民族共同体意识，维护边境地区安定团结，推动边境地区和谐富裕。本文尝试以近年来防城港市文物保护工作为例，谈谈对边境地区文物保护工作的认识。

【关键词】边境地区；文物保护；防城港市

边境地区是国家疆域的边缘区域，也是国家对外交往的重要门户，边境地区的安定团结对国家安全与边境地区的经济社会发展至关重要。文物是中华民族珍贵的历史文化遗产，在边境地区，则是各族人民共同创造的优秀历史文化遗产。做好边境地区文物保护工作，有利于增强边境地区人民的民族自信和文化自信，铸牢中华民族共同体意识，促进民族团结，汇聚磅礴力量，实现中华民族伟大复兴的中国梦。防城港市地处中国西南海陆交汇处，面向东南亚，背靠大西南，与越南海陆相连，区位优势明显，属于中国边境地区。防城港市下辖上思县、东兴市、港口区、防城区，是民族聚居区，有汉族、壮族、瑶族、京族4个世居民族，截至2022年底，全市总人口102.32万人，全市少数民族人口51.36万人。本文以防城港市为例，探讨边境地区文物保护工作的主要经验做法、存在困境及相应对策。

# 1 近年来防城港市文物保护工作概况

## 1.1 加强巡查监管，确保文物安全

### 1.1.1 常态化、制度化开展日常巡查

近年来，按照分级管理和属地管理原则，防城港市已逐步建立和形成常态化、制度化的文物巡查监管机制。市级文物部门主要对自治区级以上文物保护单位开展巡查，并对辖区各地进行抽查督查，各县（市、区）文物部门对辖区所有级别不可移动文物开展巡查监管。防城港市各级文物部门每月组织 1 ～ 2 次文物安全巡查、消防安全检查，每年累计巡查 300 余处不可移动文物，基本实现全市文物点的全覆盖。防城港市通过开展文物安全巡查及消防安全检查，及时排查和处理存在的各类安全隐患，防止发生文物安全事故和及时制止文物违法行为，保障文物安全。

### 1.1.2 部门联动，形成保护合力

防城港市地处西南边陲，沿海沿边。防城港市历史遗存丰富，已列有 324 处不可移动文物，其分布独具特色，既有古墓葬、古民居等传统常见文物，及边境地区传统的边塞海防重要设施，又有古人类遗存贝丘遗址，更有近现代边界意义的"大清国钦州界"老界碑。其中，古民居 59 处、古墓葬 90 处，主要分布于上思县；民国时期西方建筑风格的建筑 13 处，主要分布于防城区、东兴市江平镇等地；军事设施遗存古炮台遗址 6 处，分布于企沙镇、江山镇、那梭镇等沿海（近海）地区；古人类文化遗存贝丘遗址 9 处，分布于沿海地带及部分岛屿；"大清国钦州界"老界碑 20 处（界碑仍立于原地的仅有"大清国钦州界" 1 号界碑和 5 号界碑，其余均为遗址），分布于峒中镇、那良镇、东兴市等与越南接壤地区。针对文物分布的特点，防城港市主要依靠各级文物工作者，包括各乡镇文化站工作者开展日常巡查监管，同时联合海洋、海警、边防、消防等部门力量，实现部门联动，形成保护合力以开展文物保护工作。如 2013 年 3 月，防城港市文化部门与海洋部门签署了《关于合作开展防城港市管辖海域内水下文化遗产保护工作的框架协议》，定期与海监机构联合开展海域水下文化遗产分布区域的执法巡查，依法查处盗捞和破坏文化遗产的行为。2018 年，防城港市文物部门与海警部门开展联谊活动，达成共同加强全国重点文物保护单位连城要塞遗址和友谊关之白龙炮台群的日常巡查，维护文物安全的共识。防城港市文物部门每年与消防部门举行

多次消防演练、联合巡查等已成为常态化。借助消防部门的专业力量，提升了全市文物单位消防安全管理水平，同时也提高了防城港市文博工作者的消防意识和消防应急反应能力。多部门联动，有效弥补了防城港市文博力量不足的缺点，增强防城港市文物保护力量。

### 1.1.3 聘请文物协管员，协助开展监管

对重要的野外文物，为确保其安全，及时发现和处理突发情况，从 2018 年起，防城港市文物部门聘请了一批文物协管员，对白龙炮台、潭蓬运河、刘永福故居、社山遗址、罗浮恒望天主教堂、杯较墩遗址等一批野外重要文物加强巡查监管，防止出现破坏文物和安全隐患等情况。这些文物协管员均是文物点所在地的村民（居民），对文物保护很热心，责任心强。正式上岗前，文物部门专业人员对其逐一进行培训，使其掌握必要的文物知识，随时与其保持联系，为其提供政策业务咨询和指导，便于及时掌握文物保护动态情况。文物部门于年末综合研判各文物协管员的工作履职情况，决定是否予以续聘。就近聘请村民（居民）为文物协管员，协助开展文物日常巡查监管，有效增强了防城港市的文博队伍力量。

## 1.2 组织申报、公布各级文物保护单位

根据文物的历史价值、艺术价值、科学价值，积极申报各级文物保护单位，提高文物保护级别，有利于获取更多保护项目及资金等方面的支持，使文物保护工作得到充实的保障基础，从而使文物的真实性、完整性等得到有效保障。近年来，防城港市不断推动辖区内不可移动文物申报各级文物保护单位，以提高保护级别。2012 年 4 月，东兴市人民政府将"大清国钦州界"1 号界碑、"大清国钦州界"5 号界碑公布为东兴市文物保护单位。2017 年 12 月，港口区石龟头炮台遗址、防城区刘永福故居、防城区谦受图书馆旧址及东兴市"大清国钦州界"1 号界碑、"大清国钦州界"5 号界碑等成功晋级为第七批广西壮族自治区文物保护单位。2018 年，防城港市积极推荐潭蓬运河申报第八批全国重点文物保护单位。2021 年 12 月，防城港市将近年新发现的具有重要历史价值的港口区洲尾遗址公布为第三批防城港市文物保护单位。2022 年，防城港市积极申报第八批广西壮族自治区文物保护单位，推荐"三光企"革命武装起义纪念碑等 4 处市、县级文物保护单位作为申报项目。

### 1.3　划定保护范围及建设控制地带

按照《中华人民共和国文物保护法》的相关规定，根据文物保护的需要，应结合文物保护现状，划出一定保护范围和建设控制地带，以确保文物的真实性、完整性及保持文物的历史风貌。建设项目选址应尽量避开不可移动文物，如因建设需要确实无法避开的，应履行相关报批手续。文物保护范围和建设控制地带对于文物安全而言，是一处缓冲区和一道安全防线。因此，划定和公布文物保护范围和建设控制地带对文物保护工作尤为重要。2017 年 11 月，防城港市上报的白龙炮台、潭蓬运河、杯较墩遗址、社山遗址、罗浮恒望天主教堂 5 处重要文物保护单位的保护范围被自治区人民政府正式发文公布，建设控制地带划定方案也已上报。2021 年 12 月，防城港市完成石龟头炮台遗址、谦受图书馆旧址、刘永福故居、"大清国钦州界" 1 号界碑及 "大清国钦州界" 5 号界碑 5 处自治区级文物保护单位的保护范围和建设控制地带划定方案的划定及上报工作。

### 1.4　实施文物保护修缮工程

因年久失修，文物会出现不同程度的损坏现象，为确保文物的真实性、完整性和原有历史风貌，更好地传承和保护中华民族优秀文化遗产，近年来，防城港市经过努力，先后完成白龙炮台、石龟头炮台遗址、谦受图书馆旧址、刘永福故居、罗浮恒望天主教堂、陈树坤旧居、粤东书院等重要文物单位的保护修缮工程。经过修缮，防城港市重要文物得到有效保护，防止了文物自然损毁，为广大市民实现免费参观创造良好条件。特别是作为防城港市目前唯一的国家级文物保护单位，白龙炮台地处江山半岛旅游度假区南端，紧临白浪滩、怪石滩等著名景区，已成为人文景观和自然景观相交融的精品旅游景区。

### 1.5　开展相关调查和研究

防城港市历史悠久，自新石器时代始就有人类在这片土地上生存繁衍，至今保存有多处新石器时代的贝丘遗址，如社山遗址、杯较墩遗址等；西汉时马援南征曾经过这里，至今防城港市各地仍留存多处伏波庙遗址，其中规模较大、保存较完整的是东兴罗浮伏波庙旧址；唐代高骈于咸通年间凿通的潭蓬运河，现为自治区级文物保护单位，也是北部湾地区古代海上丝绸之路的重要遗址。为深入挖掘防城港市历史文化遗产，增强民族自信，传承和弘扬防城港市悠久的历史文化，防城港市博物馆近年来开展了系列调查和学术研究。

2016—2017 年，防城港市博物馆组织人员对包括上思县和峒中镇壮族民居、防城区那良镇瑶族民居、东兴市江平镇京族民居等在内的全市传统民居开展调查，并整理成《防城港传统民居》一书。2017 年，组织开展包括东兴市在内的防城港沿海地区水下考古调查，形成《防城港水下考古陆地调查研究》一书。2012—2020 年，先后开展交东贝丘遗址、皇城坳遗址、潭蓬运河、洲尾遗址、冲茶窑址、上思窑头遗址、皇帝沟运河等遗址的考古调查工作，经研究整理，先后有《潭蓬运河研究》《洲尾贸易场：汉代以后北部湾海上丝绸之路变迁与延续的历史见证》等研究专著问世，不断充实地方历史文化实物证据，丰富地方历史文化研究成果。

### 1.6　加强可移动文物的展示利用

文物分为不可移动文物和可移动文物。与古遗址、古建筑、近现代代表性建筑等不可移动文物相比较，博物馆、展览馆、纪念馆等展出的可移动文物，亦是中华民族优秀的历史文化遗产。而博物馆则是通过基本陈展、临时展览等展出具有历史价值、艺术价值、科学价值的可移动文物，宣传民族政策、弘扬民族团结进步精神的重要场所。防城港市已建成开放的博物馆有防城港市博物馆和东兴京族博物馆。其中，防城港市博物馆是广西北部湾地区首家以海洋文化为主题，展示防城港本土历史、地方文化及民族民俗，集收藏、保护、研究于一体的国家三级博物馆。自 2017 年建成开放以来，防城港市博物馆自觉将民族团结工作融入博物馆的日常工作，通过不断征集反映全市各民族历史文化、民俗文化的展品，充实馆藏，及时更新各展厅展品，提高陈展水平，以及通过引进区内外精品展览等方式，不断满足广大市民和游客日益增长的观展需求。其中，关于民族文化的常设展览有非物质文化遗产展览馆和"醉美边海——悠久丰厚的防城港历史与民俗"展厅。两个展厅全面、翔实、生动地展示了防城港市各民族悠久的历史文化和独具特色的民俗文化，深受观众喜爱。据统计，防城港市博物馆自开放以来，年均接待观众 30 万人次。此外，近年来防城港市博物馆还推出一系列具有民族和地域特色的临时展览，主要有"背上的牵挂——防城港市博物馆馆藏壮族背带展""壮锦刺绣展——防城港市博物馆三月三临时展览""银光暗烁——防城港市博物馆馆藏银器专题展""一绣宜心——绣球文化展""镂云裁月——苗绣艺术作品展"

等。防城港市博物馆通过举办系列丰富多彩的临时展览，向观众展现了优秀的民族文化、海洋文化等，深受人们欢迎。

东兴京族博物馆于 2009 年 7 月正式建成并对外开放，其与东兴京族生态博物馆、东兴非物质文化遗产馆三馆合一。它的建成开放对展示和研究跨境民族的文化变迁，推动中越民族文化研究的合作交流，增强中国与东盟各国的文化交流具有深远的国际意义。东兴京族博物馆于 2018 年进行了展览提升，展厅面貌焕然一新，对观众更具吸引力。

2019 年，为了充分发挥地理优势和展示本市瑶族聚居区瑶族优秀文化，防城区文化馆完成了那良高林村瑶族刺绣馆、大板瑶服饰及阿宝节展示馆两个项目的布展工作，宣传展示大板瑶、花头瑶的传统服饰及节庆，增强了当地瑶族同胞的自信心和自豪感，使其更加自觉地参与到传承瑶族传统服饰技艺的行列中，同时也吸引了不少外地游客前来参观。

2023 年 1 月，防城港市刘永福故居陈列馆正式建成开放。该馆依托自治区级文物保护单位刘永福故居，陈列展示刘永福生平事迹及相关物件和图片，向防城港市内外观众讲述清末抗法名将、民族英雄刘永福的不朽功勋，传承和弘扬其伟大的爱国主义精神，成为防城港市不可多得的一处人文景观。

## 1.7　加强宣传教育

除可以通过举办展览宣传和弘扬各民族的优秀历史文化遗产外，还可以通过举办各类文物宣传活动来弘扬优秀的历史文化遗产。自 2017 年建成开放以来，防城港市博物馆依托本馆民族文化资源，结合元旦、春节、壮族三月三、"5·18 国际博物馆日"、文化遗产保护成果宣传月等重大节庆、节日，开展了系列宣传教育活动。一是开展文物普法宣传、发放全市文物保护单位名单及简介、宣讲文物保护条例等，提高民众的文物保护意识。二是开展文物进校园、进社区、进机关、进军营、进企业活动，主要有"福鹿贺新春——上思舞鹿表演""京花烟云——京族烟煲手绘""壮族三月三民俗风情展""壮族三月三·桂风壮韵浓""壮族三月三·网聚也精彩""壮族三月三·边海壮韵浓""多彩民族秀一秀""民族'童'心绘""防城港世居民族民俗文化讲座进校园""贝壳里的世界——防城港市博物馆校园流动展"等。防城港市博物馆通过开展系列宣传教育活动，扩大博物馆的宣传教育影响，让广大观众在参与活动的同时，领略防城港市各民族独特的文化内涵，激发观众的民族自信心和自豪感，充分发挥了博物馆的爱国主义教育功能和作用，对民族团结也起到了重要的促进作用。

## 2　存在问题及原因分析

### 2.1　文物保护工作基础较薄弱

2009—2011 年，防城港市全面启动第三次全国文物普查工作，这是防城港市文物保护工作得到前所未有重视、步入快速发展的开端。此后，防城港市人民政府先后公布了三批市级文物保护单位和全市文物点名录，各县（市、区）也相应开展了有关工作。然而，由于起步晚、基础差，加之经费不足、人员有限诸多因素，防城港市文物保护工作的基础仍然比较薄弱。

### 2.2　文博单位人才紧缺

包括防城港市博物馆、各县（市、区）博物馆、文物管理所在内的各级文博单位要同时承担文物安全监管、场馆（遗址）正常开放、文物修缮与保护、考古调查、地方历史文化研究等职责，以及完成上级行政部门交予的其他常规工作，人员严重不足。防城港市城乡地区有 300 多处不可移动文物，大部分为野外文物，零星散布于沿海、边境乃至十万大山深处，文博单位人员短缺与工作量庞大的矛盾突出，且面临专业技术人才流动大的困境。各县（市、区）情况更为严重，从事文物保护工作的基本仅有 1 ～ 2 人，甚至可能无专人负责文物工作。

### 2.3　经费投入不足

受经济总量、财政收入等影响，长期以来防城港市、县两级文物保护经费较为紧张，以县（市、区）为例，部分县（市、区）的文物部门年度工作经费仅有数千元，难以维持工作正常开展，另有部分县（市、区）几乎没有文物保护工作经费。近年来，防城港市开展的文物修缮项目，经费多为上级部门划拨，市、县财政未将文物保护修缮经费纳入年度预算，市、县级文物保护单位及文物点因缺乏专项经费而未得到必要的修缮，部分建筑体自然破损严重。

## 3 对策与建议

### 3.1 加大力度补短板，做好文物保护基础工作

一是要全部完成防城港市各级文物保护单位的"四有"工作（有保护范围、有保护标志、有记录档案、有保管机构），这是开展文物保护的基础前提。二是有计划、分批次推进一批项目维修。建议市、县两级政府制订辖区市、县级文物保护单位的修缮规划，逐年实施，抢救性推进一批文物保护单位的修缮工作。

### 3.2 落实人员经费保障，增强文物保护力量

人员、经费是推动文物保护事业发展的两大关键要素，防城港市文物保护工作在这两个方面均较为薄弱，人员、经费成为制约文物保护事业发展的瓶颈因素，亟待解决。

经费方面，一方面市、县两级财政应在年度预算中安排能够维持文物巡查、文物调查、日常监管等最基本的工作经费，这是文博机构能够正常运作和履职、发挥保护作用的基本前提；另一方面，应设立文物保护（修缮）专项资金，逐年分批次、有计划地推进文物保护修缮工作，以点带面，推动全市各级文物保护单位的保存状况由劣向好转变，切实解决部分文物的安全问题。

人员方面，一是要加大人才引进力度，及时补充文物保护方面的专业技术人员，尤其是基层文博单位，在人才招考或引进中，应根据国家有关基层文博人才的扶持政策，提升人才引进渠道、方式的灵活性和用人单位的自主权。二是应加强现有在职人员的职业培训，不断提升文物保护工作队伍的专业化水平。三是应在市、县两级财政支持的前提下，实行和推广文物协管员制度，通过就近聘用工作人员协助开展文物保护工作，以社会力量的参与扩大全市的文物保护力量。四是继续扩大和加强部门联动，联合包括财政、海关、海洋、国土、住建、海警、边防、公安、消防、教育等部门共同发力合作，使文物保护成为各政府部门共同承担和关注的工作，改变以往文物部门"单打独斗"的工作风貌，形成合力，推动文物保护工作向前发展。

### 3.3 加大宣传力度，营造全社会关注文物、保护文物的浓厚氛围

文物保护事业是一项伟大的公益事业，为当代和子孙后代保护和传承中华民族优

秀传统文化。因此，文物保护事业是事关人民群众切身利益的长远事业，必须依靠人民、发动人民共同参与文物保护工作。各级政府部门要加大文物保护工作宣传力度，使人民群众真正认识到保护文物的重要意义。文物部门要联合教育部门组织开展系列文物保护进校园活动，教育部门要将文物保护纳入教学活动，培养学生的文物保护意识，培养文物保护事业接班人。

## 4　结语

边境地区文物保护工作是一项充满意义的工作，功在当代，利在千秋，同时也面临基础薄弱、资金缺乏、人才不足等困境。做好边境地区文物保护工作需要文物工作者不懈努力和相关部门共同发力，更需要社会各界广泛参与和支持。

## 参考文献

［1］刘延强.浅析不可移动文物的保护工作［J］.黑龙江史志，2014（19）：69-70.

［2］卢娜.浅析对不可移动文物的保护策略［J］.学理论，2013（19）：178-179.

［3］李娜.浅谈新时期不可移动文物的保护工作［J］.文物鉴定与鉴赏，2018（10）：116-117.

［4］钟燕丽.浅议基层博物馆的文物保护及人才队伍建设［J］.文物鉴定与鉴赏，2019（2）：124-125.

［5］赵兵涛.基层文物博物馆发展思考［J］.才智，2019（8）：244.

# Bobai Hakka weaving: Plant diversity, traditional culture, and a model for rural revitalization

Liufu Yongqing[1], Hu Renchuan[2], Fu Qiongyao[1], Luo Binsheng[3]

1.Natural History Museum of Guangxi, Nanning　530012, China

2.Guangxi Institute of Chinese Medicine and Pharmaceutical Science, Nanning　530022, China

3.Lushan Botanical Garden, Jiangxi Province and Chinese Academy of Sciences, Lushan　332900, China

【 Abstract 】The Hakka people, a branch of the Han nationality with their own language, culture, and customs, are one of the largest immigrant groups worldwide, primarily distributed in southern China. Bobai, a county with the largest Hakka population globally, has a thriving weaving industry that is one of the local pillar industries. This study aimed to systematically analyze the plant source, product function, and development model of Bobai Hakka weaving. The study recorded 33 plant species for weaving, which belonged to 17 families and 27 genera. The weaving plants were mainly bamboo, rattan, herbs, and wood, with herbs being the most commonly used (15 species, 45.5%). Most weaving plants were obtained locally (16 species, 48.5%) and from wild sources (13 species, 39.4%). Stems were the most commonly used plant parts (66.7%) in local weaving, followed by leaf sheaths, inflorescence stems, leaves, stem bark, leaf rachis, and female bracts. Additionally, wastes from crops

Acknowledgements: We are very grateful to Mo Chengzhen, Huang Lianjiang, Tu Chunxiao, Pang Feihong, and other locals for providing valuable information on weaving plants and related knowledge. This research was funded by the Guangxi Natural Science Foundation(2022GXNSFBA035527), Survey and Collection of Germplasm Resources of Woody & Herbaceous Plants in Guangxi, China(GXFS-2021-34), and the Special Project of Lushan Botanical Garden of the Chinese Academy of Sciences(2021ZWZX12).

such as wheat, rice, bananas, and corn, as well as invasive water hyacinths, were widely used as weaving materials by the local Hakka people. The products' functions ranged from household appliances, cultural and entertainment products, furniture, to production tools, reflecting a range of conventional cultural connotations. The study found that the Bobai Hakka weaving industry had integrated modern elements and additional use value to expand its market appeal. With the participation of the government, enterprises, and farmers, the Bobai weaving industry has formed a development model of "intangible cultural heritage+industry+poverty alleviation", which has become a successful case of poverty alleviation and rural revitalization.

【Keywords】Hakka; Plant weaving; Ethnobotany; Handicrafts; Traditional knowledge

# 1 Introduction

Hakkas are a branch of the Han nationality (Parish & Whyte, 1978) who migrated from the ancient Central Plains (present-day Henan Province of China) to southeastern China in AD 300 to escape wars and natural disasters (Luo, et al., 2019). Hakkas speak their dialects and have their own customs, beliefs, and unique culture (Au, et al., 2008). In China, Hakkas mainly distribute in southwestern Fujian, southern Jiangxi, western Guangdong, southeastern Guangxi, Hainan, and Taiwan (Constable, 1994). Bobai County in Guangxi has the largest Hakka population in the world, with more than 1.4 million Hakkas, accounting for more than 75% of the total population (Yulin Municipal Committee of the Chinese People's Political Consultative Conference, 2016). The Hakka people in Bobai have a rich history, with most of them migrating from Hakka regions of Fujian, Guangdong, and Jiangxi provinces during the Ming Dynasty, around 500 years ago (Yulin Municipal Committee of the Chinese People's Political Consultative Conference, 2016). Like other Hakkas, the Bobai Hakkas have a strong adaptability to the local natural and social environment, and have created unique culture such as folk songs, food, and weaving while adapting to the local culture.

Bobai County is located in southeastern Guangxi, China, and has a warm and rainy climate, which is ideal for the growth of wild plants used in Hakka weaving (Zhang, 2013).

Hakkas use these plants as raw materials and weave them into household items or handicrafts. In Bobai, the Hakka weaving culture has a long history, and since the 1970s, it has become one of China's earliest exports of weaving products. According to the introduction by local government officers, Bobai was awarded the title of " Capital of Chinese Weaving Handicrafts " for its excellent weaving skills in 2006; and in 2014, the local government included Bobai weaving skills in the list of Intangible Cultural Heritage of Guangxi Zhuang Autonomous Region (http: // www. gxfyb hw. cn/ dir-197.html). This background information indicates the significance of the weaving industry in Bobai.

Bamboo, rattan, and herbs are examples of non-timber forest products (NTFPs) that are widely used in various fields such as food, medicine, furniture, construction, weaving technology, and others (Arnold & Pérez, 1998; Zhang, et al., 2008). There are estimated 4000-6000 species of NTFPs of commercial importance worldwide (Ticktin, 2004). While NTFPs have been recognized for their potential to provide economic sources, employment opportunities, and ecological benefits, there is still much to be explored in terms of their potential for rural development (Feng, 2002; Rahim & Idrus, 2019). Although there have been some studies on the use of NTFPs for weaving, the literature remains limited, highlighting the novelty and significance of our study.

Recent studies have shown that the use of non-timber plants in the development of the plant weaving industry can be beneficial to the rural economy, the quality of life of ethnic minorities, and the promotion of intangible cultural heritage (Hai, et al., 2021; Luo, et al., 2020; Pazon & Del Rio, 2018; Rahayu, et al., 2020; Xia, et al., 2018). Our study focuses on the Hakka traditional weaving industry in Bobai, Guangxi, and examines how it has adapted to the modern market and become a pillar industry. By conducting an ethnobotanical investigation on plant weaving in the Bobai area in 2021-2022, we aim to contribute to the existing literature on NTFPs and rural development, and shed light on the potential of NTFPs in supporting the well-being of local communities.

Our study has two main objectives: to rescue and document the plant-based sources of Hakka weaving practice and to clarify how the local weaving industry adapts to the changing times. By achieving these objectives, we hope to support the inheritance and development of local weaving culture and provide a reference for other areas to develop traditional handicrafts and use local resources for poverty alleviation and rural revitalization.

# 2    Methods

## 2.1    Study area

Bobai County, home to 1.82 million people, of which more than 1.4 million are Hakkas, is situated in the southeastern part of Guangxi (Yulin Municipal Committee of the Chinese People's Political Consultative Conference, 2016). The county falls within the monsoon climate zone where the southern subtropical region meets the tropics, with plentiful sunshine, high temperatures, abundant rainfall, and high humidity. Bobai County is located southwest of the Liuwan Mountain and southeast of the Yunkai Mountain, and boasts 43 large and small rivers, including the Nanliu, Yu, Jiuzhou, and Najiao rivers. The region is rich in certain plant species such as *Bambusa chungii* McClure, *Dicranopteris pedata* (Houtt.) Nakaike, and *Schoenoplectus triqueter* (L.) Palla, which serve as excellent weaving materials (Zhang, 2013). The abundance of wild plant resources provides a solid foundation for developing the weaving industry.

Between 2021 and 2022, we conducted an ethnobotanical investigation on weaving plants across several towns in Bobai County, including Langping, Bobai, Shuiming, Yashan, Jiangning, Dungu, Dongping, Shahe, and Nabu (refer to Figure 1). The study employed the ethnobotanical interview method to obtain information. We selected 50 information reporters (27 female, 23 male), of which 20 key informants were composed of local government officials, bamboo weaving intangible cultural inheritors, dealers, and village leaders. The remaining 30 regular informants were selected through snowball sampling, all of whom were local residents and practiced plant weaving.

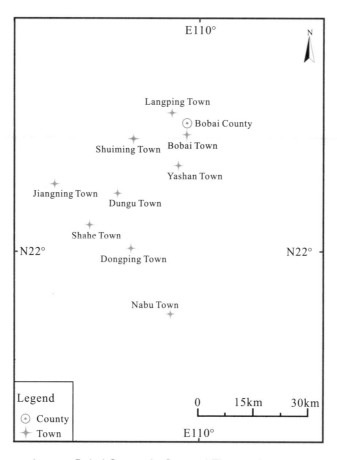

Figure 1    The study area: Bobai County in Guangxi Zhuang Autonomous Region, China

In the process of the interview, semi-structured interviews and unstructured interviews are mainly used, and the interview contents include: (1) What plant species are used? (2)What are the uses of weaving products? (3) What changes have occurred in the weaving process and industry compared with the past? (4) Where do those weaving materials come from?

## 2.2    Taxonomic identification

Aside from conducting interviews, we also visited production workshops, markets, and villages, and actively engaged in weaving to gain first-hand knowledge of the materials and processes. We were able to take photographs of weaving products and raw materials, with the help of the locals. To identify weaving plants and natural materials, we utilized electronic taxonomic databases such as https: // www. cvh. ac. cn/, http: // www. iplant. cn/, and www. world flora online. org, based on their morphological characteristics and geographical origin. Any plant specimens obtained were deposited in Natural History Museum of Guangxi.

## 2.3　Quantitative Indicators

The relative frequency of citation (RFC) was utilized to assess and compare the significance of weaving plants used by the Hakka community in Bobai. The RFC was calculated using the formula:

$$RFC = \frac{FC}{N}$$

where FC represents the number of respondents who mentioned a specific weaving plant, and $N$ represents the total number of participants who participated in the survey (Tardío & Pardo-de-Santayana, 2008; Vitalini, et al., 2013).

# 3　Results and discussion

## 3.1　Diversity of weaving plants

Based on the ethnobotanical analysis of Hakka weaving plants in Bobai, our findings demonstrate that 33 species (listed in Table 1) from 17 families and 27 genera are used in weaving practices. Poaceae (9 species) and Arecaceae (4 species) represent the families with the largest number of species (as shown in Figure 2). Other families, however, are represented by only 1-2 species, indicating a distinctive diversity. This suggests that the Hakka people in Bobai County possess a deep understanding of the surrounding plant species and their distinct material properties.

The weaving plants identified in this study primarily come from locally cultivated plants (16 species, 48.5%) and wild plants (13 species, 39.4%), with a few imported plants also used (10 species, 30.3%) (see Table 2).

Table 1　Inventory of weaving plants in Bobai

| Species name | Family | Vernacular name | Used part | Characteristics | Life form | Source type | Process method | Function | RFC | Specimen no. |
|---|---|---|---|---|---|---|---|---|---|---|
| *Agave sisalana* Perr. ex Engelm. | Asparagaceae | Jiànmá | Leaf | Flexible, soft | Herb | Cultivated | Scutch, filter residue. wash, sun-cure and rope | Utensils | 0.52 | LFYQ792 |
| *Alpinia hainanensis* K. Schumann | Zingiberaceae | Cǎoguǒmá, Shānjiāngmá | Leaf sheath | Flexible, soft | Herb | Cultivated, introduced | Sun-cure | Utensils | 0.12 | LFYQ807 |
| *Alpinia zerumbet* (Pers.) B. L. Burtt & R. M. Sm. | Zingiberaceae | Cǎoguǒmá, Shānjiāngmá | Leaf sheath | Flexible, soft | Herb | Wild, introduced | Sun-cure | Utensils | 0.08 | LFYQ808 |
| *Bambusa chungii* McClure | Poaceae | Dānzhú | Stem | Flexible, solid | Bamboo | Cultivated | Scrape and split | Production tools, utensils, furniture, culture and entertainment | 0.92 | LFYQ781 |
| *Bambusa ramispinosa* L. C. Chia et H. L. Fung | Poaceae | Huángnízhú | Stem | Flexible, solid | Bamboo | Cultivated | Scrape and split | Production tools, utensils, furniture, culture and entertainment | 0.16 | LFYQ800 |
| *Bambusa textilis* McClure | Poaceae | Qīngpízhú | Stem | Flexible, solid | Bamboo | Cultivated | Scrape and split | Production tools, utensils, furniture, culture, and entertainment | 0.24 | LFYQ798 |
| *Calamus* sp. | Arecaceae | Yìnníténg | Stem | Flexible, solid | Rattan | Introduced | Peel, sun-cure, and water softening | Production tools, utensils, furniture, culture, and entertainment | 0.82 | LFYQ785 |

Table 1 ( continued )

| Species name | Family | Vernacular name | Used part | Characteristics | Life form | Source type | Process method | Function | RFC | Specimen no. |
|---|---|---|---|---|---|---|---|---|---|---|
| *Calamus simplicifolius* C. F. Wei | Arecaceae | Dānyèshēngténg | Stem | Flexible, solid | Rattan | Wild, introduced | Peel, sun-cure, and water softening | Production tools, utensils, furniture, culture, and entertainment | 0.12 | LFYQ787 |
| *Calamus tetradactylus* Hance | Arecaceae | Báiténg | Stem | Flexible, solid | Rattan | Wild, introduced | Peel, sun-cure, and water softening | Production tools, utensils, furniture, culture, and entertainment | 0.18 | LFYQ786 |
| *Cocos nucifera* L. | Arecaceae | Yēzishù | Leaf, leaf sheath | Flexible, soft | Herb | Introduced | Slice up and sun-cure | Culture and entertainment, utensils | 0.44 | LFYQ790 |
| *Corchorus capsularis* L. | Malvaceae | Máshéng | Stem bark | Flexible, soft | Herb | Cultivated | Peel, water soften, scutch, sun-cure, and rope | Utensils | 0.32 | LFYQ793 |
| *Cunninghamia lanceolata* (Lamb.) Hook | Cupressaceae | Shānmù | Stem | Solid | Wood | Cultivated | Peel, slice up, and sun-cure | Furniture, utensils | 0.28 | LFYQ788 |
| *Cyperus malaccensis* subsp. *monophyllus* (Vahl) T.Koyama | Cyperaceae | Xícǎo | Stem | Flexible, soft | Herb | Wild | Sun-cure and rope | Utensils | 0.6 | LFYQ795 |
| *Dendrocalamus latiflorus* Munro | Poaceae | Mázhú | Stem | Flexible, solid | Bamboo | Cultivated | Scrape and split | Production tools, utensils, furniture, culture, and entertainment | 0.66 | LFYQ812 |

Table 1 ( continued )

| Species name | Family | Vernacular name | Used part | Characteristics | Life form | Source type | Process method | Function | RFC | Specimen no. |
|---|---|---|---|---|---|---|---|---|---|---|
| *Dicranopteris pedata* (Houttuyn) Nakaike | Gleicheniaceae | Mángjī | Rachis | Flexible, soft | Herb | Wild | Peel and sun-cure | Utensils, culture, and entertainment | 0.58 | LFYQ782 |
| *Pontederia crassipes* Mart. | Pontederiaceae | Shuǐhúlú | Stem | Flexible, soft | Herb | Wild, introduced | Sun-cure | Production tools, utensils, furniture, culture, and entertainment | 0.78 | LFYQ783 |
| *Juncus effusus* L. | Juncaceae | Dēngxīncǎo | Stem | Flexible, soft | Herb | Wild | Sun-cure | Utensils | 0.46 | LFYQ796 |
| *Lycopodiastrum casuarinoides* Spring | Lycopodiaceae | Téngshísōng | Stem | Flexible | Rattan | Wild | Air-dry | Utensils, culture, and entertainment | 0.1 | LFYQ809 |
| *Lygodium japonicum* (Thunb.) Sw. | Lygodiaceae | Jīnsīténg | Stem | Flexible, solid | Rattan | Wild | Sun-cure and water soften | Culture and entertainment | 0.14 | LFYQ805, LFYQ228 |
| *Musa nana* Lour. | Musaceae | Xiāngjiāo | Leaf sheath | Flexible, soft | Herb | Cultivated | Slice up and sun-cure | Utensils | 0.64 | LFYQ811 |
| *Musa basjoo* Siebold & Zucc. ex Iinuma | Musaceae | Bājiāo | Leaf sheath | Flexible, soft | Herb | Cultivated | Slice up and sun-cure | Utensils | 0.68 | LFYQ791 |
| *Oryza sativa* L. | Poaceae | Hégǎn | Inflorescence stem | Flexible, soft | Herb | Cultivated | Sun-cure | Utensil, culture, and entertainment | 0.56 | LFYQ808 |
| *Palhinhaea cernua* (L.) Vasc. & Franco | Lycopodiaceae | Sōngjīncǎo | Stem | Flexible | Rattan | Wild | Air-dry | Utensils, culture, and entertainment | 0.06 | LFYQ810 |
| *Pericampylus glaucus* (Lam.) Merr. | Menispermaceae | Qīngténg | Stem | Flexible | Rattan | Wild | Peel and sun-cure | Utensils | 0.18 | LFYQ804 |

Table 1 ( continued )

| Species name | Family | Vernacular name | Used part | Characteristics | Life form | Source type | Process method | Function | RFC | Specimen no. |
|---|---|---|---|---|---|---|---|---|---|---|
| *Phyllostachys edulis* J.Houz. | Poaceae | Máozhú | Stem | Flexible, solid | Bamboo | Cultivated | Scrape and split | Production tools, utensils, furniture, culture, and entertainment | 0.74 | LFYQ801 |
| *Pinus massoniana* Lamb. | Pinaceae | Sōngmù | Stem | Solid | Wood | Cultivated | Peel, slice up, and sun-cure | Furniture, utensils | 0.34 | LFYQ789 |
| *Salix suchowensis* W.C. Cheng ex G. Zhu | Salicaceae | Liǔtiáo | Stem | Flexible, solid | Wood | Introduced | Peel, slice up, and sun-cure | Furniture, utensils, culture, and entertainment | 0.58 | LFYQ797 |
| *Schizostachyum pseudolima* McClure | Poaceae | Shízhú | Stem | Flexible, solid | Bamboo | Cultivated | Scrape and split | Production tools, utensils, furniture, culture, and entertainment | 0.34 | LFYQ799 |
| *Schoenoplectus triqueter* (L.) Palla | Cyperaceae | Sānléngcǎo | Stem | Flexible, soft | Herb | Wild | Strip and sun-cure | Utensils | 0.52 | LFYQ794 |
| *Smilax glabra* Roxb. | Smilacaceae | Tǔfúlíng | Stem | Flexible, solid | Rattan | Wild, introduced | Peel, dry, and water softening | Culture and entertainment | 0.12 | LFYQ803 |
| *Taxodium distichum* var. *imbricatum* (Nutt) Croom | Cupressaceae | Shuǐshāmù | Stem | Solid | Wood | Cultivated | Peel, slice up, soften, and sun-cure | Furniture, utensils | 0.26 | LFYQ802 |
| *Triticum aestivum* L. | Poaceae | Màigǎn | Inflorescence stem | Flexible, soft | Herb | Introduced | Sun-cure and water soften | Utensils | 0.4 | LFYQ806 |
| *Zea mays* L. | Poaceae | Yùmǐ | Female inflorescent bracts | Flexible, soft | Herb | Cultivated | Sun-cure | Utensils | 0.72 | LFYQ784 |

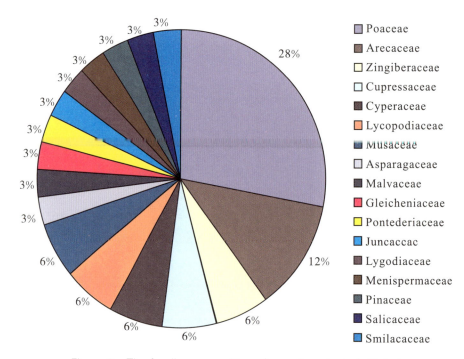

Figure 2　The family composition of weaving plants in Bobai

Table 2　Source type of weaving plants in Bobai

| Source type | Species | Percentage/% |
| --- | --- | --- |
| Wild | 13 | 33.3 |
| Introduced | 10 | 25.6 |
| Cultivated | 16 | 41.0 |
| Total | 39 | |

Various plant species possess distinct morphological and physical characteristics, which influence their suitability for weaving (Dharsono, et al., 2021; Luo, et al., 2020; Rahim & Idrus, 2019). The Hakkas in Bobai County utilize different parts of plants for weaving, depending on their unique features (Figure 3). Among the different plant parts, stems (66.7%) are the most frequently used, followed by leaf sheath, inflorescence stem, leaf, stem bark, leaf rachis, and female bracts. The chosen plant parts are typically characterized by good toughness and moderate hardness, which ensure that they are not prone to breakage during the weaving process.

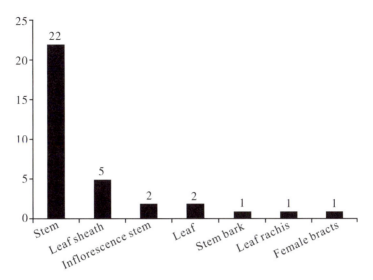

Figure 3    Statistics on the use of plant parts

Weaving plants in Bobai include bamboo, rattan, herbs, and wood, with herbs being the most diverse group (15 species, 45.5%) (see Figure 4). The use of herbs is mainly for soft products, such as dinner cushions, cushions, and fans. They can also serve as decorative elements for hard-woven products, such as rattan and bamboo. The majority of herbaceous weaving plants are common in Bobai and are readily available.

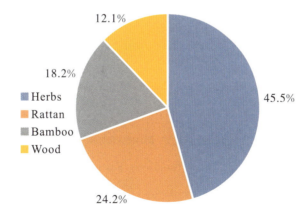

Figure 4    Life forms of Hakka weaving plants in Bobai

Table 1 outlines the various processing methods required for different braided plant materials. Generally, herbaceous materials can be utilized for weaving after being dried and peeled. However, bamboo plants must undergo a more complicated process, including scraping and cutting into strips. Wood must be peeled, sliced, and smoked, while vines require peeling, smoking, soaking, and softening (Table 1). To ensure the durability and aesthetic appeal of the woven products, they must be rinsed with water and then soaked in Gelsemium juice (*G. elegans* decocted in boiling water for 3 h) to prevent mildew and repel insects. Subsequently, the products are dried and brushed with turpentine to ensure a smooth finish. These procedures guarantee the ease of weaving braided materials, produce durable and aesthetically pleasing products, and deter insect infestation.

## 3.2  The transformation of braiding function: from traditional to modern

According to their function, woven products can be divided into four categories: production tools, utensils, furniture, and cultural and entertainment products (Table 1).

Historically, most of the Hakka weaving products in Bobai were practical tools, such as grain baskets, dustpans, vegetable baskets, and fish baskets (Figure 5 a-d). The Hakka people of Bobai valued convenience, sturdiness, and durability in their woven goods. Although the weaving process was time-consuming, the demand for weaving products was minimal, making it challenging to sell them at a reasonable price. Therefore, local weaving tools were mainly used for their specific production and daily needs.

With the rapid development of society, the weaving products in Bobai have undergone significant changes. Today's weaving products are more artistic, diverse, and functional, as shown in Figure 5 e-r. Compared to the past, people now pay more attention to promoting the aesthetic aspect of the products. Even for practical products, they add artistic elements to their design, such as incorporating animal shapes into fruit bowls, storage baskets, and flower shapes into lighting decorations (Figure 5 f, i). Moreover, some traditional production and life tools have been developed with additional functions. For example, the dustpan used in the past for making food is now used as painting tools, and the fishing basket is now used as a prop for performances. By developing more valuable products, the local weaving industry has gained a broader market, overcoming the bottleneck of low demand for traditional handicrafts.

In addition to the practicability, the woven products of Bobai Hakka carry rich and specific cultural connotations, such as the region's food culture. For instance, the Hakkas in Bobai are fond of eating cakes made from rice, cassava, and vegetables, known as "bǎn"locally. To facilitate food production, people weave practical items such as dustpans and food baskets.

As cultural carriers, these traditional woven products hold the cultural memory of Bobai Hakka. If they disappear, the traditional knowledge of weaving will be lost, making it difficult to inherit and protect local Hakka culture. Therefore, it is essential to continue producing and using traditional woven products while promoting the development of new weaving products. This will ensure the preservation of local cultural heritage and promote the sustainable development of the weaving industry in Bobai.

Bamboo weaving: a-e, a—paddy basket (*Bambusa chungii*), b—dustpan (*B. chungii*), c—fruit basket (*B. ramispinosa*), d—weel (*B. chungii*), e—bamboo lamp (*Phyllostachys edulis*);

rattan weaving: f-j, f—rattan lamp (*Calamus* sp.), g—chair (*Calamus* sp.), h—festival decoration (*Lygodium japonicum*), i—animal-shaped basket (plastic vine), j—fan and basket (plastic vine);

herb weaving: k-q, k—vase (*Dicranopteris pedata*), l—storage basket (*Schoenoplectus triqueter*), m—wall clock (*Juncus effusus*), n—storage basket (*Agave sisalana*), o—mirror (*Corchorus capsularis*), p—lampshade (*Pontederia crassipes*), q—mat (*Alpinia hainanensis*);

wood weaving: r—picnic basket (*Taxodium distichum* var. *imbricatum*).

Figure 5　Weaving products in Bobai

### 3.3 The RFC value of plant materials

Based on the statistics of the relative frequency of citation, *B. chungii* (RFC=0.92) and *Calamus* sp. (RFC=0.82) have the highest RFC value (Table 1). *B.chungii* is known for its strong toughness, long and flat internodes, and thinness, making it a popular choice for weaving locally (Jia & Feng, 1996). *Calamus* sp. is preferred for its flexibility and tensile strength, which prevents cracking or destruction while bending, unlike bamboo or hardwoods (Rahim & Idrus, 2019; Xu, et al., 2002). There are 14 species whose RFC value is higher than 0.5, including *B. chungii*, *Calamus* sp., *Pontederia crassipes*, *Phyllostachys edulis*, *Zea mays*, *Musa basjoo*, *Dendrocalamus latiflorus*, *Musa nana*, *Cyperus malaccensis* subsp. *monophyllus*, *Dicranopteris pedata*, *Salix suchowensis*, *Oryza sativa*, *Schoenoplectus triqueter*, *Agave sisalana*, which suggests their relative abundance as weaving materials in Bobai. On the other hand, species like *Palhinhaea cernua* (RFC = 0.06), *Alpinia zerumbet* (RFC = 0.08), and *Lycopodiastrum casuarinoides* (RFC = 0.10) have a lower citation rate, indicating that they may not be the most suitable weaving materials in the region or that knowledge related to their use may be fading away.

We have also found some species that have rarely been reported to be used as weaving materials, like *D. pedata*, *S. glabra*, *A. hainanensis*, and *A. zerumbet*. The stem of *D. pedata*, which is small and unjointed, can grow up to about 2 m, and is flexible, making it suitable for weaving baskets and storage baskets. The stem of *S. glabra*, with its smooth, thornless, and resilient branches that can grow up to 4 m in length, is used by locals to weave bird nests, garlands, and other products. *A. hainanensis* and *A. zerumbet* plants can be up to 3 m in height, and the leaf sheaths are rich in fibers (Wu & Chen, 1981), which can be used to weave daily necessities such as baskets and mats. Although these species are not commonly reported to be used in weaving, their potential for weaving products should not be overlooked.

### 3.4 The choice of plant materials

The selection of weaving materials is influenced by factors such as material availability, weaver preference, and intended product use (Pazon & Del Rio, 2018). For instance, bamboo and rattan are preferred for products that require high load-bearing capacity, while soft and flexible herbs are used for items that need to be folded. Weavers also employ different colors and materials to enhance the durability and aesthetics of their products.

Our survey revealed that the majority of weaving plants are utilized to create utensils (30), followed by cultural and entertainment products (16), furniture (14), and production tools (10). Remarkably, bamboo and rattan are versatile materials that can be employed in the production of various products, whereas wood is primarily used for furniture and household appliances. Herbs, on the other hand, are commonly utilized in weaving household appliances and some cultural and entertainment products.

It is worth noting that, based on our interviews, local weaving companies in Bobai offer customized services to their customers. The weaver first creates a skeleton model using iron wire based on the customer's product demand, and then selects a specific plant for weaving. This highlights the flexibility, adaptability, and vitality of Bobai's Hakka weaving process, which caters to the modern market.

However, we found that plastic is frequently used to imitate rattan products due to its excellent anti-mildew and insect-resistant properties, eliminating the need for treatments such as drying or fumigation. This saves both human resources and production costs. Nevertheless, non-degradable materials such as plastics pose a significant threat to the environment and human health (Borrelle, et al., 2020).

## 3.5 Turning waste into treasure

According to our interviews, over 90% of weaving products in Bobai were made from locally abundant bamboo and *D. pedata* in the past. With the continuous expansion of the weaving industry, bamboo and *D. pedata* can no longer meet the growing demand of local weaving companies for raw materials, and people have sought alternative weaving materials. Rice stalks, wheat straws, corn bracts, banana leaf sheaths are the residual wastes of crops after harvest. Traditionally, these wastes are disposed of by incineration or in situ decay (Dharsono, et al., 2021), which wastes many resources and seriously pollutes the environment. In this study, the RFC values of wheat straws, rice stalks, banana leaf sheaths, and corn bracts were 0.4–0.72, indicating that many local people know the weaving uses of these plant materials. In addition, the RFC of *P. crassipes* was also very high (0.78), second only to *B. chungii*, *Calamus* sp. *P. crassipes* is one of the world's most common invasive aquatic plants (Villamagna & Murphy, 2010). Because of its solid reproductive ability, it is easy to flood the water. Hakkas in Bobai turn these residual wastes and invasive plants into treasures for weaving, protecting the environment and providing more materials for the local weaving industry.

## 3.6　The development model

To support the growth of the local weaving industry, the Bobai region has implemented the "intangible cultural heritage+industry+poverty alleviation" model. This approach involves leveraging the cultural heritage of weaving to boost economic development and alleviate poverty in the area. To facilitate market access for local weaving products, the government has invested in the construction of highways and high-speed railways to improve transportation infrastructure. This has enabled more woven products to reach both domestic and foreign markets. Additionally, the provincial government provides support to weaving enterprises by offering training programs for weaving and management personnel, guiding companies in setting up e-commerce platforms, and promoting the development of weaving-related e-commerce. These initiatives aim to expand the scope and scale of cooperation in the weaving industry.

The development of the weaving industry in Bobai has created employment opportunities for local households and other vulnerable groups, which is particularly important in the context of the COVID-19 epidemic. During our visit, we observed many villagers weaving products for the local weaving enterprises at home. According to the head of one of the weaving industries, his company attracted more than 120 poor households in 2020, each of which can earn a monthly income of 2000-3000 *yuan* (CNY). The weaving industry has become one of the largest pillar industries in Bobai County, with 386 weaving enterprises and a total output value of 683 million *yuan* in 2020 (http: // www. bobai. gov. cn/ xxgk/ bdgk/ bdnj/ t8204 982. shtml).

The success of the Bobai weaving industry in promoting rural revitalization, poverty alleviation, and the protection of traditional knowledge can be attributed to the business model of "non-heritage+industry+poverty alleviation". This model has been successfully applied in other traditional handicrafts, such as Sansui bamboo weaving in Guizhou (Luo et al., 2020), Nimu Tibetan incense (Song, et al., 2011), and Vietnam bang (Truyen, et al., 2014), and has achieved positive results. Therefore, this model is worth extending to the industrial development of other conventional handicrafts.

## 4　Suggestions and prospects

There are inherent contradictions in the process of balancing the preservation and innovation of Bobai weaving. Weaving companies are pressured to increase their profits by minimizing costs and innovating products, which could undermine the protection of traditional weaving knowledge. To address this issue, the government can consider introducing incentive policies to encourage weaving enterprises to use eco-friendly plant materials and promote sustainable weaving products among consumers.

To attract more young people to engage in the preservation and protection of traditional weaving knowledge, we can take the following steps: (1) strengthen the development of weaving courses, research activities, and recreational events to generate interest and facilitate knowledge transfer; (2) leverage the Internet, media, fairs, and museums to promote and raise public awareness and appreciation of local weaving culture.

Ensuring the sustainability of weaving materials is a pressing challenge faced by most weaving companies (Kotze & Traynor, 2011). Our investigation found that local wild and cultivated plants, such as *A. zerumbet*, *C. simplicifolius*, *C. tetradactylus*, *P. crassipes*, and *A. hainanensis*, are insufficient to meet the demand for weaving production in Bobai. Consequently, weaving companies must import a significant amount of raw materials from other regions. Additionally, the Bobai weaving industry has a high demand for rattan, but due to the shortage of local rattan resources, woven rattan is primarily imported from abroad. Notably, most of the vines traded globally are from wild populations in Southeast Asia, with few exceptions (Peters, et al., 2007; Yulianto, et al., 2021). Rattan resources are decreasing rapidly due to a lack of conservation resources and a high harvest rate (Hirschberger, 2011; Yulianto, et al., 2021). Plants play a crucial role in people's recognition of cultures, traditions, and lifestyles (Shebitz, 2005). Once the resources necessary for practices are unavailable, traditions may change significantly (Shebitz & Kimmerer, 2005). Therefore, the protection of cultural diversity and biodiversity are inextricably linked.

China is rich in plant resources available for weaving (Xu, et al., 1993; Zhai, et al., 2009; Zhou, et al., 2013), and some species have been commercially developed in some other countries (Cunningham & Milton, 1987; Kotze & Traynor, 2011). By identifying more alternative materials that can be used for weaving, the dependence on any particular species can be reduced, thereby enhancing the sustainability of the weaving industry. In addition, promoting the cultivation of weaving plants with high demand, such as rattan and bamboo, can help support the industry's sustainable development in Bobai County. Many achievements have been made in the artificial planting of weaving plants in China, for example, *A. katsumadi*, *C. tetradactylus*, *C. nambariensis* var. *xishuangbannaensis* and reed (Gan, 2005; Li, et al., 2013; Su, et al., 2006). Given Bobai's subtropical location, which is characterized by a hot and humid climate, many plant species can thrive in the area (Zeng, et al., 1993). Growing weaving plants locally can alleviate pressure on the industry's raw material supply and provide additional benefits such as beautifying the environment, enhancing ecological services, and safeguarding local biodiversity and traditional culture.

## 5　Conclusion

In this study, we recorded 33 species of plants used for Hakka weaving, belonging to 17 families and 27 genera. Different plants can be processed into various products. Among the plants used for weaving, herbs are the most abundant, while respondents mention bamboo and Indonesian vines (*Calamus* sp.) most frequently. Bobai weaving turns crop waste and invasive species such as water hyacinth into treasures as weaving materials, making it more environmentally friendly. Bobai weaving products contain a variety of traditional cultural connotations. By integrating modern elements and more use value, Bobai Hakka weaving has realized the transformation from conventional to modern and won broad markets. With the joint participation of the government, enterprises, and farmers, the Bobai weaving industry has formed a model of "non-heritage+industry+poverty alleviation", which has become a successful case of poverty alleviation and rural revitalization and is worth popularizing.

# References

[1] ARNOLD J E, PÉREZ, M R. The role of non-timber forest products in conservation and development.In E. Wollenberg & A. Ingles (Eds.), Incomes from the forest: Methods for the development and conservation of forest products for local communities (pp. 17–42). CIFOR/ IUCN.

[2] AU D T, WU J, JIANG Z, et al. Ethnobotanical study of medicinal plants used by Hakka in Guangdong, China[J]. Journal of Ethnopharmacology, 2008, 117 (1), 41–50. https: // doi. org/10. 1016/j. jep. 2008. 01. 016.

[3] BORRELLE S B, RINGMA J, LAW K. L, et al. Predicted growth in plastic waste exceeds efforts to mitigate plastic pollution[J/OL]. *Science*, 2020, 369: 1515–1518. https: // doi. org/ 10. 1126/ scien ce. aba3656.

[4] CONSTABLE, N. Christian souls and Chinese spirits: A Hakka community in Hong Kong. University of California Press, 1994.

[5] CUNNINGHAM A B, MILTON S J. Effects of basket-weaving industry on mokola palm and dye plants in northwestern Botswana[J/OL]. Economic Botany, 1987, 41 (3), 386–402. https: // doi. org/ 10. 1007/BF02859055.

[6] DHARSONO D, SUMARNO S, ATMAJA N A C D. Utilization of straw in furniture design[J/ OL].ARTISTIC: International Journal of Creation and Innovation, 2021, 2 (1), 69–81. https: // doi. org/ 10.33153/ artistic. v2i1. 3413.

[7] FENG C. The present situation and the development trends of non-timber forest products in the world[J/OL]. World Forestry Research, 2002, 15 (1): 43–52. https: // doi. org/ 10. 3969/j. issn. 1001–4241. 2002. 01.006.

[8] GAN, B. Cultivation and utilization of *Alpinia katsumadi* Hayata[J/OL]. Resource Development and Market, 2005, 21 (2): 144–145. https: // doi. org/ 10. 3969/j. issn. 1005–8141. 2005. 02. 023.

[9] HAI N T, DUONG N T, HUY D T N, et al. Sustainable business solutions for traditional handicraft product in the northwestern provinces of Vietnam[J/OL]. Management, 2021, 25 (1): 209–233.https: // doi. org/ 10. 2478/ manme nt-2019–0067.

[10] HIRSCHBERGER, P. Global rattan trade: Pressure on forest resources, analysis and challenges. Vienna: WWF-Austria, 2011.

[11] JIA L, FENG X. Bambusa. In B. Geng & Z. Wang (Eds.), Flora Reipublicae Popularis Sinicae 9 (1), 120. Berlin: Science Press, 1996.

[12] KOTZE D C, TRAYNOR C H. Wetland plant species used for craft production in Kwazulu-Natal, south Africa: Ethnobotanical knowledge and environmental sustainability[J]. Economic Botany, 2011, 65: 271–282.

[13] LI D, SUN D C, HU Y L. Cultivation and management of reed[J/OL]. Wetland Science and Management, 2013, 9 (2): 42–44. https: // doi. org/ 10. 3969/j. issn. 1673–3290. 2013.02. 11.

[14] LUO B, AHMED S, LONG C. Bamboos for weaving and relevant traditional knowledge in Sansui, southwest China[J/OL]. Journal of Ethnobiology and Ethnomedicine, 2020, 16 (1): 1–9. https: // doi. org/10. 1186/ s13002–020–00418–9.

[15] LUO B, LI F, AHMED S, LONG C. Diversity and use of medicinal plants for soup making in traditional diets of the Hakka in west Fujian, China[J/OL]. Journal of Ethnobiology and Ethnomedicine, 2019, 15 (1): 1–15. https: // doi. org/ 10. 1186/ s13002–019–0335–y.

[16] PARISH W L, WHYTE M K. Village and family in contemporary China. University of Chicago Press, 1978.

[17] PAZON A N R, DEL RIO J M P. Materials, functions and weaving patterns of Philippine indigenous baskets[J]. Asian Journal of Multidisciplinary Studies, 2018, 1 (2): 107–118.

[18] PETERS C M, HENDERSON A, MAUNG U M, et al. The rattan trade of northern Myanmar: Species, supplies, and sustainability[J/OL]. Economic Botany, 2007, 61 (1): 3–13.https: // doi. org/ 10. 1663/ 0013–0001 (2007) 61[3: TRTONM] 2.0. CO; 2.

[19] RAHAYU M, KUNCARI E S, MAHDAWIA, et al. Short communication: Ethnobotanical

study of *Lygodium circinnatum* and its utilization in crafts weaving in Indonesia[J/OL]. *Biodiversitas*, 2020, 21 (2): 617–621. https: // doi. org/ 10. 13057/ BIODIV/ D210225.

[20] RAHIM W R W A, IDRUS R M. Importance and uses of forest product bamboo and rattan: Their value to socio-economics of local communities[J/OL]. International Journal of Academic Research in Business and Social Sciences, 2019, 8 (12): 1484–1497. https: // doi. org/ 10. 6007/ IJARB SS/ V8-I12/ 5252.

[21] SHEBITZ D. Weaving traditional ecological knowledge into the restoration of basketry plants[J]. Journal of Ecological Anthropology, 2005, 9 (1): 51–68. https: // doi. org/ 10. 5038/ 2162–4593.9. 1.4.

[22] SHEBITZ D J, KIMMERER R W. Reestablishing roots of a Mohawk community and a culturally significant plant: Sweetgrass[J/OL]. Restoration Ecology, 2005, 13 (2): 257–264. https: // doi. org/ 10. 1111/j.1526–100X. 2005. 00033.x.

[23] SONG Z, XU Y, LI X. A probe into protective development of national cultural heritage tourism: A case study of Tunba, Nimu County Tibetanincense is produced[J/OL]. Journal of Minzu University of China (philosophy and Social Sciences Edition), 2011, 38 (01): 55–60. https: // doi. org/ 10.15970/j. cnki. 1005–8575. 2011. 01. 025.

[24] SU J, YIN J, WANG D, et al. Trials on the introduction and cultivation of *Calamus tetradactylus* and *Calamus nambariensis* var. *xishuangbannaensis*[J/OL]. Journal of Fujian Forestry Science and Technology, 2006, 33 (3): 155–157. https: // doi. org/ 10. 3969/j. issn. 1002–7351. 2006. 03. 038.

[25] TARDÍO J, PARDO-DE-SANTAYANA M. Cultural importance indices: A comparative analysis based on the useful wild plants of southern Cantabria (northern Spain)[J/OL]. Economic Botany, 2008, 62 (1): 24–39.https: // doi. org/ 10. 1007/ s12231–007–9004–5.

[26] VILLAMAGNA A M, MURPHY B R. Ecological and socio-economic impacts of invasive water hyacinth (*Eichhornia crassipes*): A review[J/OL]. Freshwater Biology, 2010, 55 (2): 282–298. https: // doi. org/ 10.1111/j. 1365–2427. 2009. 02294.x.

[27] VITALINI S, IRITI M, PURICELLI C, et al. Traditional knowledge on medicinal and food plants used in valsangiacomo (Sondrio, Italy): An alpine ethnobotanical study[J/OL]. Journal of Ethnopharmacology, 2013, 145 (2): 517–529. https: // doi. org/ 10. 1016/j. jep.

2012.11. 024.

[28] WU T, CHEN S. ALPINIA. In T. Wu (Ed.), Flora Reipublicae Popularis Sinicae. Science Press, 1981.

[29] XIA F, PAN W, BIAN X, et al. Research on straw and willow plaiting in Shandong and traditional craft[J/OL]. 5th International Conference on Education, Management, Arts, Economics and Social Science (ICEMAESS 2018) (pp. 933–936). Atlantis Press, 2018. https: // doi. org/ 10. 2991/ icemaess-18.2018. 183.

[30] XU H, YIN G, LI Y, et al. The natural distribution and utilization of rattan resources in China[J/OL]. Forest Research, 1993, 6 (4): 380–389. https: // doi. org/ 10. 3321/j. issn: 1001–1498. 1993. 04. 017.

[31] XU H, YIN G, SUN Q, et al. Research and development of rattan in China[J/OL]. Scienta Silvae Sinicae, 2002, 38: 135–143. https: // doi. org/ 10. 11707/j. 1001–7488. 20020223.

[32] YULIANTO, NOGUCHI R, SOEKMADI R, et al. Reconciling livelihoods and conservation for rattan sustainable harvesting in Lore Lindu National Park, Indonesia[J/OL]. Small-Scale Forestry, 2021, 20: 175–197. https: // doi. org/ 10. 1007/ s11842–020–09463–4.

[33] YULIN MUNICIPAL COMMITTEE OF THE CHINESE PEOPLE'S POLITICAL CONSULTATIVE CONFERENCE. Yulin Kejia. Guangxi Normal University Press, 2016.

[34] ZENG B, XU H, YIN G. Study on the division of rattan cultivation[J]. Forest Research, 1993, 6 (5): 547–555.

[35] ZHAI S, CHEN Z, ZHANG G, et al. Survey of wild fiber plant resources in Shilin County of Yunnan Province[J/OL]. Journal of Kunming University, 2009, 31 (3): 53–59. https: // doi. org/ 10. 3969/j. issn.1674–5639. 2009. 03. 018.

[36] ZHANG A, XIE Y, WEN Y, et al. Current situation and countermeasures of exploitation and utilization on the NWFPs in China[J/OL]. Journal of Beijing Forestry University (Social Sciences), 2008, 7 (3): 47–51. https: // doi. org/ 10. 3969/j. issn. 1671–6116. 2008. 03. 010.

[37] ZHANG Y. On the knitting technology and its industrialization development of Bobai Hakka[J/OL]. Journal of Yulin Normal University, 2013, 34 (3): 23–27. https: // doi. org/ 10. 13792/j. cnki. cn45–1300/z. 2013.03. 001.

[38] ZHOU X, WAN W, WANG J. The species and distribution of wild fiber plants in Hebei

Bobai Hakka weaving: Plant diversity, traditional culture, and
a model for rural revitalization
105

Province[J/OL]. Hebei Journal of Forestry and Orchard Research, 2013, 28 (3): 307–313. https: // doi. org/ 10. 3969/j. issn. 1007–4961. 2013.03. 020.

原载*Environment, Development and Sustainability* 2024年第26期第17335–17352页。

# Feed plants, ethnoveterinary medicine, and biocultural values: Insights on the Luchuan pig from Hakka communities in China

Liufu Yongqing[1], Zhou Jilong[2], Fu Qiongyao[1], Shao Min[1], Xie Yaozhang[1], Luo Binsheng[3]

1. Natural History Museum of Guangxi, Nanning　530012, China

2. Luchuan Livestock Station, Luchuan　537700, China

3. Lushan Botanical Garden, Jiangxi Province and Chinese Academy of Sciences, Lushan　332900, China

【 Abstract 】 **Background**: The Luchuan pig is an indigenous breed from Luchuan County, China, with cultural and genetic significance. However, traditional knowledge and conservation status have not been systematically documented.

**Methods**: Using ethnobiological methods, we surveyed 72 Luchuan pig farmers in 7 townships during 2021-2023. Semi-structured interviews and participant observation were conducted to document traditional knowledge and management practices.

**Results**: The locals reported 51 plant species used as pig feed, with 30 wild species. Growth-stage-specific feeding and seasonal adjustment practices were documented. We recorded 62 ethnoveterinary plant uses, mainly for treating pigs' heat stress and skin conditions. Luchuan pigs play central roles in local Hakka customs, rituals, and cuisine. Additionally, the new ecological farming models minimize the environmental

Funding: This study was supported by the Natural Science Foundation of Guangxi Zhuang Autonomous Region（Project No. 2022GXNSFBA035527）, the National Natural Science Foundation of China（Project No. 41662002; Project No. 32300325）, the Talents Program of Jiangxi Province of China（Project No. jxsq2020104003）and the Special Project of the Lushan Botanical Garden of the Chinese Academy of Sciences（Project No. 2021ZWZX12）.

Feed plants, ethnoveterinary medicine, and biocultural values:
Insights on the Luchuan pig from Hakka communities in China

107

impacts to the local community. However, there are still some challenges remained for conserving and promoting Luchuan pigs.

**Conclusions**: The Luchuan Hakka people possess rich traditional knowledge and management experience in raising Luchuan pigs. Our study provides extensive documentation of traditional knowledge and recommends integrating cultural and genetic aspects for sustaining this biocultural heritage. Findings can inform initiatives supporting local breed conservation globally.

【Keywords】Luchuan pig; Local breed; Feed plants; Veterinary plants; Genetic breeding; Traditional knowledge; Hakka

# 1　Introduction

Livestock and poultry genetic resources provide quality animal products and promote farmer income, sustainable resource use, and ecological and cultural heritage protection, establishing a foundation for food security, rural revitalization, biodiversity conservation, and ecological construction. [1-3]Native breeds of livestock and poultry are populations adapted to local traditional farming systems and environments. [4] Originating from specific regions where they are frequently utilized, native breeds are adapted to the local conditions. [4] They often have advantageous traits like coarse feed tolerance, disease resistance, delicious taste, good meat quality, and stable genetics, making them important genetic resources for developing new breeds and promoting sustainable animal husbandry. [5-7]

As a major livestock producer, China possesses the world's richest livestock and poultry genetic resources, accounting for about 1/6 of the global total. [8, 9] However, the rise of intensive farming and economic growth has led to the replacement of some native breeds with faster-growing varieties, driving rapid decline and even extinction of local breeds. [10-12] Statistics indicate that 30% of existing animal genetic resources are threatened, endangered, vulnerable, or extinct. [13] Alarmingly, nearly 800 livestock breeds have been documented as lost in the past century. [13] Surveys reveal that 55 local Chinese breeds are endangered and 22 critically endangered. [14] Additionally, 15 documented breeds were not found, making their extinction status unclear. [14] In total, endangered and critically endangered breeds account for approximately 14% of local breeds in China. [14] Thus, the attention and protection of traditional animal breeds in China are imperative.

Luchuan County in Guangxi is a major settlement area for the Hakka people, with approximately 700, 000 residents, constituting about two-thirds of the total population [15]. The Luchuan pig, named after its place of origin, is primarily raised by Hakka people in the region and has become a representative indigenous breed in China. Compared to Western domestic pigs, Luchuan pigs exhibit distinct characteristics, including superior meat quality, early maturity, high reproductive capacity, stable maternal lineage, adaptability to coarse feed, and strong disease resistance. [16–18] Recognized as one of China's excellent local pig breeds, the Luchuan pig was listed in the "National Catalogue of Livestock and Poultry Genetic Resources" and "Geographical Indication Protection for Agricultural Products" [19]. Studies report that Luchuan pig meat is tender, delicious, and rich in essential amino acids like glutamic acid and lysine, as well as vitamins, saturated fatty acids, and monounsaturated fatty acids, contributing to its unique flavor and high nutritional value. [20–22] However, Luchuan pigs also exhibit some physiological limitations, such as small body size, slow growth rate, and low lean meat percentage. [23] Moreover, their higher market price compared to other pig breeds has led to limited market capacity. These factors pose challenges to the reproductive production of Luchuan pigs. Despite being recognized as an important genetic breeding strategic resource, the conservation of Luchuan pigs remains a complex task, drawing significant attention from the local government.

Researches have shown that the conservation of genetic resources cannot be dissociated from their natural and cultural environments. [11, 24] In numerous indigenous regions around the world, the utilization of natural resources is embedded within local traditional knowledge and culture. Traditional knowledge serves as a valuable source of information concerning local wild forage resources, their nutritional characteristics, as well as veterinary and plant resources. [25] It can significantly contribute to the development of novel and sustainable approaches to natural resource management. [26, 27]

The Hakka people in Luchuan have accumulated a vast amount of traditional knowledge

Feed plants, ethnoveterinary medicine, and biocultural values:
Insights on the Luchuan pig from Hakka communities in China

109

regarding breeding Luchuan pigs through their long-standing production practices. Alongside this knowledge, they have also developed various traditional cultures and customs related to pigs, such as dietary customs, social rituals, and festive traditions. Despite the crucial significance of this knowledge in the conservation of Luchuan pigs, there is a lack of systematic documentation and record keeping of these traditional practices. Therefore, we conducted multiple investigations in Luchuan County with the objective of: (1) documenting the traditional breeding and management experiences of Luchuan pigs, including the utilization of feed and veterinary medicinal plants; (2) evaluating and identifying key plant species used in feeding Luchuan pigs through a scoring system for feed plants; (3) assessing the current status of the local Luchuan pig-related industry's conservation and development and providing feasible improvement suggestions; and(4) elucidating the importance of Luchuan pig-related traditional customs and culture in the conservation efforts. This investigation aims to provide insights into the development of plant-based feed and veterinary medicine and also serve as a case reference for the conservation and industrial development of local livestock and poultry breeds.

## 2　Study area and methodologies

Luchuan County, Guangxi Zhuang Autonomous Region, is situated in the hilly region of south China and represents a typical agricultural area characterized by hills. The land in this region is fertile, with a substantial organic matter content(3. 21%) and a considerable presence of iron elements, and the pH level ranges from 5.4 to 6.7. The climate is mild, with abundant sunlight, plentiful rainfall, and a long frost-free period, providing highly favorable conditions for the growth and reproduction of various flora and fauna. These conditions also benefit the cultivation and propagation of agricultural and forage crops, which offer an excellent natural geographical environment for breeding and raising Luchuan pigs. [28]

From 2021 to 2023, we conducted ethnobiological research using the ethnobotanical approach in seven townships known for their significant Luchuan pig farming activities, including Gucheng, Qinghu, Liangtian, Wushi, Daqiao, Wenquan, and Mapo(Figure 1).

Subsequently, purposive sampling was employed to select respondents with abundant traditional knowledge of pig farming for interviews. [3, 29] A total of 72 respondents participated in the study, comprising 25 females and 47 males, with an average age of 55.8 years and an average pig farming experience of 26.9 years.

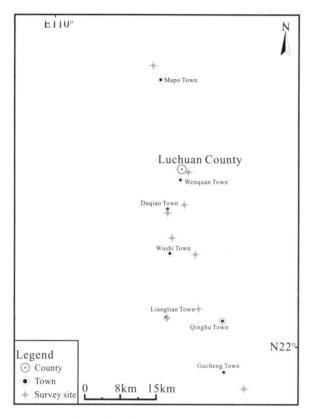

Figure 1　Map of the study area

Data collection employed a semi-structured interview method and participatory observation. [3, 24, 30] During the semi-structured interviews, respondents were asked basically around the questions listed in annex(Additional file 1). The participatory observation was conducted during the free-range grazing of Luchuan pigs and the collection of feed and veterinary medicinal plants by farmers. Specimens were collected, and records of the plant species and related knowledge on their utilization were made. Plant identification was carried out using taxonomic electronic databases, such as https: // www. cvh. ac. cn/; http: // www. iplant. cn/; www. world flora online. org, based on morphological characteristics and geographical origins of the plants. Voucher specimens of all the feed plants and veterinary medicinal plants were

Feed plants, ethnoveterinary medicine, and biocultural values:
Insights on the Luchuan pig from Hakka communities in China
111

collected and deposited in the herbarium of the Natural History Museum of Guangxi.

Furthermore, 2-3 individuals, totaling 25 key informants, including farmers, farm caretakers, veterinarians, and intangible cultural heritage inheritors, were selected at each survey site for group discussions and scoring. [31] Five aspects were quantitatively scored for the feed plants: nutritional value, pig preference level, availability of resources, digestibility, and frequency of use. Each aspect was rated on a scale from 1 to 5, with 5 indicating the highest score and 1 the lowest. For instance, regarding the nutritional value of feed plants, the scoring criteria were as follows: Excellent(5 points), Good(4 points), Moderately Good(3 points), Fair(2 points), and Poor(1 point) [30]. The scoring criteria for the frequency of use were as follows: used more than once per week(5 points), used once per week(4 points), used once per month(3 points), used less than once per month but more than once per year(2 points), and used once or less per year(1 point). The overall utilization value of feed plants was assessed based on the total scores. A higher score indicated a higher comprehensive utilization value of the feed plant, indicating greater development prospects.

## 3　Results and discussion

### 3.1　The traditional feed of Luchuan pigs

A total of 51 feed plants were reported by the respondents, belonging to 21 families and 43 genera(Table 1). Among these feed plants, the Asteraceae, Poaceae, and Amaranthaceae families were the most represented, with 11, 6, and 5 species, respectively. Various parts of the plants were utilized as feed, including aboveground parts, whole plants, leaves, fruits, seeds, seed coats, rice husks, stems, and tubers, with aboveground parts and whole plants being the primary components, accounting for 37.7% and 22.6%, respectively. More than half of the feed plants used for Luchuan pigs were wild plants(accounting for 56.6% of the total) (some images are shown in Figure 2), while cultivated plants accounted for 41.5%. The results showed that the comprehensive utilization scores of Luchuan pig feed plants ranged from 10 to 24 points. Rice(*Oryza sativa*), corn(*Zea mays*), *Pennisetum purpureum*, sweet

Table 1　The inventory of feed plants for Luchuan pigs

| Specimen no. | Family name | Scientific name | Local name | Used part | Harvesting season | Resource type | Life form | Integrated score |
|---|---|---|---|---|---|---|---|---|
| LFYQ23146 | Amaranthaceae | *Beta vulgaris* L. | tóng sháo mài, zhū má cài | Leaf | Spring, summer, winter | Cultivated | Herb | 20 |
| LFYQ23157 | Amaranthaceae | *Alternanthera philoxeroides* (Mart.) Griseb. | jiǎ kōng xīn cài | Overground part | Spring, summer | Wild | Herb | 16 |
| LFYQ23164 | Amaranthaceae | *Amaranthus viridis* L. | gǒu sè xiàn | Whole plant | Spring, summer, fall | Wild | Herb | 16 |
| LFYQ23034 | Amaranthaceae | *Cyathula prostrata* (L.) Blume | xī yàng mǎ biān cǎo, dì dǎn | Whole plant | Whole year | Wild | Herb | 12 |
| LFYQ23019 | Amaranthaceae | *Celosia argentea* L. | qīng xiāng | Overground part | Spring, summer, fall | Wild | Herb | 11 |
| LFYQ23144 | Araceae | *Colocasia esculenta* (L.) Schott. | yù tóu miáo, yàng yù | Petiole | Whole year | Cultivated or wild | Herb | 21 |
| LFYQ23068 | Asteraceae | *Ixeris polycephala* Cass. ex DC. | mǎi cài | Leaf | Spring, winter | Cultivated | Herb | 21 |
| LFYQ23154 | Asteraceae | *Lactuca sativa* L. | yóu mǎi cài | Leaf | Whole year | Cultivated | Herb | 17 |
| LFYQ23159 | Asteraceae | *Lactuca sativa* var. *ramosa* Hort. | shēng cài | Leaf | Spring, winter | Cultivated | Herb | 16 |
| LFYQ22018 | Asteraceae | *Emilia sonchifolia* (L.) DC. | yī diǎn hóng | Whole plant | Whole year | Wild | Herb | 16 |
| LFYQ23161 | Asteraceae | *Lactuca sativa* var. *angustata* Irish ex Bremer | wō sǔn | Leaf | Spring, winter | Cultivated | Herb | 15 |
| LFYQ23111 | Asteraceae | *Erechtites valerianifolius* (Link ex Spreng.) DC. | guò cháo cài | Overground part | Whole year | Wild | Herb | 15 |
| LFYQ23048 | Asteraceae | *Gamochaeta pensylvanica* (Willd.) Cabrera | é ài | Whole plant | Whole year | Wild | Herb | 15 |

Feed plants，ethnoveterinary medicine，and biocultural values：
Insights on the Luchuan pig from Hakka communities in China

113

Table 1（continued）

| Specimen no. | Family name | Scientific name | Local name | Used part | Harvesting season | Resource type | Life form | Integrated score |
|---|---|---|---|---|---|---|---|---|
| LFYQ22009 | Asteraceae | *Bidens pilosa* L. | yī bāo zhēn | Overground part | Whole year | Wild | Herb | 14 |
| LFYQ23054 | Asteraceae | *Crassocephalum crepidioides* S. Moore | guò cháo cài, gé míng cài | Overground part | Spring, summer, fall | Wild | Herb | 14 |
| LFYQ22172 | Asteraceae | *Eclipta prostrata* (L.) L. | mò cǎo | Overground part | Whole year | Wild | Herb | 12 |
| LFYQ23164 | Asteraceae | *Erigeron canadensis* L. | xiǎo péng cǎo | Overground part | Whole year | Wild | Herb | 10 |
| LFYQ23150 | Brassicaceae | *Raphanus raphanistrum* subsp. *sativus* (L.) Domin | luó bo | Whole plant | Winter | Cultivated | Herb | 18 |
| LFYQ23151 | Brassicaceae | *Brassica rapa* var. *glabra* Regel | huǒ tǒng cài, bái cài | Leaf | Winter | Cultivated | Herb | 18 |
| LFYQ23155 | Brassicaceae | *Brassica oleracea* var. *botrytis* L. | yē zǐ cài | Overground part | Spring, winter | Cultivated | Herb | 17 |
| LFYQ23156 | Brassicaceae | *Brassica oleracea* L. | bāo cài | Overground part | Spring, winter | Cultivated | Herb | 17 |
| LFYQ23160 | Caricaceae | *Carica papaya* L. | mù dōng guā | Fruit | Fall | Cultivated | Tree | 15 |
| LFYQ23020 | Caryophyllaceae | *Stellaria aquatica* Scop. | má sī cǎo, é, cháng cài | Overground part | Whole year | Wild | Herb | 12 |
| LFYQ23151 | Commelinaceae | *Commelina diffusa* Burm.f. | ròu cǎo, zhú gāo cǎo | Whole plant | Whole year | Wild | Herb | 18 |
| LFYQ23142 | Convolvulaceae | *Ipomoea batatas* (L.) Lam. | hóng shǔ téng, hóng shǔ téng, fān shǔ | Whole plant | Whole year | Cultivated | Herb | 24 |

Table 1 ( continued )

| Specimen no. | Family name | Scientific name | Local name | Used part | Harvesting season | Resource type | Life form | Integrated score |
|---|---|---|---|---|---|---|---|---|
| LFYQ23158 | Convolvulaceae | *Ipomoea aquatica* Forssk. | kōng xīn cài | Overground part | Summer | Cultivated | Herb | 16 |
| LFYQ23100 | Costaceae | *Hellenia speciosa* (J.Koenig) S. R. Dutta | fú shǒu gùn | Overground part | Spring, summer, fall | Wild | Herb | 11 |
| LFYQ23148 | Cucurbitaceae | *Cucurbita moschata* Duchesne | nán guā | Fruit | Summer, fall | Cultivated | Herb | 19 |
| LFYQ23153 | Cucurbitaceae | *Benincasa hispida* Cogn. | dōng guā | Fruit | Summer, fall | Cultivated | Herb | 18 |
| LFYQ23145 | Euphorbiaceae | *Manihot esculenta* Crantz | mù shǔ | Root | Fall, winter | Cultivated | Shrub | 21 |
| LFYQ23143 | Fabaceae | *Glycine max* (L.) Merr. | dòu pò | Seed | Fall | Cultivated | Herb | 23 |
| LFYQ23147 | Fabaceae | *Arachis hypogaea* L. | huā shēng fū | Seed coat | Summer | Cultivated | Herb | 20 |
| LFYQ23149 | Moraceae | *Broussonetia papyrifera* (L.) Vent. | gòu shù | Tender leaf | Whole year | Wild | Tree | 19 |
| LFYQ23148 | Onagraceae | *Ludwigia adscendens* (L.) H. Hara | guò táng shé | Whole plant | Whole year | Wild | Herb | 19 |
| LFYQ23021 | Onagraceae | *Ludwigia hyssopifolia* (G. Don) Exell. | / | Overground part | Spring, winter | Wild | Herb | 12 |
| LFYQ22784 | Poaceae | *Zea mays* L. | yù mǐ | Seed, stem | Fall | Cultivated | Herb | 24 |
| LFYQ22808 | Poaceae | *Oryza sativa* L. | zhōu, mǐ kāng, xǐ mǐ shuǐ | Seed, husk | Summer, fall | Cultivated | Herb | 24 |
| LFYQ23052 | Poaceae | *Pennisetum purpureum* Schumach. | tián xiàng cǎo, jiǎ gān zhè | Overground part | Whole year | Cultivated or wild | Herb | 24 |
| LFYQ22806 | Poaceae | *Triticum aestivum* L. | mài pí | Seed coat | / | Introduced | Herb | 23 |

Feed plants, ethnoveterinary medicine, and biocultural values:
Insights on the Luchuan pig from Hakka communities in China

115

Table 1 ( continued )

| Specimen no. | Family name | Scientific name | Local name | Used part | Harvesting season | Resource type | Life form | Integrated score |
|---|---|---|---|---|---|---|---|---|
| LFYQ23152 | Poaceae | *Cenchrus flaccidus* (Griseb.) Morrone | huáng zhú cǎo | Overground part | Whole year | Wild | Herb | 18 |
| LFYQ23018 | Poaceae | *Eleusine indica* Gaertn. | niú jīn cǎo | Overground part | Whole year | Wild | Herb | 13 |
| LFYQ23050 | Polygonaceae | *Rumex crispus* L. | jiǎ mài cài | Overground part | Spring, summer, fall | Wild | Herb | 16 |
| LFYQ23015 | Polygonaceae | *Persicaria maculosa* Gray | xiǎo là liǎo | Whole plant | Whole year | Wild | Herb | 15 |
| LFYQ23006 | Polygonaceae | *Persicaria lapathifolia* (L.) Delarbre | jiǎ là liǎo | Overground part | Whole year | Wild | Herb | 15 |
| LFYQ23002 | Polygonaceae | *Polygonum plebeium* R. Br. | wū yíng yì, páng xiè yǎn | Whole plant | Whole year | Wild | Herb | 13 |
| LFYQ23152 | Pontederiaceae | *Pontederia crassipes* Mart. | shuǐ piāo, fú shuǐ lián | Overground part | Spring, summer | Wild | Herb | 18 |
| LFYQ23066 | Portulacaceae | *Portulaca oleracea* L. | mǎ chǐ xiàn | Whole plant | Spring, summer, fall | Wild | Herb | 16 |
| LFYQ23163 | Sapindaceae | *Litchi chinensis* Sonn. | lì zhī | Leaf | Whole year | Cultivated | Tree | 10 |
| LFYQ23013 | Saururaceae | *Houttuynia cordata* Thunb. | yú xīng cǎo | Whole plant | Whole year | Wild | Herb | 16 |
| LFYQ23157 | Solanaceae | *Solanum americanum* Mill. | bái huā cài | Stem and leaf | Spring, summer, fall | Wild | Herb | 17 |
| LFYQ23162 | Solanaceae | *Physalis angulata* L. | dēng lóng cài | Overground part | Whole year | Wild | Herb | 12 |

a−*Celosia argentea*; b−*Pennisetum purpureum*; c−*Commelina diffusa*; d−*Polygonum plebeium*; e−*Persicaria lapathifolia*; f−*Portulaca oleracea*; g−*Stellaria aquatica*; h−*Pontederia crassipes*; i−*Erechtites valerianifolius* (All photographs were taken by Yongqing Liufu).

Figure 2　Part of wild feed plants for Luchuan pigs

potato(*Ipomoea batatas*), wheat(*Triticum aestivum*), and soybean(*Glycine max*) obtained relatively high scores, indicating their significant comprehensive utilization value in Luchuan pig farming. Apart from wheat, which needs to be introduced, all these plants are commonly cultivated locally. *P. purpureum*, on the other hand, is both harvested from the wild and cultivated by some individuals.

This study shows that Luchuan pig feed plants are mainly herbaceous plants(accounting for 92.2%). This result is similar to other ethnobotanical cases in Europe and other regions of Guangxi. [30, 32] The wild herbaceous plants we recorded are mainly weeds, among which *Pennisetum purpureum*, *Colocasia esculenta*, *Commelina diffusa*, *Pontederia crassipes*, *Solanum americanum*, *Emilia sonchifolia*, *Portulaca oleracea* are the most favorite forage

Feed plants，ethnoveterinary medicine，and biocultural values：
Insights on the Luchuan pig from Hakka communities in China

117

plants harvested by local Hakka people. On the one hand, these plants are commonly found in the wastelands and ditches near their homes, which provide a convenient source of feed during periods of feed shortage. On the other hand, for local Hakka people, these plants are well-known and have multiple uses: *S. americanum*, *E. sonchifolia*, and *P. oleracea* are commonly used as wild vegetables and medicinal plants. *P. crassipes* is a commonly used weaving plant by Hakka people. *P. purpureum* and *C. diffusa* serve as fodder plants for local cattle and other livestock. The leafstalk of *C. esculenta* is utilized by locals to make pickled food, while its root is a commonly used starchy edible plant.

Among the 51 feed plants, the farmers classified rice, corn, soybean, peanut bran, and wheat, which have relatively high nutritional content, as concentrate feed. The remaining 46 feed plants, including *P. purpureum*, sweet potato(*I. batatas*), and taro(*C. esculenta*), were categorized as roughage. Different species of concentrate and roughage supplements are provided to Luchuan pigs during different growth stages. During the gestation period, it is essential to balance the nutritional needs of pregnant sows. For piglets aged 0 to 2 months, their protein requirements are high, and they primarily rely on maternal milk supplemented with appropriate solid food. They should be fed 4 to 5 times a day with a diet consisting mainly of porridge, corn(*Z. mays*) flour, soybean(*G. max*) meal, and wheat(*T. aestivum* subsp. *spelta*) bran, mixed with small amounts of fish meal and bone meal. After reaching a weight of 7.5 kg, roughage feed should be gradually introduced. Piglets can be kept in confinement after weaning or gradually switched to free-range feeding. When confined, they should be fed twice a day, with roughage as the main component and a small amount of concentrate feed. During free-range feeding, they can be fed once in the morning or evening, with the rest of the time spent foraging on wild plants.

The favorable weather and unique geographical environment have nurtured abundant feed plant resources in Luchuan. The survey results reveal that a large variety of plants are available year-round to feed Luchuan pigs. Among the feed plants used for Luchuan pigs, 23 species can be harvested throughout the year, accounting for 45.10% of the total; 16 species are harvested in spring(31.37%), 14 species in summer(27.45%), 13 species in fall(25.49%), and 10 species in winter(19.61%). During late winter and early spring, farmers mainly compensate for the insufficient feed by strengthening the cultivation of melons, fruits, and vegetables. Some farmers also utilize fermentation techniques to preserve plant feed, such as fermenting *P. purpureum*. They rarely use artificial feed, as they believe that feeding artificial feed may lead to issues such as fever, constipation, and digestive problems in Luchuan pigs.

During our participatory survey of free range pigs, we found that Luchuan pigs consume a greater variety of wild plants than that the respondents reported, such as *Eleusine indica*, *Ludwigia adscendens*, *Erigeron canadensis*. The respondents who raised free-range pigs mentioned that they were familiar with certain plants but did not know their specific names. However, when we interviewed the handlers of captive-bred Luchuan pigs, they were able to name the commonly used feed plants and their other functions. A study from Nigeria also found that farmers who kept confined animals had a greater knowledge about the resources compared with farmers who raised animals free in the pasture. [33]

Compared to the present, in the past, farmers used more wild plants to feed Luchuan pigs, especially during times of grain scarcity when people had no choice but to rely on wild plants. However, with improvements in living standards and changes in feeding practices, many traditional wild-feed plants have been replaced by fermented feed and cultivated plants. Similar to other Chinese local pig breeds[29], the traditional knowledge about the utilization and management of wild-feed plants is facing significant risks of extinction in the local community.

## 3.2 The traditional veterinary medicine for Luchuan pigs

Traditional herbal medicine is an important source of medication used by farmers to treat ailments in Luchuan pigs. The results of this study show that a total of 62 species of herbal medicines were reported by the respondents for treating diseases in Luchuan pigs(Table 2, Figure 3). Common diseases in Luchuan pigs include cold, cough, wheezing, constipation, anorexia, indigestion, internal heat, and diarrhea.

Pig farmers mentioned that feeding Luchuan pigs with rice(*O. sativa*) bran, soybean(*G. max*) meal, and peanut(*Arachis hypogaea*) bran can easily lead to internal heat and associated issues such as anorexia, constipation, and wheezing. Therefore, they place great emphasis

Feed plants, ethnoveterinary medicine, and biocultural values:
Insights on the Luchuan pig from Hakka communities in China

119

Table 2　The inventory of veterinary plants for Luchuan pigs

| Specimen ID | Family name | Scientific name | Local name | Part used | Processing method | Medicinal effect | Life form | Resource type |
|---|---|---|---|---|---|---|---|---|
| LYFQ21020 | Acanthaceae | *Dicliptera chinensis* Juss. | qīng shé | Overground part | Cook fully and feed | Clear heat, treat cold, treat jaundice | Herb | Wild |
| LFYQ23170 | Acanthaceae | *Strobilanthes cusia* Kuntze | bǎn lán gēn | Root | Make herbal decoction and drink; sun-dry, grind into powder, and mix into feed | Clear heat, treat jaundice | Herb | Introduced |
| LFYQ23175 | Acanthaceae | *Andrographis paniculata* (Burm. f.) Wall. | chuān xīn lián | Overground part | Sun-dry, grind into powder, and mix into feed | Clear heat, cool blood, reduce swelling, treat cold, reduce fever | Herb | Introduced |
| LYFQ21121 | Anacardiaceae | *Mangifera indica* L. | máng guǒ mù yè | Leaf | Make herbal decoction and drink | Improve digestion | Tree | Cultivated |
| LYFQ21027 | Apiaceae | *Hydrocotyle sibthorpioides* Lam. | xì yàng léi gōng gēn | Whole plant | Cook fully and feed | Treat cold, treat cough | Herb | Wild |
| LFYQ23177 | Apiaceae | *Saposhnikovia divaricata* (Turcz.) Schischk. | fáng fēng | Root | Sun-dry, grind into powder, and mix into feed | Treat cold | Herb | Introduced |
| LYFQ21007 | Apiaceae | *Centella asiatica* (L.) Urb. | yú sè cǎo | Whole plant | Cook fully and feed | Treat jaundice, clear heat | Herb | Wild |
| LFYQ22348 | Aquifoliaceae | *Ilex rotunda* Thunb. | róng dǎn mù | Root | Make herbal decoction and drink | Clear heat, treat cold | Tree | Wild |

Table 2（continued）

| Specimen ID | Family name | Scientific name | Local name | Part used | Processing method | Medicinal effect | Life form | Resource type |
|---|---|---|---|---|---|---|---|---|
| LFYQ22021 | Asteraceae | *Elephantopus scaber* L. | di dǎn tóu | Whole plant | Make herbal decoction and drink | Clear heat, treat cold, treat jaundice | Herb | Wild |
| LYFQ21157 | Asteraceae | *Ageratum conyzoides* L. | chòu cǎo | Overground part | Make herbal decoction for bath | Kill bacterial, relieve itching, treat skin diseases | Herb | Wild |
| LYFQ21002 | Asteraceae | *Emilia sonchifolia* (L.) DC. | yī diǎn hóng | Overground part | Cook fully and feed | Clear heat | Herb | Wild |
| LFYQ23054 | Asteraceae | *Taraxacum mongolicum* Hand.-Mazz. | pú gōng yīng | Whole plant | Cook fully and feed | Relieve inner heat | Herb | Introduced |
| LFYQ23174 | Asteraceae | *Artemisia annua* L. | qīng hāo | Overground part | Make herbal decoction and drink | Treat gastrointestinal illnesses | Herb | Introduced |
| LYFQ21084 | Asteraceae | *Artemisia indica* Willd. | ài | Overground part | Herbal soak or decoction for bathing | Relieve itching, expel parasites, treat skin diseases | Herb | Wild |
| LFYQ23183 | Asteraceae | *Artemisia argyi* H. Lév. & Vaniot | ài | Overground part | Herbal soak or decoction for bathing | Relieve itching, expel parasites, treat skin diseases | Herb | Wild |

Feed plants，ethnoveterinary medicine，and biocultural values：
Insights on the Luchuan pig from Hakka communities in China

121

Table 2（continued）

| Specimen ID | Family name | Scientific name | Local name | Part used | Processing method | Medicinal effect | Life form | Resource type |
|---|---|---|---|---|---|---|---|---|
| LYFQ21242 | Caprifoliaceae | *Lonicera confusa* DC. | jīn yín huā | Branch and leaf; flower | Flower or branch and leaf: make herbal decoction and drink; branch and leaf: herbal soak or decoction for bathing | Herbal drink: treat cold, clear heat; medicinal bath: relieve itching, expel parasites, treat skin diseases | Liana | Wild |
| LFYQ23182 | Celastraceae | *Tripterygium wilfordii* Hook. f | léi gōng téng | Root | Herbal soak or decoction for bathing | Relieve itching, expel parasites, treat skin diseases | Shrub | Wild |
| LYFQ21217 | Convolvulaceae | *Cuscuta australis* R.Br. | tú sī zǐ | Whole plant | Cook fully and feed | Alleviate constipation | Herb | Wild |
| LYFQ21297 | Dioscoreaceae | *Schizocapsa plantaginea* Hance | shuǐ tián qī | Whole plant | Make herbal decoction and drink | Clear heat, treat pink eye | Herb | Wild |
| LFYQ23181 | Dryopteridaceae | *Dryopteris crassirhizoma* Nakai | guàn zhòng | Root | Make herbal decoction and drink | Clear heat, stimulate urination, alleviate inflammation | Herb | Introduced |
| LFYQ23178 | Ephedraceae | *Ephedra equisetina* Bunge | má huáng | Stem | Sun-dry, grind into powder, and mix into feed | Clear heat, treat asthma, treat lung fever | Shrub | Introduced |
| LYFQ21159 | Euphorbiaceae | *Breynia fruticosa* (L.) Müll. Arg | guǐ huà fú | Branch and leaf | Make herbal decoction and drink | Stimulate urination, treat dysentery | Shrub | Wild |
| LFYQ22341 | Euphorbiaceae | *Ricinus communis* L. | hóng bì má | Branch and leaf | Herbal soak or decoction for bathing | Relieve itching, expel parasites, treat skin diseases | Herb | Cultivated |

Table 2（continued）

| Specimen ID | Family name | Scientific name | Local name | Part used | Processing method | Medicinal effect | Life form | Resource type |
|---|---|---|---|---|---|---|---|---|
| LYFQ21038 | Fabaceae | *Grona styracifolia* (Osbeck) H. Ohashi & K. Ohashi | jīn qián cǎo | Whole plant | Make herbal decoction and drink | Improve digestion | Herb | Wild |
| LFYQ23171 | Fabaceae | *Glycyrrhiza uralensis* Fisch. | gān cǎo | Root | Sun-dry, grind into powder, and mix into feed; make herbal decoction and drink | Treat asthma | Herb | Introduced |
| LFYQ23172 | Fabaceae | *Astragalus mongholicus* Bunge | huáng qí | Root | Make herbal decoction and drink | Treat gastrointestinal illnesses | Herb | Introduced |
| LFYQ23166 | Gentianaceae | *Gentiana scabra* Bunge | dǎn cǎo | Whole plant | Sun-dry, grind into powder, and mix into feed | Clear heat, treat cold | Herb | Wild |
| LYFQ21192 | Lamiaceae | *Clerodendrum fortunatum* L. | hóng dēng lóng | Overground part | Make herbal decoction and drink | Alleviate swine fever | Herb | Wild |
| LYFQ21046 | Lamiaceae | *Mentha canadensis* L. | bò hé | Overground part | Crush and mix into feed; cook fully and feed | Treat cold | Herb | Wild |
| LFYQ23176 | Lamiaceae | *Schizonepeta tenuifolia* Briq. | jīng jiè | Overground part | Sun-dry, grind into powder, and mix into feed | Treat cold | Herb | Introduced |
| LYFQ21094 | Lamiaceae | *Leonurus japonicus* Houtt. | yì mǔ cǎo | Overground part | Cook fully and feed | Prevent miscarriage | Herb | Wild |

Feed plants, ethnoveterinary medicine, and biocultural values:
Insights on the Luchuan pig from Hakka communities in China

123

Table 2 ( continued )

| Specimen ID | Family name | Scientific name | Local name | Part used | Processing method | Medicinal effect | Life form | Resource type |
|---|---|---|---|---|---|---|---|---|
| LYFQ21064 | Lygodiaceae | *Lygodium japonicum* (Thunb.) Sw. | niú dòu xū | Branch and leaf | Make herbal decoction for bath; place fresh plants in pigpen as bedding | Kill bacterial | Herb | Wild |
| LYFQ21172 | Melastomataceae | *Melastoma dodecandrum* Lour. | di niè | Whole plant | Cook fully and feed | Stop diarrhea | Herb | Wild |
| LFYQ22427 | Meliaceae | *Melia azedarach* L. | kǔ liàn mù | Bark | Herbal soak or decoction for bathing | Relieve itching, expel parasites, treat skin diseases | Tree | Wild |
| LFYQ23137 | Menispermaceae | *Fibraurea recisa* Pierre | shān dà wáng, shān huáng lián | Root, stem | Make herbal decoction and drink | Clear heat | Liana | Wild |
| LFYQ22811 | Musaceae | *Musa acuminata* Colla | jiāo xīn | Leaf sheath | Cook fully and feed | Relieve constipation, treat heat heat syndrome of the eyes, clear heat | Herb | Cultivated |
| LFYQ23036 | Myrtaceae | *Psidium guajava* L. | fān táo | Tender leaf | Make herbal decoction and drink | Stop diarrhea | Tree | Cultivated |
| LFYQ23028 | Myrtaceae | *Baeckea frutescens* L. | sào bǎ | Tender branch and leaf | Herbal soak or decoction for bathing | Relieve itching, expel parasites, treat skin diseases | Shrub | Wild |
| LFYQ22745 | Myrtaceae | *Eucalyptus robusta* Sm. | dà yè ān | Branch and leaf | Herbal soak or decoction for bathing | Relieve itching, expel parasites, treat skin diseases | Tree | Cultivated |

Table 2 ( continued )

| Specimen ID | Family name | Scientific name | Local name | Part used | Processing method | Medicinal effect | Life form | Resource type |
|---|---|---|---|---|---|---|---|---|
| LFYQ23180 | Oleaceae | *Forsythia suspensa* Vahl | lián qiào | Fruit | Sun-dry, grind into powder, and mix into feed | Clear heat | Shrub | Introduced |
| LFYQ23148 | Onagraceae | *Ludwigia adscendens* (L.) H.Hara | guò táng shé | Whole plant | Cook fully and feed | Clear heat, treat cold, relieve constipation | Herb | Wild |
| LFYQ23167 | Oxalidaceae | *Averrhoa carambola* L. | yáng táo mù yè | Branch and leaf | Make herbal decoction and drink | Improve digestion | Tree | Wild |
| LYFQ21143 | Pandanaceae | *Pandanus tectorius* Parkinson ex Du Roi | gāo jiǎo lǜ gǔ tóu | Fruit | Make herbal decoction and drink | Clear heat | Shrub | Wild |
| LFYQ23095 | Pinaceae | *Pinus massoniana* Lamb. | sōng zhēn | Branch and leaf | Herbal soak or decoction for bathing | Relieve itching, expel parasites, treat skin diseases | Tree | Wild |
| LYFQ21022 | Plantaginaceae | *Plantago major* L. | zhú kè cài | Whole plant | Cook fully and feed | Stimulate urination | Herb | Wild |
| LYFQ21166 | Poaceae | *Lophatherum gracile* Brongn. | dàn zhú yè | Whole plant | Make herbal decoction and drink | Improve digestion, clear heat, treat cold | Herb | Wild |
| LYFQ21278 | Poaceae | *Cymbopogon citratus* Stapf | xiāng máo | Leaf | Make herbal decoction for bath; place fresh plants in pigpen as bedding | Sterilize, kill bacterial, expel evil | Herb | Wild |
| LFYQ23169 | Poaceae | *Bambusa blumeana* Schult. f. | lè zhú xīn | Tender leaf | Make herbal decoction and drink | Clear heat | Herb | Cultivated |

Feed plants, ethnoveterinary medicine, and biocultural values:
Insights on the Luchuan pig from Hakka communities in China

125

Table 2 ( continued )

| Specimen ID | Family name | Scientific name | Local name | Part used | Processing method | Medicinal effect | Life form | Resource type |
|---|---|---|---|---|---|---|---|---|
| LYFQ21071 | Poaceae | *Panicum repens* L. | yìng gǔ cǎo shǔ | Root | Make herbal decoction and drink | Alleviate stomach distension | Herb | Wild |
| LFYQ23173 | Poaceae | *Phragmites australis* (Cav.) Steud. | wěi gēn | Root | Sun-dry, grind into powder, and mix into feed; make herbal decoction and drink | Treat gastrointestinal illnesses | Herb | Wild |
| LFYQ22184 | Polygonaceae | *Polygonum chinense* L. | huǒ zhì tàn chā | Branch and leaf | Cook fully and feed; make herbal decoction for bathing | Feed: clear heat and swine fever, prevent miscarriage, treat jaundice; decoction for bathing: relieve itching, treat skin diseases | Herb | Wild |
| LFYQ23066 | Portulacaceae | *Portulaca oleracea* L. | mǎ chǐ xiàn | Whole plant | Cook fully and feed | Relieve constipation | Herb | Wild |
| LFYQ23165 | Primulaceae | *Maesa perlarius* (Lour.) Merr. | jì yú dǎn | Branch and leaf | Make herbal decoction and drink | Clear heat, treat cold, treat jaundice | Shrub | Wild |
| LFYQ23083 | Primulaceae | *Embelia laeta* (L.) Mez | suān téng mù yè | Leaf, root | Make herbal decoction and drink | Leaf: improve digestion, stop diarrhea, treat jaundice, clear heat; root: clear heat | Liana | Wild |

Table 2（continued）

| Specimen ID | Family name | Scientific name | Local name | Part used | Processing method | Medicinal effect | Life form | Resource type |
|---|---|---|---|---|---|---|---|---|
| LFYQ23168 | Rosaceae | *Prunus persica* (L.) Stokes | máo táo yè | Branch and leaf | Make herbal decoction for bathing; place fresh plants in pigpen as bedding | Sterilize, kill bacterial, expel evil | Tree | Cultivated |
| LFYQ23179 | Rosaceae | *Prunus sibirica* L. | kǔ xìng rén | Seed | Sun-dry, grind into powder, and mix into feed | Clear heat, treat asthma, treat lung heat | Shrub | Introduced |
| LFYQ23123 | Rubiaceae | *Psychotria serpens* L. | shàng mù shé | Whole plant | Cook fully and feed | Clear heat, treat cold | Liana | Wild |
| LFYQ22015 | Rubiaceae | *Mussaenda pubescens* W.T.Aiton | xiǎo liáng téng | Whole plant | Make herbal decoction and drink | Treat cold, clear heat | Shrub | Wild |
| LYFQ21005 | Saururaceae | *Houttuynia cordata* Thunb. | yú xīng cǎo | Whole plant | Cook fully and feed; or crush and mix into feed | Treat cold, treat cough | Herb | Wild |
| LYFQ21021 | Solanaceae | *Solanum americanum* Mill. | bái huā cài | Overground part | Cook fully and feed | Clear heat, treat jaundice | Herb | Wild |
| LFYQ23010 | Urticaceae | *Boehmeria nivea* Gaudich. | zhù má yè | Branch and leaf | Make herbal decoction and drink | Prevent miscarriage, alleviate heat syndrome in sows | Shrub | Wild |
| LYFQ21149 | Verbenaceae | *Clerodendrum cyrtophyllum* Turcz. | dà qīng yè | Root | Make herbal decoction and drink | Antibacterial, stimulate urination, treat jaundice, clear heat | Tree | Wild |

Feed plants, ethnoveterinary medicine, and biocultural values:
Insights on the Luchuan pig from Hakka communities in China

127

a—*Ricinus communis*; b—*Cymbopogon citratus*; c—*Mussaenda pubescens*; d—*Emilia sonchifolia*; e—*Prunus persica*; f—*Averrhoa carambola*; g—*Mangifera indica*; h—*Solanum americanum*; i—*Baeckea frutescens* (All photographs were taken by Yongqing Liufu).

Figure 3　Part of veterinary plants for Luchuan pigs

on preventing internal heat in the process of pig farming. They use 27 species of crushed or grinded herbs decocted and mixed into the feed as a preventive and treatment measure for internal heat in Luchuan pigs. Locally, these herbal concoctions are referred to as "cooling teas". Additionally, they adjust the daily diet of Luchuan pigs to prevent and treat internal heat. For instance, when symptoms of internal heat occur in Luchuan pigs, the feeders reduce the proportion of rice(*O. sativa*) bran, soybean(*G. max*) meal, and peanut(*Arachis hypogaea*) bran in their food while increasing the proportion of wheat(*T. aestivum* subsp. *spelta*) bran, sweet potato(*I. batatas*) shoots, and *Musa acuminata*. These plants promote gastrointestinal motility in pigs, thereby alleviating symptoms such as constipation and indigestion.

According to the interviewees, newborn piglets and pigs raised under forested conditions are prone to skin diseases. To address this, the local people use 14 species of plants, such as *Pinus massoniana*, *Melia azedarach*, *Eucalyptus robusta*, *Tripterygium wilfordii*, and *Cymbopogon citratus*, for pig bathing. They believe that these plants have excellent therapeutic effects and can treat and prevent approximately 95% of skin diseases. Research results indicate that active ingredients in plants like *E. robusta* and *T. wilfordii* have vermifugal, insecticidal, and antibacterial effects. [34-36] In traditional Chinese medicine, *T. wilfordii* is also used for treating autoimmune diseases like rheumatoid arthritis, glomerulonephritis, and systemic lupus erythematosus. [36] During the survey, it was observed that farmers prefer placing *C. citratus*, *Prunus persica* leaves, and *Lygodium japonicum* directly inside the pigsty for pigs to sleep on. According to their accounts, this practice effectively repels mosquitoes, parasites and prevents skin diseases in piglets. *C. citratus* emits a strong aroma and is reported to have effective chemical components with antibacterial and insect-repelling properties. [37-39]

It is worth noting that among the medicinal plants we have documented, three of them have been reported to possess toxicity. For example, *M. azedarach* has been reported that the bark of *M. azedarach* has cytotoxic effects and may result in gastrointestinal, cardiovascular, respiratory, or neurological effects, and death in severe cases. [40, 41] Also, the commonly used industrial plant *Ricinus communis* is also used locally; it contains highly toxic compounds such as *Ricinus communis* agglutinin and the alkaloid ricinine. [42] Besides, *Tripterygium wilfordii* has toxicity and adverse reactions, especially the hepatotoxicity. [43] These plants are mainly used by local people to relieve itching, repel insects, and treat other skin diseases in Luchuan pigs. The toxic herbal species can be potentially lethal, but their effects are closely tied to their processing methods, usage, and dosage. [41, 44] In the context of animal health, knowledge of various toxic and poisonous species is a prerequisite for safe grazing as grazing on such species could be fatal resulting in economic loss. [45, 46] Therefore, the utilization and scientific validation of these related plants should also draw the attention of local residents, local governments, and researchers.

In the past, the treatment of Luchuan pigs' illnesses mainly relied on herbal medicine. With the development of modern medical technology, modern farmers now primarily depend on vaccines and Western medicine to treat pig diseases. Indeed, animal vaccination has

Feed plants, ethnoveterinary medicine, and biocultural values:
Insights on the Luchuan pig from Hakka communities in China

129

significantly contributed to the prevention and control of severe animal diseases. However, this shift toward modern medical practices may have adversely affected the traditional knowledge system concerning livestock health and welfare, as vaccines have become readily available for most farmers, and disease prevention is now the primary focus. [1] Nonetheless, in treating less severe health issues and in more isolated regions, traditional ethnic veterinary practices may still serve as an essential low-cost alternative to "Western" veterinary methods. [1] Therefore, effective measures should be taken to promote the use of traditional herbal remedies. For instance, utilizing pig farming association platforms to disseminate common knowledge about traditional Chinese veterinary medicine among farmers.

### 3.3 Luchuan pig farming models

In our investigation, we observed a historic transformation in the Luchuan pig farming industry, achieved through collaborative efforts among the government, enterprises, and farmers, transitioning from traditional confinement systems to more environmentally friendly and sustainable practices: ecological farming and free-range in the forest(Figure 4).

In the ecological farming model, farms are typically established within artificial economic and fruit forests, accompanied by fish ponds. The pigpens are equipped with innovative features such as slatted floors, automated feeding and watering systems, and centralized manure treatment pools. The use of automated equipment significantly reduces feed and labor costs. Moreover, the slatted floors in the pigpens enhance ventilation, reducing the risks of harmful gases for the pigs and lowering the likelihood of diseases among Luchuan pigs. To mitigate environmental pollution from pig feces and urine, farmers primarily employ techniques such as solid-liquid separation and biogas fermentation to treat the excrement in an eco-friendly manner. The processed pig manure serves as a natural fertilizer for fruit trees, forest plants, and pasture within the farm, while the biogas slurry is used to raise fish or irrigate crops. This "pig farming+fish farming" and "pig farming+cultivation" ecological farming model not only minimizes environmental pollution from waste but also promotes sustainability and generates additional economic income for the farmers.

In the free-range in the forest model, Luchuan pig farmers divide the mountainous

a—free-range farming on mountain areas (by Song Li); b—free-range farming in fruit ranch (by Guixin Chen); c—the ecological farming base (by Jinming Li); d—Luchuan pigs on slatted floors (by Song Li).

Figure 4　The ecological farming and free-range farming of Luchuan pigs

area into several sections and practice low-density rotational grazing to allow for free-range feeding. This method helps reduce the potential threats to the ecological environment caused by overgrazing. To manage Luchuan pigs more efficiently during the night and provide shelter during adverse weather conditions(such as rain or high temperatures), farmers often build simple houses on the mountain. Luchuan pigs in the forest are familiar with their owner's voice or whistle and can return to designated areas based on specific signals. Under this model, Luchuan pigs are only fed once a day, which reduces feed costs. Due to the minimal input required and low economic risks, free-range pig farming is gaining popularity and plays a significant role in the livelihoods of many rural families worldwide. [47–49]

In the wild, pigs are active during the day and spend 75% of their active time on foraging activities. [50] Their increased activity contributes to better health and improved meat quality compared to typical domestic pigs. [3, 30, 51, 52] Research indicates that free-range pigs living in

Feed plants, ethnoveterinary medicine, and biocultural values:
Insights on the Luchuan pig from Hakka communities in China

131

vast, comfortable natural environments have enhanced immunity and disease resistance. [3]

## 3.4　Breeding utilization and industrial development of Luchuan pigs

Luchuan pigs may have limited market share due to their small size, slow growth, and low lean meat percentage. However, they possess valuable genetic traits such as high prolificacy, tolerance to coarse feed, high reproductive capacity, early maturation, and easy fattening, making them of significant genetic breeding value. For instance, crossbreeding Luchuan sows with Danish Landrace boars produces hybrid offspring, and further crossing these hybrids with Duroc boars creates three-way crossbred pigs. Likewise, crossbreeding Luchuan sows with Duroc boars yields black pig offspring, and crossing these offspring with Danish Landrace boars results in three-way crossbred pigs(Figure 5). The hybrid pigs exhibit excellent adaptability, high productivity, and superior meat quality, giving them a competitive edge in the market[53].

In southern China, Luchuan pig is recognized as an ideal hybrid female parent. In the past, Hakka people primarily raised Luchuan pigs to meet their family's protein needs. Currently, due to increasing recognition of the genetic breeding value of Luchuan pigs, many farmers are rearing them with the intention of acquiring more female pigs and subsequently attaining greater economic benefits through hybrid breeding. This practice not only satisfies people's demand for traditional diets but also successfully achieves economic benefits. This farming practice objectively promotes the protection of Luchuan pigs and has a positive significance for safeguarding both the biological and cultural diversity of Luchuan County. Therefore, in the future, while conducting rescue and protection work for traditional knowledge, there should be a focused effort on preserving the genetic resources of local varieties.

The Luchuan pig farming industry is a distinctive sector in Luchuan County. According to statistics, in 2016, the total output value of Luchuan pigs reached 5-billion-*yuan*, accounting for 70% of the counties' total agricultural output. [54] In recent years, the government has undertaken significant efforts to protect and breed Luchuan pigs. These efforts include establishing a national-level Luchuan pig conservation center, setting up Luchuan pig

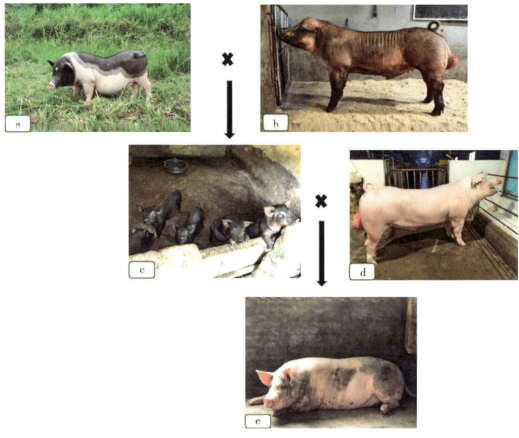

a—Luchuan pig (by Song Li); b—Duroc boar (by Shichong Wang); c—Hybrid black pigs (by Yongqing Liufu); d—Danish Landrace boar (by Shichong Wang); e—Hybrid black-spotted white pig (by Yongqing Liufu).

Figure 5　The breeding application of Luchuan pigs

protection areas in five different towns, providing financial subsidies to Luchuan pig breeders, and promoting the Luchuan pig brand, etc.

Despite these measures, the production and utilization of Luchuan pigs still face several challenges. Firstly, the current sales market for Luchuan pigs mainly relies on local consumption. However, with the impact of lowcost, high-yield pork from Europe and America, it is difficult for Luchuan pigs to fetch competitive prices in the market. Secondly, due to insufficient consumer awareness of Luchuan pigs, fraudulent practices in the pork market led to a significant negative impact on the sales of genuine Luchuan pork. Although the government is working toward building the Luchuan pig brand, there are currently only few Luchuan pig specialty chain stores in Yulin, Guigang, and Nanning in Guangxi, which is insufficient for promoting and disseminating Luchuan pigs. Additionally, epidemics have always posed the most significant obstacle to pig farming [55]. In 2018, African swine fever was introduced into China, resulting in an outbreak. According to disease prevention policies, all deceased pigs, culled pigs, their products, potentially contaminated feed, equipment, and waste materials were subject to safe disposal. Similar to other pigbreed in China [3], during the outbreak of African swine fever, Luchuan pigs suffered significant losses, with the number decreasing from over 1.31 million to 235, 000, causing substantial economic damage to breeders [54]. While some interviewees mentioned the effectiveness of strict epidemic prevention measures and feeding " liangcha " (cooling herbal tea) to pigs to reduce the occurrence and spread of African swine fever, most pig breeders lack experience in epidemic prevention and control, leading them to avoid pig farming risks.

Therefore, to promote and protect Luchuan pigs, government agencies, related companies and non-governmental organizations need to take proactive measures, such as(1) increasing the promotion of breeding and farming methods; (2) utilizing the pig farming association platform to educate farmers on preventing and treating common diseases; (3) enhancing research and development in pork processing to expand Luchuan pig meat products in domestic and international markets; (4) conducting effective publicity through museums, promotional events, media, etc. , to increase consumer awareness of Luchuan pigs; and(5) attracting investment to establish more specialty chain stores.

### 3.5   Folk culture and customs related to Luchuan pigs

Luchuan pigs play a significant role in the local Hakka traditional dietary culture, social rituals, festive celebrations, and customary practices(Figure 6). Among the Hakka community, Luchuan pigs are regarded as symbols of kindness, good fortune, and blessings. The locals adhere to feeding Luchuan pigs with natural feeds. Luchuan pig meat is highly valued for its delicious taste and nutritional benefits, making it a precious ingredient in both culinary and medicinal practices. Additionally, in the Hakka culture of worship and offerings, pigs are considered the most sincere and meaningful tribute to the deities.

a—Luchuan pig cuisine cooking competition (by Yongqing Liufu); b—Luchuan pig cuisine (by Wu Weicui).

Figure 6　Luchuan pig cultural festival and Luchuan pig cuisine

### 3.5.1　Dietary culture

The traditional practice of feeding Luchuan pigs with natural feed is closely related to the lifestyle habits of the Luchuan Hakka people. In the past, the Luchuan Hakka people relished "Lao Fan", which was a dish made by boiling a large quantity of water with rice in a wok, then scooping out the cooked rice with a ladle. They would mix the leftover rice broth with other plant fodder to feed pigs. Until now, many farmers in rural areas still maintain this traditional method of feed production.

Luchuan pigs belong to the fatty-type breed, characterized by tender, aromatic, crisp, and sweet meat. Locals prepare various pork dishes to entertain guests, creating a rich culture centered around consuming pork. Commonly enjoyed dishes include white cut pig's feet, roasted suckling pig, braised pork, cured pork, sausage, and preserved meat. For the Hakka community in Luchuan, Luchuan Pigs' meat serves not only as a source of nutritional food but also as an important medicinal resource for preventing and treating illnesses.

Through long-term practical experience, they have developed the concept of "Doctrine of Signature", using specific parts of the pig to address corresponding health issues. Such as consuming pig's blood to replenish blood, pig's kidneys to nourish the kidneys, and pig's feet to strengthen the feet. Local Hakka people use pig liver, and gǒu qǐ(*Lycium chinense*) leaves together to make soup with the effects of liver clearing and vision improvement. Stewed pig's ears with *Combretum alfredii* are used to treat tinnitus, while a soup made from

Feed plants, ethnoveterinary medicine, and biocultural values:
Insights on the Luchuan pig from Hakka communities in China

135

*Tinospora sinensis* and pig's feet is employed to alleviate rheumatic bone pain and other ailments.

### 3.5.2　Folk festivals and traditional customs

The Luchuan pigs play a significant role in the local Hakka traditional customs. Locally, when a Hakka man gets married, it is customary to present a pig's head and tail to the matchmaker as a gesture of gratitude. Additionally, the Luchuan pig is an essential offering in the worship of deities and ancestors during traditional festivals and important customs among the Hakka people. Particularly during the Qingming Festival and the Double Ninth Festival, affluent Hakka families often use a roasted suckling pig as an offering to their ancestors(Figure 6b). The Hakka people of Luchuan believe that pigs are easy to raise and bring good fortune. Therefore, if a child is weak and prone to illness, his parents may offer a Luchuan pig or a pig's head to the local earth god, praying for the child to be as healthy and fortunate as a pig.

Amid urbanization and changing lifestyles, many traditional ceremonies are gradually fading from people's view. However, the cultural significance related to pigs remains well-preserved in the Hakka region of Luchuan County. The Luchuan pig not only holds an important place in Hakka culture but also serves as a medium for reflecting the distinct characteristics of the local Hakka people. The Hakka people of Luchuan are known for their kindness, warmth, hospitality, gratitude, and reverence for deities and ancestors. They share the best pork with guests to express hospitality and gratitude and offer pork as the finest tribute to deities and ancestors, conveying their reverence and fond remembrance. These cultural values likely serve as a vital driving force in preserving the local traditional customs and culture. Therefore, while safeguarding the genetic resources of the Luchuan pig, equal emphasis should be placed on the conservation of the associated traditional customs and of Hakka culture.

### 3.5.3　Luchuan pig cultural festival

In recent years, local governments have frequently organized cultural festivals related to the Luchuan pig industry to promote its development. During these cultural festivals, various artists and food enthusiasts utilize the pig as a medium to showcase and celebrate the local

Hakka culture, which includes Hakka opera, Hakka folk songs, and Hakka cuisine, among other elements. They employ various forms of expression such as calligraphy, photography, theatrical performances, and culinary demonstrations to promote the Luchuan pig.

Simultaneously, domestic and international pig farming experts, entrepreneurs, and government officials are invited to participate in these cultural festivals. They share and exchange experiences related to Luchuan pig breeding, management, product processing, sales, promotion, and conservation. The rich heritage of Hakka traditional customs and culture infuses cultural elements into the promotion and preservation of the Luchuan pig, further propelling the development of the Luchuan pig industry.

## 4 Conclusion

The Luchuan Hakka people possess rich traditional knowledge and management experience in raising Luchuan pigs. However, with improved living standards, changes in farming practices, and developments in medical technology, many traditional wild feed plants have been replaced by fermented feed and cultivated crops, while traditional Chinese veterinary medicine has been substituted by vaccines and Western medicine. The traditional knowledge about using and managing wild feed plants and veterinary plants faces a significant risk of disappearing, and effective measures are needed to preserve it. The ecological farming and under forest grazing models of Luchuan pigs have reduced environmental pollution and potential threats caused by pig farming, promoting the sustainable development of Luchuan pig farming. These models are worthy of promotion. The genetic advantages are an important driving force for the conservation and breeding of Luchuan pigs. Currently, there are still some challenges in raising Luchuan pigs that need to be further improved and protected. As an important local cultural species, efforts should also be made to strengthen the preservation of traditional customs and culture related to Luchuan pigs while protecting their genetic resources.

Feed plants，ethnoveterinary medicine，and biocultural values：
Insights on the Luchuan pig from Hakka communities in China

137

Supplementary Information

The online version contains supplementary material available at https: // doi. org/ 10. 1186/ s13002–023–00613–4.

Additional file 1: Table S2. The inventory of feed plants for Luchuan pigs.

# References

[1] BRUSCHI P, URSO V, SOLAZZO D, et al. Traditional knowledge on ethno-veterinary and fodder plants in South Angola: An ethnobotanic field survey in Mopane woodlands in Bibala, Namibe Province. J Agric Environ Int Dev. 2017; 111: 105–21. https: // doi. org/ 10. 12895/ jaeid. 20171. 559.

[2] CHAND S, KUMAR N, ROY SD. Livestock production challenges and strategies for tropical agro-ecosystem, Andaman and Nicobar Islands, India. Basic Res J Agric Sci Rev. 2013; 2: 195–201.

[3] CHU Y, LIN C, CHENG Z, et al. A Biocultural study on Gaoligongshan pig(Sus scrofa domesticus), an important hog land race, in Nujiang Prefecture of China. Biology. 2022; 11: 1603. https: // doi. org/ 10. 3390/ biology11111603.

[4] FAO. Report of a consultation on the definition of breed categories. In: Intergovernmental technical working group on animal genetic resources for food and agriculture. Rome, Italy: Commission on Genetic Resources for Food and Agriculture; 2012.

[5] HALIMANI TE, MUCHADEYI FC, CHIMONYO M, et al. Opportunities for conservation and utilisation of local pig breeds in low-input production systems in Zimbabwe and South Africa. Trop Anim Health Prod. 2012; 45: 81–90. https: // doi. org/ 10. 1007/ s11250–012–0177–2.

[6] YANG Y, HE Y, CHEN X, et al. Current status and measures for development of Nixi chicken breeding in the Shangri-La area. Anim Husb Vet Med. 2021; 53: 141–4.

[7] PAN D. Research on effective measures for protection, development and utilization of livestock and poultry genetic resources. Chin J Vet Med. 2022: 92–94.

[8] WANG Q, WANG H, GUO Z, et al. Strengthening protection of livestock and poultry genetic resources, promoting development of animal breed industry in China. Bull Chin Acad Sci.

2019; 34: 174–9. https: //doi. org/ 10. 1007/ s11250–012–0177–2.

[9] FU R. Suggestions for sustainable development of animal husbandry in China. Henan Agric Sci. 2008. https: // doi. org/ 10. 3969/j. issn. 1004–3268. 2008. 12. 042.

[10] ZHANG G. Thoughts about development and sustainable utilization of animal genetic resources in China. J Agric Sci Technol. 2014; 16: 23–8. https: //doi. org/ 10. 13304/j. nykjdb. 2013. 472.

[11] OVASKA U, BLÅ UER A, KROLØKKE C, et al. The conservation of native domestic animal breeds in Nordic countries: From genetic resources to cultural heritage and good governance. Animals. 2021; 11: 2730. https: // doi. org/ 10. 3390/ ani11092730.

[12] IKEYA K. Biodiversity, native domestic animals, and livelihood in Monsoon Asia: Pig pastoralism in the Bengal Delta of Bangladesh. In: Traditional wisdom and modern knowledge for the earth's future: lectures given at the plenary sessions of the international geographical Union Kyoto regional conference, 2013. 2014; 51–77.

[13] SCHERF B D. World watch list for domestic animal diversity food and agriculture organization of the United Nations. Rome: FAO Corporate Document Repository; 2000.

[14] RESOURCES CNCOAG. Pigs. Beijing: China Agriculture Press; 2011; 486.

[15] CONFERENCE YCCOTCPSPC. YulinKejia. Guilin, Guangxi, Guangxi Normal University Press; 2016.

[16] YANG Y, LIAN J, XIE B, et al. Chromosome-scale de novo assembly and phasing of a Chinese indigenous pig genome. BioRxiv. 2019. https: // doi. org/ 10. 1101/ 770958.

[17] LIAO G. Breeding technology and development prospect of Luchuan pig. Livest Poult Ind. 2017; 28: 2.

[18] MO C, XIE R, ZHOU J, et al. Technical scheme for the protection of germplasm resources of Luchuan pig. Guangxi J Anim Husb Vet Med. 2012; 28: 4. https: // doi. org/ 10. 3969/j. issn. 1002–5235. 2012. 05. 013.

[19] HUANG Y N, LAN G Q, JIANG Q Y. Research progress on molecular biology of Guangxi Luchuan pigs and Bama miniature pigs[J]. China Anim Husb Vet Med. 2014; 41: 79–84.

[20] HUANG YQ, JIANG YQ, LIANG WQ, et al. A review of biological characteristics and performance in Luchuan pig. Acta Ecol Anim Domastici. 2013. https: // doi. org/ 10. 3969/j.

Feed plants，ethnoveterinary medicine，and biocultural values：
Insights on the Luchuan pig from Hakka communities in China

139

issn. 1673–1182. 2013. 05. 018.

[21] ZHANG J, HE R, JIANG Y, et al. Studies on carcass and meat quality of Luchuan pig. Swine Prod. 2010. https: // doi. org/ 10. 3969/j. issn. 1002–1957. 2010. 06. 016.

[22] GUAN Y Y. Review on the conservation and breeding techniques of Luchuan pig germplasm resources[J]. J Guangxi Agric. 2020. https: // doi. org/10. 3969/j. issn. 1003–4374. 2020. 05. 019.

[23] HUANG YQ, JIANG YQ, LIANG WQ, et al. Developmental status on national-class protected species Luchuan pig[J]. Heilongjiang Anim Sci Vet Med. 2013. https: // doi. org/ 10. 13881/j. cnki. hljxm sy. 2013. 07. 013.

[24] FAN Y, CHENG Z, LIU B, et al. An ethnobiological study on traditional knowledge associated with black-boned sheep(*Ovis aries*) in Northwest Yunnan. China J Ethnobiol Ethnomed. 2022; 18: 39. https: // doi. org/ 10. 1186/ s13002–022–00537–5.

[25] SHAHEEN H, QURESHI R, QASEEM M F, et al. The fodder grass resources for ruminants: an indigenous treasure of local communities of Thal desert Punjab, Pakistan[J]. PLoS ONE. 2020; 15: 4061. https: // doi. org/ 10. 1101/796227.

[26] BIRÓ M, MOLNÁR Z, BABAI D, et al. Reviewing historical traditional knowledge for innovative conservation management: A re-evaluation of wetland grazing[J]. Sci Total Environ. 2019; 666: 1114–25. https: // doi. org/ 10. 1016/j. scito tenv. 2019. 02. 292.

[27] MOLNÁR Z, KELEMEN A, KUN R, et al. Knowledge co-production with traditional herders on cattle grazing behaviour for better management of species-rich grasslands[J]. J Appl Ecol. 2020; 57: 1677–87. https: // doi. org/ 10. 1111/ 1365–2664. 13664.

[28] COUNTY MOTCOLCOL. Luchuan County Record National Library of China publishing House 1993.

[29] YANG J, LUO J, GAN Q, et al. An ethnobotanical study of forage plants in Zhuxi County in the Qinba mountainous area of central China[J]. Plant Divers. 2021; 43: 239–47.

[30] HU R, HU Q, NONG Y, et al. Ethnobotanical study on forage plants of Baiku Yao in China. Guihaia. 2023; 43: 21–31. https: // doi. org/ 10. 11931/ guiha ia. gxzw2 02111076.

[31] CHAMBERS R. Participatory rural appraisal(PRA): Analysis of experience. World Dev. 1994; 22: 1253–68. https: // doi. org/ 10. 1016/ 0305–750X(94)90003–5.

[32] MOLNAR Z, SZABADOS K, KIS A, et al. Preserving for the future the—once widespread but now vanishing—knowledge on traditional pig grazing in forests and marshes(Sava-Bosut floodplain, Serbia). J Ethnobiol Ethnomed. 2021; 17: 56. https: // doi. org/ 10. 1186/s13002–021–00482–9.

[33] OKOLI LC, EBERE CS, UCHEGBU MC, et al. A survey of the diversity of plants utilized for small ruminant feeding in south-eastern Nigeria[J]. Agric Ecosyst Environ. 2003; 96: 147–54. https: // doi. org/ 10. 1016/S0167–8809(02) 00172–X.

[34] ZHOU YE. Chemical constituents of the essential oil from the leaves of Eucalyptus robusta and its antimicrobial activity[J]. J Fujian Coll For. 2007. https: // doi. org/ 10. 3969/j. issn. 1001–389X. 2007. 01. 011.

[35] LUO D Q, ZHANG X, FENG J T. Research development of an insectidal plant *Tripterygium wilfordii* Hook. Acta Univ Agric Boreali-occidentalis[J]. 2000; 28: 86–9. https: // doi. org/ 10. 3321/j. issn: 1671–9387. 2000. 03. 018.

[36] HUANG M L, MA Z. The research progress of *Tripterygium wilfordii*[J]. Chem Bioeng. 2012. https: // doi. org/ 10. 3969/j. issn. 1672–5425. 2012. 07. 001.

[37] LIN S, QIU S, ZHENG K, et al. Composition analysis and antibacterial activity of the essential oil from *Cymbopogon citratus*[J]. J Agric Sci Technol. 2017; 19: 89–95. https: // doi. org/ 10. 13304/j. nykjdb. 2016. 756.

[38] HONGMEI X, KANG T. Effects of *Cymbopogon winterianus* oil on two stored grain insect adults[J]. Grain Storage. 2008; 37: 8–11.

[39] LI H M, WU S J, LI S S, et al. Inhibiting effect of citronella essential oil on fungi in the air[J]. Fujian Agric Sci Technol. 2021; 52: 42–5. https: // doi. org/ 10. 13651/j. cnki. fjnykj. 2021. 03. 009.

[40] WU S B, BAO Q Y, WANG W X, et al. Cytotoxic triterpenoids and steroids from the bark of *Melia azedarach*[J]. Planta Med. 2011; 77: 922–8. https: // doi. org/ 10. 1055/s–0030–1250673.

[41] PHUA D H, TSAI W-J, GER J, et al. Human *Melia azedarach* poisoning[J]. Clin Toxicol. 2008; 46: 1067–70. https: // doi. org/ 10. 1080/15563650802310929.

[42] WORBS S, KÖ HLER K, PAULY D, et al. *Ricinus communis* intoxications in human and

Feed plants，ethnoveterinary medicine，and biocultural values：
Insights on the Luchuan pig from Hakka communities in China

141

veterinary medicine: A summary of real cases. Toxins. 2011; 3: 1332–72. https: // doi. org/ 10. 3390/toxin s3101332.

[43] LI X X, DU F Y, LIU H X, et al. Investigation of the active components in *Tripterygium wilfordii* leading to its acute hepatotoxicty and nephrotoxicity[J]. J Ethnopharmacol. 2015; 162: 238–43. https: // doi. org/ 10. 1016/j. jep. 2015. 01. 004.

[44] TIAN Y G, SU X H, LIU L L, et al. Overview of hepatotoxicity studies on *Tripterygium wilfordii* in recent 20 years[J]. China J Chin Mater Med. 2019; 44: 3399–405. https: // doi. org/ 10. 19540/j. cnki. cjcmm. 20190 527. 408.

[45] RIVERA D, VERDE A, FAJARDO RODRÍGUEZ J, et al. Ethnoveterinary medicine and ethnopharmacology in the main transhumance areas of Castilla-La Mancha(Spain)[J]. Front Vet Sci. 2022; 9: 866132. https: // doi. org/ 10. 3389/fvets. 2022. 866132.

[46] UPRETY Y, KARKI S, POUDEL RC, et al. Ethnoveterinary use of plants and its implication for sustainable livestock management in Nepal[J]. Front Vet Sci. 2022; 9: 930533. https: // doi. org/ 10. 3389/ fvets. 2022. 930533.

[47] DE A K, JEYAKUMAR S, KUNDU M S, et al. Farming practices and genetic characterization of Nicobari pig, an indigenous pig germplasm of Nicobar group of islands, India[J]. Trop Anim Health Prod. 2014; 46: 655–61. https: // doi. org/ 10. 1007/ s11250–014–0547–z.

[48] CARTER N, DEWEY C, MUTUA F, et al. Average daily gain of local pigs on rural and peri-urban smallholder farms in two districts of Western Kenya[J]. Trop Anim Health Prod. 2013; 45: 1533–8. https: // doi. org/10. 1007/ s11250–013–0395–2.

[49] MUTUA F K, DEWEY C, ARIMI S, et al. A description of local pig feeding systems in village smallholder farms of Western Kenya[J]. Trop Anim Health Prod. 2012; 44: 1157–62. https: // doi. org/ 10. 1007/s11250–011–0052–6.

[50] DELSART M, POL F, DUFOUR B, et al. Pig farming in alternative systems: Strengths and challenges in terms of animal welfare, biosecurity, animal health and pork safety[J]. Agriculture. 2020; 20: 261. https: // doi. org/10. 3390/ agriculture10070261.

[51] KONGSTED A, JAKOBSEN M. Effect of genotype and level of supplementary concentrate on foraging activity and vegetation cover in an organic free-range pig system[J]. Acta Agric Scand Sect A Anim Sci. 2015; 65: 139–47. https: // doi. org/ 10. 1080/ 09064702.

2016. 1156152.

[52] LAHRMANN H, BREMERMANN N, KAUFMANN O, et al. Health, growing performance and meat quality of pigs in indoor and outdoor housing—a controlled field trial. DTW Deutsche tierarztlicheWochenschrift. 2004; 111: 205–8. https: // doi. org/ 10. 1016/j. cimid. 2003. 11. 004.

[53] HE R, LI Q, DUAN F, et al. Study on breed characteristic of Luchuan pig heterosis selective breed. In: Guangxi Animal husbandry and veterinary society pig science branch 2007 annual meeting 2008; 37–41.

[54] TENG F, LUO T, LV Q, et al. Investigation and analysis of the current situation of Luchuan pig industry in Guangxi[J]. Chin Livest Poult Breed. 2022; 18: 5–7. https: // doi. org/ 10. 3969/j. issn. 1673–4556. 2022. 08. 002.

[55] SHEN S, WILKES A, RONNIE V. The importance of ethnoveterinary treatments for pig illnesses in poor, ethnic minority communities: A case study of Nu people in Yunnan, China[J]. Int J Appl Res Vet Med. 2010; 8: 53–9.

原载*Journal of Ethnobiology and Ethnomedicine* 2023年第19卷第40篇。

# A new titanosaurian sauropod from the Upper Cretaceous of Jiangxi Province, southern China

Mo Jinyou[1], Fu Qiongyao[1], Yu Yilun[2], Xu Xing[2, 3, 4]

1. Geological Department, Natural History Museum of Guangxi, Nanning, China;

2. Key Laboratory of Vertebrate Evolution and Human Origins of Chinese Academy of Sciences,

Institute of Vertebrate Paleontology and Paleoanthropology, Chinese Academy of Sciences, Beijing,

China;

3. Centre for Vertebrate Evolutionary Biology, Yunnan University, Kunming, China;

4. College of Paleontology, Paleontological Museum of Liaoning, Shenyang Normal University,

Shenyang, China

【Abstract】 *Jiangxititan ganzhouensis* gen. et sp. nov. is a new titanosaurian sauropod recovered from the Upper Cretaceous (Maastrichtian) Nanxiong Formation of Jiangxi Province, southern China. It is characterised by: (1) posterior cervical and anterior dorsal centra strongly compressed dorsoventrally; (2) accessory horizontal laminae present within the anterior dorsal pleurocoels; (3) posterior cervical and anterior dorsal neural arches low; (4) posterior cervical and anterior dorsal neural spines deeply bifurcated and widely separated; (5) inverted 'V' lamina formed by the left and right medial spinoprezygapophyseal laminae present at the anterior margin of the bifid point in posteriormost cervical and anteriormost dorsal neural spines; (6) triangular fossa formed by the metapophysis, medial and lateral spinoprezygapophyseal laminae

Funding: J-YM was supported by the Natural Science Foundation of Guangxi [2023GXNSFAA026496], China; XX was supported by the Natural Science Foundation of China [grant number 42288201] and the Yunnan Revitalization Talent Support Program (202305AB350006).

present at the anterior margins of the posteriormost cervical and anteriormost dorsal neural spines; (7) postzygapophyses in the posterior cervical vertebrae fan-shaped; (8) medial and lateral spinopostzygapophyseal laminae present in the anterior dorsal vertebrae and; (9) anterior dorsal rib short and gracile. Our phylogenetic analysis places *Jiangxititan* within the deeply-nested titanosauriform clade Lognkosauria and the sympatric *Gannansaurus* in a much earlier-diverging lineage. This new discovery thus demonstrates the presence of both early-diverging and late-diverging titanosauriform sauropods in the Late Cretaceous Ganzhou dinosaur fauna.

【 Keywords 】 Titanosauria; Upper Cretaceous; Nanxiong Formation; Jiangxi Province; *Jiangxititan ganzhouensis*

# 1 Introduction

The Upper Cretaceous Nanxiong Formation of Jiangxi Province, southern China has yielded a diverse array of vertebrates in recent years, including theropods (Xu and Han, 2010; Wang, et al. , 2013; Wei, et al. , 2013; Lü, et al. , 2013a, 2014, 2015, 2016, 2017; Mo and Xu, 2015), ornithopods (Xing, et al. , 2021, 2022), crocodiles (Li, et al. , 2019), turtles (Tong and Mo, 2010), lizards (Mo, et al. , 2010, 2012), and mammals (Jin, et al. , 2022), as well as a vast number of dinosaur eggs (Sato, et al. , 2005; Cheng, et al. , 2008; Ji, 2009; Shao, et al. , 2014; Zhao, et al. , 2015; Wang, et al. , 2016; Jin, et al. , 2019; Bi, et al. , 2021; Fang, et al. , 2022). Only one sauropod taxon, *Gannansaurus sinensis*, has been recorded in this area (Lü, et al. , 2013b).

Here we described another new sauropod dinosaur taxon, *Jiangxititan ganzhouensis*, which consists of seven articulated posterior cervical and anterior dorsal vertebrae, some articulated cervical and dorsal ribs. The specimen was collected from the latest Cretaceous deposits (i. e. Nanxiong Formation) in Tankou Town, Nankang County, southwest of Ganzhou City, Jiangxi Province, which is about five kilometres away from Longling Town, the locality of *Gannansaurus* (Figure 1). The Nanxiong Formation, or its equivalents, is found across several provinces in southeastern China and represented by an extensive sequence of red

mudstones, sandstones and conglomerates (Bureau of Geology and Mineral Resources of
Guangdong Province, 1988). The presence of *Truncatella maxima* and *Rubeyella carinate*
suggests that the Nanxiong Formation was deposited towards the end of the Late Cretaceous
(Maastrichtian) (Bureau of Geology and Mineral Resources of Jiangxi Province, 1984; Wang,
et al. , 2013). *Jiangxititan* preserves some distinct characters, such as neural spines deeply
bifurcated, neural arches very low, centra strongly compressed dorsoventrally, etc., very
different from some other Cretaceous of titanosauriforms from Asia. The discovery of the new
taxon adds a new element not only to the poorly preserved sauropod dinosaurs in the Late
Cretaceous of Jiangxi, but also to the diversity of titanosauriforms in the Late Cretaceous of
Asia. Nomenclature for vertebral laminae and pneumatic fossae follows Wilson (1999) and
Wilson, et al. (2011).

Figure 1　Map showing the fossil locality of the holotype of *Jiangxititan*

*ganzhouensis* (NHMG 034062)

## 2　Anatomical abbreviations

ACDL, anterior centrodiapophyseal lamina; CDF, centrodiapophyseal fossa; CeA, antepenultimate cervical vertebra; CeP, penultimate cervical vertebra; CeU, ultimate cervical vertebra; CPOL, centropostzygapophyseal lamina; CPRL, centroprezygapophyseal lamina; cr, cervical rib; D, dorsal vertebra; di, diapophysis; dr, dorsal rib; epi, epipophysis; EPRL, epipophyseal-prezygapophyseal lamina; hl, horizontal lamina; lSPOL, lateral spinopostzygapophyseal lamina; lSPRL, lateral spinoprezygapophyseal lamina; met, metapophysis; mSPOL, medial spinopostzygapophyseal lamina; mSPRL, medial spinoprezygapophyseal lamina; pa, parapophysis; PACD-F, parapophyseal centrodiapophyseal fossa; PCDL, posterior centrodiapophyseal lamina; pd, dorsolaterally facing platform of diapophysis; pl, pleurocoel; POCD-F, postzygapophyseal centrodiapophyseal fossa; PODL, postzygodiapophyseal lamina; POSD-F, postzygapophyseal spinodiapophyseal fossa; poz, postzygapophysis; PPDL, paradiapophyseal lamina; PRCD-F, prezygapophyseal centrodiapophyseal fossa; PRDL, prezygodiapophyseal lamina; PRPAD-F, prezygapophyseal paradiapophyseal fossa; PRPL, prezygoparapophyseal lamina; PRSD-F, prezygapophyseal spinodiapophyseal fossa; prz, prezygapophysis; SPDL, spinodiapophyseal lamina; SPOL, spinopostzygapophyseal lamina; SPRL, spinoprezygapophyseal lamina; TPOL, intrapostzygapophseal lamina; TPRL, intraprezygapophyseal lamina.

## 3　Systematic palaeontology

Dinosauria Owen (1842)

Sauropoda Marsh (1878)

Neosauropoda Bonaparte (1986)

Somphospondyli Wilson & Sereno (1998)

Titanosauria Bonaparte and Coria (l993)

*Jiangxititan ganzhouensis* gen. et sp. nov.　(Figures 2-9; Table 1)

urn: lsid: zoobank. org: pub: C8DF4A1E-AD82-40DE-9F41-A60454A412D4 urn: lsid: zoobank. org: act: 9AB6A0EF-87E5-4564-A197-2F7B9FC54F58

urn: lsid: zoobank. org: act: 379B8F91-2396-40E6-9F8C-898D20B4C27E

## 3.1 Holotype

NHMG 034062, seven articulated vertebrae including three posteriormost cervicals and
the first four dorsals (D1-D4), two articulated cervical ribs, three articulated dorsal ribs
(Figures 2-9; Table 1). The specimen is housed in the Natural History Museum of Guangxi
Zhuang Autonomous Region.

## 3.2 Etymology

The generic name *Jiangxi*, pinyin, is in reference to the fossil locality in Jiangxi
Province, southern China, *titan*, in Greece, means giant dragon. The specific name *ganzhou*,
pinyin, is from the fossil locality of Nankang County, Ganzhou City, Jiangxi Province.

## 3.3 Locality and horizon

The specimen was collected in Tankou Town, Nankang County, Ganzhou City, Jiangxi
Province, southern China. Upper Cretaceous (Maastrichtian), Nanxiong Formation (Bureau of
Geology and Mineral Resources of Jiangxi Province, 1984; Bi, et al. , 2021).

## 3.4 Diagnosis

*Jiangxititan ganzhouensis* can be diagnosed on the basis of the following unique
combination of character states: posterior cervical and anterior dorsal centra strongly
compressed dorsoventrally; accessory horizontal laminae present within the anterior dorsal
pleurocoels; posterior cervical and anterior dorsal neural arches low; posterior cervical and
anterior dorsal neural spines deeply bifurcated and widely separated; inverted 'V' lamina
present at the anterior margin of the bifid point in posteriormost cervical and anteriormost
dorsal neural spines; both the EPRL and SPDL present in posterior cervical vertebrae;
triangular fossa formed by the metapophysis, medial and lateral SPRLs present at the anterior
margin of the posteriormost cervical and anteriormost dorsal neural spines; postzygapophyses

in the posterior cervical vertebrae fan-shaped; medial and lateral SPOLs present in the anterior dorsal vertebrae; anterior dorsal rib short and gracile.

### 3.5    Ontogenetic assessment

The *Jiangxititan* specimen preserved seven articulated posterior cervical and anterior dorsal neural arches. The neural arches and centra are fully fused, some of the cervical and dorsal ribs are attached. The right side of the cervical rib in CeP is preserved, but is deformed and obscured by the rock. The left side of the cervical rib in CeU is partly fused with the parapophysis. The left sides of the dorsal ribs in D1, D3 and D4 are attached with the parapophyses and diapophyses. This indicates that *Jiangxititan* probably represents a morphologically mature individual (Wedel and Taylor, 2013; Griffin, et al. , 2021).

### 3.6    Description and comparisons

The holotype was recovered during construction work, with the first and the last vertebrae of the series being broken during the field work (Figures 2-4). The right side of the neural arches of the seven articulated vertebrae was relatively complete, whereas the left side was deformed during its fossilisation. The anterior dorsal pleurocoels are visible in ventral view, partly due to the deformation. For description, the three cervical vertebrae will be designated as CeA (antepenultimate cervical vertebra), CeP (penultimate cervical vertebra) and CeU (ultimate cervical vertebra), respectively, and the four dorsal vertebrae will be designated as D1-D4. The identification of the first dorsal vertebrate (D1) is based on the following features: the distal end of the articulated dorsal rib directs mainly laterally and slightly posteriorly (Figures 2 and 4); the capital and tubercular heads are nearly coplanar; the parapophysis is positioned at the anteroventral margin of the pleurocoel (Figure 3); the parapophysis is oval in shape, and differs from that of the posteriormost cervical which is anteroposteriorly elongated; the lack of oblique septum within the pleurocoel, differs from that of the posteriormost cervical where three accessory laminae are present within the pleurocoel; the length of centrum in D1 decreases dramatically than that of the posterior most cervical (Table 1).

The CeA preserves its posterior half of the centrum and fragmentary postzygapophysis, while the fourth dorsal vertebra (D4) preserves its anterior part of the centrum and some neural arch. The cervical vertebrae CeP and CeU have fused cervical ribs, while D1, D3 and D4 have articulated dorsal ribs. All the cervical and dorsal ribs are incomplete.

### 3.6.1　Posterior cervical vertebrae (Figures 2–6; Table 1)

#### 3.6.1.1　Centra

The centra in CeP and CeU are nearly complete, the anterior part of the centrum in CeA is missing. The centra are strongly opisthocoelous, with a convex anterior articulation and corresponding concave posterior articulation, as indicated by the exposed margins of some intercentrum articulations (Figures 3 and 4). The centrum is relatively elongated in CeP, and decreases in length in CeU (Table 1). In lateral view, the ventral surfaces of the cervical centra are concave anteroposteriorly. In ventral view, the ventral surfaces of the cervical centra in CeP and CeU are markedly constructed transversely, posterior to the parapophyses (Figure 4). The ventral surfaces of the cervical centra in CeP and CeU are slightly concave transversely between the parapophyses, no ventral ridges or excavations present at the ventral surfaces. The camellate internal structures can be seen from the broken ventral surfaces of the centra. The centra in CeP and CeU are strongly compressed dorsoventrally (Table 1), with the ratio of mediolateral width to dorsoventral height of posterior articular surfaces being greater than 2.3, similar to *Mendozasaurus neguyelap* (González Riga, et al. , 2018).

The pleurocoels are preserved in CeA-CeU, though the anterior part of the pleurocoel in CeA is broken (Figure 3). The cervical pleurocoels in CeP and CeU are deep and large, occupying almost their lateral surfaces of the centra, and are divided into numerous separate chambers by subvertical laminae. All the pleurocoels have deep excavations that ramify into the centra.

The parapophyses are preserved in CeP and CeU (Figure 3). They lie at the anteroventral margins of the centra, projecting ventrolaterally. The parapophyses are anteroposteriorly elongated, similar to some derived titanosaurs, such as *Malawisaurus*, *Saltasaurus*, and *Alamosaurus* (D'Emic, 2012). The parapophyses extend posteriorly and reach nearly the midlength of the centra. They project primarily laterally, and slightly ventrally. No excavations present on the dorsal surfaces of the parapophyses.

### 3.6.1.2  Neural arches

The neural arches in CeP and CeU are preserved, with the anterior part of CeP being damaged (Figure 2). The neural arch is low, with the upper margin of the neural canal being level with the TPRL or TPOL (Figures 6 and 7), although the neural canal is obscured due to the preservation and preparation, similar to the conditions in *Ligabuesaurus*, *Rukwatitan*, *Mendozasaurus* and other titanosaurs (Bonaparte, et al. , 2006; Gorscak, et al. , 2014; Gonzàlez Riga, et al. , 2018). The total heights of the cervical vertebrae are less than 30 cm due to the low neural arches and the laterally directed metapophyses (Table 1). The ratio of the posterior cervical neural arch (arch height measured from dorsal surface of the centrum to base of prezygapophyses) to centrum dorsoventral height is less than 0.5, similar to other titanosaurs, such as *Malawisaurus*, *Saltasaurus*, and *Alamosaurus* (Mannion, et al. , 2013, 2019a).

### 3.6.1.3  Diapophyses

The diapophyses are preserved in CeP and CeU, with the right side of the diapophyses being preserved better than the left side (Figures 2-4; Table 1). The diapophyses direct laterally, rather than dorsolaterally. The articular surfaces of the diapophyses are rugose, pointing ventrally, and slightly laterally (Figure 4). In ventral view, the articular surface of the diapophysis is subtriangular in outline. The diapophysis is low in CeU, nearly level with the ventral margin of the centrum. The camellate internal structures can be seen from the broken surfaces of the diapophyses. Muscle scars are developed on the dorsolateral end of the diapophysis, forming a distinct platform (Figures 2 and 3).

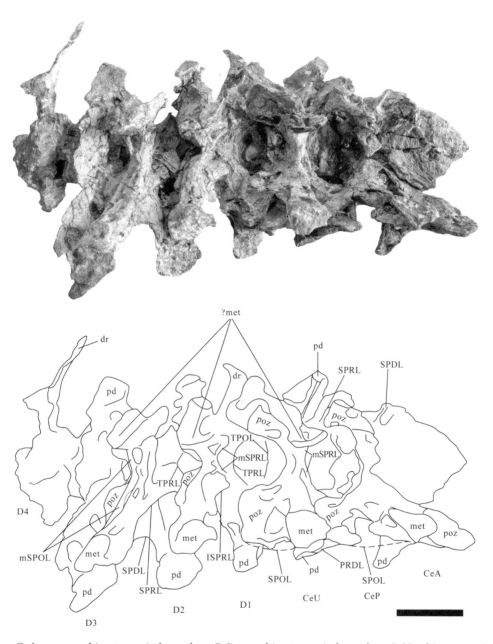

CeA—antepenultimate cervical vertebra; CeP—penultimate cervical vertebra; CeU—ultimate cervical vertebra; D—dorsal vertebra; dr—dorsal rib; lSPRL—lateral spinoprezygapophyseal lamina; met—metapophysis; mSPOL—medial spinopostzygapophyseal lamina; mSPRL—medial spinoprezygapophyseal lamina; pd—dorsolaterally facing platform of diapophysis; PODL—postzygodiapophyseal lamina; poz—postzygapophysis; PRDL—prezygodiapophyseal lamina; SPRL—spinoprezygapophyseal lamina; TPOL—intrapostzygapophseal lamina; TPRL—intraprezygapophyseal lamina. Scale bar equals 20 cm.

Figure 2    Holotype of *Jiangxititan ganzhouensis* (NHMG 034062) in dorsal view with interpreted outline below

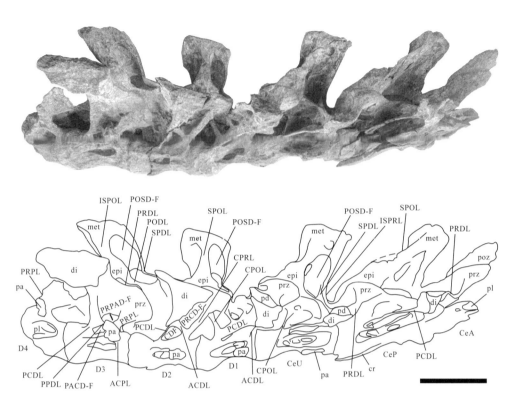

ACDL−anterior centrodiapophyseal lamina; CeA−antepenultimate cervical vertebra; CeP−penultimate cervical vertebra; CeU−ultimate cervical vertebra; CPOL−centropostzygapophyseal lamina; CPRL−centroprezygapophyseal lamina; cr−cervical rib; D−dorsal vertebra; di−diapophysis; epi−epipophysis; lSPOL−lateral spinopostzygapophyseal lamina; lSPRL−lateral spinoprezygapophyseal lamina; met−metapophysis; pa−parapophysis; PACD-F−parapophyseal centrodiapophyseal fossa; PCDL−posterior centrodiapophyseal lamina; pd−dorsolaterally facing platform of diapophysis; pl−pleurocoel; PODL−postzygodiapophyseal lamina; POSD-F−postzygapophyseal spinodiapophyseal fossa; poz−postzygapophysis; PRCD-F−prezygapophyseal centrodiapophyseal fossa; PRDL−prezygodiapophyseal lamina; PRPAD-F−prezygapophyseal paradiapophyseal fossa; PRPL−prezygoparapophyseal lamina; prz−prezygapophysis; SPDL−spinodiapophyseal lamina; SPOL−spinopostzygapophyseal lamina. Scale bar equals 20 cm.

Figure 3　Holotype of *Jiangxititan ganzhouensis*（NHMG 034062）
in right lateral and slightly ventral view, with interpreted outline below

Table 1　Measurements (in cm) of the vertebrae in the holotype of *Jiangxititan ganzhouensis* (NHMG 034062)

| Vertebra | Centrum length (without convex) | Centrum posterior width | Centrum posterior height | Width across diapophyses | Width of right metapophysis | Total height |
|---|---|---|---|---|---|---|
| CeA | 20+ | 23 | 10 | ? | ? | 10+ |
| CeP | 27 | 24 | 10 | 46+ | 29 | 25 |

Table 1 ( continued )

| Vertebra | Centrum length (without convex) | Centrum posterior width | Centrum posterior height | Width across diapophyses | Width of right metapophysis | Total height |
|----------|--------------------------------|------------------------|-------------------------|--------------------------|----------------------------|--------------|
| CeU | 22 | 23 | 9 | 59+ | 31 | 27 |
| D1 | 18 | 22 | 10 | 60+ | 31 | 28 |
| D2 | 19 | 21 | 11 | 63+ | 32 | 29 |
| D3 | 18 | 21 | 12 | 65+ | ? | 23+ |
| D4 | 13+ | ? | ? | ? | ? | 18+ |

Width of right metapophysis: measured from the distal end of the right metapophysis to the notch; '+' denotes a measurement based on an incomplete element.

### 3.6.1.4 Zygapophyses

The prezygapophyses and postzygapophyses in CeP and CeU, and the right side of the postzygapophysis in CeA are preserved (Figures 2 and 3). The medial margins of the postzygapophyses are relatively complete, while the lateral and dorsal margins are broken away during the fieldwork (Figure 2). The prezygapophyses are positioned slightly beyond the anterior margin of the anterior convex articulation. The postzygapophysis extends posteriorly and slightly ventrally well beyond the posterior margin of the centrum to contact the prezygapophysis of the succeeding vertebrate. In dorsal view, the postzygapophysis in CeU is large and fan-shaped, with a transverse width of 17 cm, and an anteroposterior length of 14 cm, respectively, though the postzygapophsis is somewhat broken. Fan-shaped postzygapophysis is also present in CeP, with the width of 14 cm, and the length of 17 cm, respectively. The left and right sides of the pre-and postzygapophyses are widely positioned from each other, well exceeding the width of the centrum, similar to the basal titanosaur *Rukwatitan*, in which the interprezygapophyseal distance is approximately twice the width of the centrum (Gorscak, et al. , 2014). For example, the distance between the lateral margins of the left and right postzygapophyses in CeP is greater than 48 cm, though the left postzygapophysis is incomplete. The epipophyses are present in CeA-CeU, which protrude the lateral margins of the postzygapophyses (Figures 3 and 5), unlike most of other sauropods such as *Euhelopus* (Wilson and Upchurch, 2009), *Silutitan* (Wang, et al. , 2021), in which the epipophyses primarily protrude the posterior margin of the postzygapophyses.

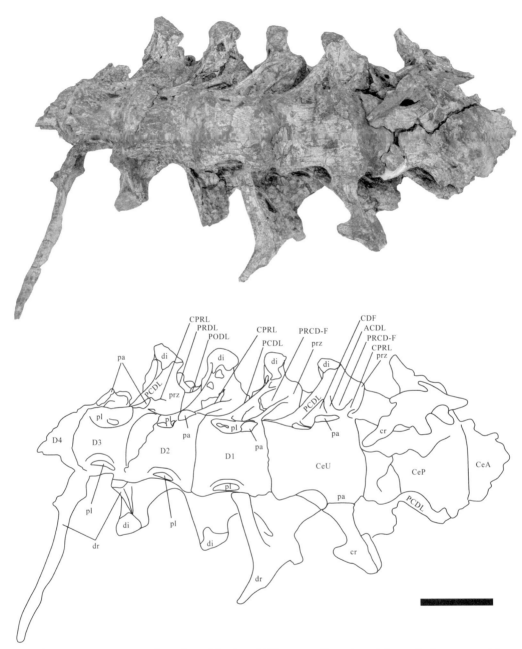

ACDL—anterior centrodiapophyseal lamina; CDF—centrodiapophyseal fossa; CeA—antepenultimate cervical vertebra; CeP—penultimate cervical vertebra; CeU—ultimate cervical vertebra; CPRL—centroprezygapophyseal lamina; cr—cervical rib; D—dorsal vertebra; di—diapophysis; dr—dorsal rib; pa—parapophysis; PCDL—posterior centrodiapophyseal lamina; pl—pleurocoel; PODL—postzygodiapophyseal lamina; PRCD-F—prezygapophyseal centrodiapophyseal fossa; PRDL—prezygodiapophyseal lamina; prz—prezygapophysis. Scale bar equals 20 cm.

Figure 4　Holotype of *Jiangxititan ganzhouensis* (NHMG 034062) in ventral view with interpreted outline below

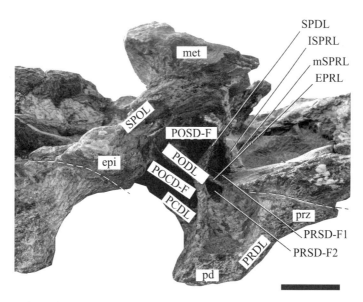

EPRL—epipophyseal-prezygapophyseal lamina; lSPRL—lateral spinoprezygapophyseal lamina; met—
metapophysis; mSPRL—medial spinoprezygapophyseal lamina; PCDL—posterior centrodiapophyseal lamina;
pd—dorsolaterally facing platform of diapophysis; POCD-F—postzygapophyseal centrodiapophyseal fossa;
PODL—postzygodiapophyseal lamina; POSD-F—postzygapophyseal spinodiapophyseal fossa; PRDL—
prezygodiapophyseal lamina; PRSD-F—prezygapophyseal spinodiapophyseal fossa; prz—prezygapophysis;
SPDL—spinodiapophyseal lamina; SPOL—spinopostzygapophyseal lamina. Scale bar equals 5 cm.

Figure 5　The neural arch of the posterior most cervical vertebra (CeU) of *Jiangxititan
ganzhouensis* (NHMG 034062) in right lateral view

### 3.6.1.5　Neural spines

The most striking feature of the cervicals is their deeply bifurcated neural spines and
widely positioned metapophyses (Figure 2). The right sides of the metapophyses are well-
preserved in CeP and CeU, while the left sides suffered from deformation. The transverse
width of the metapophysis (width from the bifid point to the distal margin of metapophysis)
well exceeds its centrum width or centrum height (Table 1). The metapophyses are relatively
straight and direct laterodorsally, forming an angle of about 30 degree to the horizontal
level, with the distal ends of the metapophyses well beyond the lateral margins of the centra,
differing from *Opisthocoelicaudia*, in which the metapophyses direct dorsally (Borsuk-
Bialynicka, 1977). The dorsal surface of the notch separating the metapophyses in CeP
is smooth, and somewhat flat in CeU, no median tubercles are positioned between the

metapophyses, differing from *Euhelopus* which has trifid posterior cervical neural spines. The dorsal surfaces of the distal parts of the metapophyses are rugose, directing dorsally, slightly medially. Large internal concavities can be seen from the broken surfaces of the metapophyses. The deep bifurcation of the posterior cervical neural spines in *Jiangxititan* is much more developed than in *Euhelopus*, *Phuwiangosaurus*, *Dongbeititan* (Wang, et al., 2007), and other titanosauriforms with bifid neural spines from Asia, but less than most dicraeosaurids, such as *Dicraeosaurus hansemanni* from Africa (Janensch, 1929).

3.6.1.6　Cervical laminae and fossa system

The cervical laminae and fossae are well developed, although some of them are damaged during the fieldwork, especially in their left sides.

The ACDL is well preserved in CeU. It projects anteromedially from the diapophysis to contact the anterolateral margin of the centrum, and is across between the nearly paralleled PCDL and CPRL, resulting in two subtriangular fossae in front and behind it, naming PRCD-F and CDF respectively, at the lateral aspect of the diapophysis (Figure 4). The CPRL seems bifurcated, with marked excavation present at the posterior margin of it.

The PCDLs are present in CeP and CeU. The right side of the PCDL in CeU is complete, projects posteromedially from the diapophysis to contact the lateral margin of the centrum, exceeding the posterior margin of the pleuroceol (Figure 4).

The CPOL can be seen in CeU, while it is broken in CeP (Figure 3). It extends medioventrally from the postzygapophysis to contact the posterior part of the PCDL.

The PRDLs are present in CeP and CeU, and are relatively complete in their right sides (Figure 3). In lateral view, the PRDL is oriented posteroventrally from the prezygapophysis to contact the diapophysis. The length of the PRDL in CeU is shorter than that of CeP, but is more robust than the latter.

The PODLs are present in CeP and CeU (Figures 3 and 5). The right side of the PODL in CeU is relatively complete. It is oriented posterodorsally from the diapophysis to contact the SPDL, then keep extending posterodorsally to contact the anterior margin of the postzygapophysis (Figure 5), forming the POSD-F and POCD-F above and below the PODL, respectively.

An EPRL is present in CeU, projecting posterodorsally from the prezygapophysis to contact the SPDL and merge with the upper part of the PODL, resulting two deep fossae, naming PRSD-F1 and PRSD-F2, respectively (Figure 5). The EPRL is oblique, unlike *Euhelopus* and *Silutitan* in which the EPRL is nearly horizontal. The EPRL is unknown in the preceding cervical due to the preservation.

The SPDLs are present in CeP and CeU, though some of them are broken away. The SPDL is complete in CeU (Figure 5), extending dorsally from the diapophysis to contact the anterior margin of the metapophysis, although the dorsal part of the SPDL is somewhat broken.

The SPRLs are present in CeP and CeU, though some of them are broken. The SPRL in CeU is divided into two laminae: lateral SPRL and medial SPRL (Figures 2, 5 and 6). The lateral SPRL projects dorsolaterally from the lateral margin of the prezygapophysis to contact the anterior margin of the metapophysis, while the medial SPRL projects dorsomedially from the medial margin of the prezygapophysis to contact its partner, forming an inverted 'V' lamina at the anterior margin of the bifid point (Figure 6). This inverted V-shaped lamina is not seen in CeP, in which only lateral SPRL is present. The prespinal and postspinal laminae are absent.

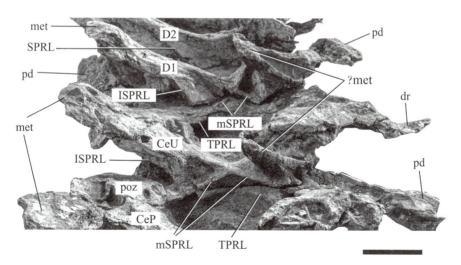

CeP—penultimate cervical vertebra; CeU—ultimate cervical vertebra; D—dorsal vertebra; dr—dorsal rib; lSPRL—lateral spinoprezygapophyseal lamina; met—metapophysis; mSPRL—medial spinoprezygapophyseal lamina; pd—dorsolaterally facing platform of diapophysis; poz—postzygapophysis; SPRL—spinoprezygapophyseal lamina; TPRL—intraprezygapophyseal lamina. Scale bar equals 10 cm.

Figure 6    The CeP-D2 of *Jiangxititan ganzhouensis* (NHMG 034062) in anterodorsal view

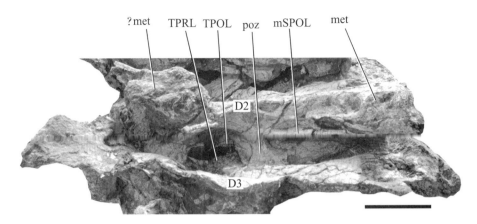

D−dorsal vertebra; met−metapophysis; mSPOL−medial spinopostzygapophyseal lamina; poz−postzygapophysis; TPOL−intrapostzygapophseal lamina; TPRL−intraprezygapophyseal lamina. Scale bar equals 10 cm.

Figure 7　The second dorsal vertebra (D2) of

*Jiangxititan ganzhouensis* (NHMG 034062) in posterodorsal view

The SPOLs are present in CeP and CeU (Figures 2, 3 and 5). The SPOL extends posteroventrally from the posteroventral margin of the metapophysis to contact the posterolateral margin of the postzygapophysis. In lateral view, the SPOL is long in CeP, and relatively short in CeU, though they are somewhat broken during the fieldwork.

3.6.1.7　Cervical ribs

The right side of the cervical rib in CeP and the left one in CeU are preserved, but are damaged during the fieldwork (Figure 4). In ventral view, the rib shaft in CeU points posteriorly, though its distal shaft is broken.

3.6.2　Anterior dorsal vertebrae (Figures 2-4, and 6-9; Table 1)

3.6.2.1　Centra

The centra of the dorsal vertebrae are opisthocoelous. The length of the centrum decreases compared to the preceding cervical (Table 1). In lateral view, the ventral surfaces of the dorsal centra are markedly concave anteroposteriorly. In ventral view, the ventral surfaces of the dorsal centra are slightly constricted and somewhat flat transversely between the parapophyses (Figure 4). The dorsal centra are strongly compressed dorsoventrally as in the preceding cervical centra (Table 1), with the ratio of mediolateral width to dorsoventral height of posterior articular surfaces of the anteriormost dorsal centra (D1-D3) being greater than 1.90, compared to *Ligabuesaurus*, *Mierasaurus*, and *Opisthocoelicaudia* which are 2.22, 1. 80, and 1. 48, respectively (Mannion, et al. , 2019a). This ratio is much less in *Yongjinglong* and *Dongbeititan* (Wang, et al. , 2007; Li, et al. , 2014).

The pleurocoels are preserved in D1-D4, though the posterior margin of the pleurocoel in D4 are broken (Figure 3). The posterior margins of the dorsal pleurocoels are acute, as in most other macronarians (Upchurch, 1998; Mannion, et al. , 2013). The pleurocoels in D1-D3 are large, pointing ventrolaterally, and are visible in ventral view (Figure 4). These pleurocoels are set within the fossae, similar to most other titanosaurs (Upchurch, et al. , 2004). Accessory horizontal laminae are present within the pleurocoel in D3 (Figure 8).

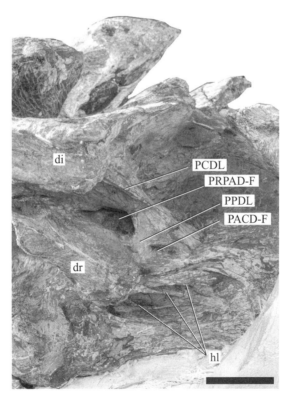

di—diapophysis; dr—dorsal rib; hl—horizontal lamina; PACD-F—parapophyseal centrodiapophyseal fossa; PCDL—posterior centrodiapophyseal lamina; PPDL—paradiapophyseal lamina; PRPAD-F—prezygapophyseal paradiapophyseal fossa. Scale bar equals 5 cm.

Figure 8　The third dorsal vertebra (D3) of *Jiangxititan ganzhouensis*

(NHMG 034062) in left lateral view, showing the horizontal laminae within the pleurocoel

The paraphyses are preserved in D1-D4 (Figure 3). From D1 to D4, the positions of the parapophyses vary. It positioned at the anteroventral corner of the pleurocoel in D1, located on the anterior margin of the pleurocoel in D2, then lay slightly dorsally to the pleurocoels in D3 and D4. The parapophyses are elliptical in outline, though the posterior part of the parapophysis in D4 is broken.

### 3.6.2.2　Neural arches

The neural arches in D1-D3 are preserved, with the posterior part of D3 being damaged. The neural arches are low as in the preceding cervicals, with the upper margins of the neural canals being level with the TPRLs (Figure 6), although the neural canals are obscured due to the preservation. The total heights of the dorsal vertebrae are less than 30 cm due to the low neural arches and the laterally directed metapophyses, as in the preceding cervical (Table 1).

### 3.6.2.3　Diapophyses

The diapophyses are preserved in D1-D4, with the right side of the diapophyses being preserved better than the left side (Figures 2-4; Table 1). The diapophyses direct slightly dorsally in the dorsal vertebrae, other than laterally as in the cervical series. The articular surfaces of the diapophyses are rugose, pointing ventrally, and slightly laterally as in the preceding cervical. In ventral view, the articular surfaces of the diapophyses are subtriangular in outline, increasing in diameter from 7 cm in CeU to 13 cm in D3. The diapophyses are positioned slightly dorsally to those of the preceding cervicals, and nearly to the level of upper margin of the centrum in D3. As in the preceding cervicals, the diapophyses of the dorsals developed a dorsally, slightly laterally facing platform (Figure 2).

### 3.6.2.4　Zygapophyses

The prezygapophyses and postzygapophyses in D1 and D2, and the prezygapophyses in D3 are preserved, though some of them are broken (Figures 2-4). The prezygapophyses and postzygapophyses are relatively complete in their right sides, while their left sides are damaged. As in the preceding cervicals, the left and right sides of the pre-and postzygapophyses are widely positioned from each other, well exceeding the width of the corresponding centrum. The anterior margin of the prezygapophysis in D1 and D2 is well beyond the anterior margin of the corresponding centrum, and slightly beyond the anterior margin in D3. In ventral view, the transverse width of the articular surface of the prezygapophysis in CeP to D3 increases backward (10 cm in CeP and 16 cm in D3). Accordingly, the transverse width of the articular surface of the postzygapophysis in CeP to D2 increases backward (14 cm in CeP and 20 cm in D2). In dorsal view, the distance between the medial margins of the left and right postzygapophyses in CeP to D2 decreases backward (22 cm in CeP and 9 cm in D2). The epipophyses are present in D1 and D2, and protrude the lateral margins of the postzygapophyses as in the cervical series.

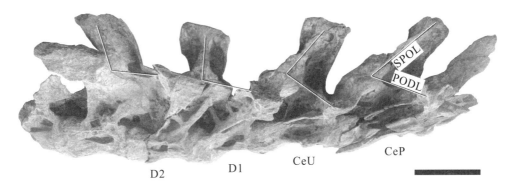

SPOL—spinopostzygapophyseal lamina; PODL—postzygodiapophyseal lamina. Scale bar equals 20 cm.

Figure 9  Holotype of *Jiangxititan ganzhouensis* (NHMG 034062)
in right lateral and slightly ventral view, showing the variation of the angle between the
SPOL and PODL along the cervical and dorsal series

Table 2  Phylogenetic coding for *Jiangxititan* and *Gannansaurus*

| *Jiangxititan*(40/556) | | | | | | |
|---|---|---|---|---|---|---|
| ?????????? | ??????010? | 1????????? | ?????????? | ?????????? | ?????????? | ?????????? |
| ?????????? | ?????????? | ?????????? | ?????????? | ???????100 | 12???0101? | ?10??1?0?? |
| ??1111???? | ??00?????0 | ?????????? | 1????????? | ?????????? | ?????????? | ?????????? |
| ?????????? | ?????????? | ?????????? | ?????????? | ?????????? | ?????????? | ?????????? |
| ?????????? | ?????????? | ?????????? | ?????????? | ??01???00? | ?0???0??? | ?????????? |
| ?????????? | ?????????? | ?????????? | ?????????? | ?????????? | ?????1???? | ??????1??? |
| ?????????? | ?????????? | ?????????? | ?????00??? | ??00??1?00 | ?????????? | ?????????? |

Table 2（continued）

| *Jiangxititan*(40/556) | | | | | | |
|---|---|---|---|---|---|---|
| ?????????? | ?????????? | ?????????? | ?????????? | ?????????? | ?????????? | ????? |
| *Gannansaurus*(25/556) | | | | | | |
| ?????????? | ?????????? | ???????11? | ?????????? | ?????????? | ?????????? | ?????????? |
| ?????????? | ?????????? | ?????????? | ?????????? | ?????????? | ?????????? | ?????????? |
| 20111??1?? | 0?????0??? | ?????????? | ?????????0 | ??00?????? | ?0???????? | ?????????? |
| ?????????? | ?????????? | ?????????? | ?????????? | ?????????? | ?????????? | ?????????? |
| ?????????? | ?????????? | ???0????01 | ?????????? | ?????????? | ?????????? | ?????????? |
| ?????????? | ?????????? | ?????????? | ?????????? | ?????????? | ?????????? | ?????????? |
| ?????????? | ?????????? | ?????????? | ?????????? | ?????????? | ?10???0??? | ?????????? |
| ?????????? | ?????0000? | ?????????? | ?????????? | ?????????? | ??????0??? | ????? |

### 3.6.2.5 Neural spines

The dorsal neural spines are deeply bifurcated as in the preceding cervicals (Figure 2). They are well preserved in the right sides of D1 and D2, while their left sides suffered from deformation. In lateral view, the metapophysis inclines slightly posteriorly, rather than anteriorly as in the cervical series. The dorsal surfaces of the bifid points are smooth as in the preserved cervical, no median tubercles are positioned between the metapophyses. In dorsal view, the dorsal surface of the bifid point in D1 is U-shaped, with a concave posterior margin. The dorsal surfaces of the distal parts of the metapophyses are rugose, directing dorsally, slightly medially. As in the cervical series, the deep bifurcation of the neural spines is much more developed than in those of titanosauriforms (*Opisthocoelicaudia*, for example) with bifid neural spines from Asia, but less than that of *Dicraeosaurus hansemanni* from Africa.

### 3.6.2.6 Dorsal laminae and fossa system

The dorsal laminae and fossae are well developed as in the preceding cervical. Because the left lateral sides of the dorsal neural arches are incompletely preserved, the descriptions of the laminae and fossae are mainly based on the right lateral, dorsal, and ventral aspects.

The ACDLs are present in D1 and D2, but are absent and replaced by the rudimentary PPDL and very short but robust ACPL in D3 (Figure 3). The ACDLs in D1 and D2 are crossed between the nearly paralleled PCDL and CPRL, resulting two fossae in front and behind them, named PRCD-F and CDF, respectively (Figures 3 and 4). There are also two fossae in the lateral aspect of the diapophysis in D3, named PRPAD-F and PACD-F above and below the rudimentary PPDL, respectively (Figure 3). The PACD-F is relatively small, and is positioned at the posterior margin of the parapophysis. The PRPAD-F is large, shallow dorsally and deep ventrally, with a weakly developed, anteroventrally oblique bony strut and two resulting concavities present at the ventral part of the PRPAD-F.

The PCDLs are present in D1-D3, but less developed than those in the cervical series (Figures 3 and 4). They oriented posteromedially, and slightly ventrally from the diapophyses to contact the posterolateral margins of the centra.

The CPOLs can be seen in D1, and obscured in D2 and D3 (Figure 3). The CPOL in D1 is robust, directing anteromedially and ventrally from the postzygapophysis to contact the posterior part of the PCDL.

The PRDLs are present in D1-D3 (Figure 3). In lateral view, the PRDL is short and robust in D1, and is relatively elongated in D2 and D3. It is oriented posteroventrally, and slightly laterally from the prezygapophysis in D1, and posterolaterally in D2 and D3 to contact the diapophysis.

The PODLs are present in D1 and D2 (Figure 3). The PODL is oriented posteriorly and gradually dorsally to contact the anterior margin of the postzygapophysis, as the diapophysis raised up dorsally in the dorsal vertebrae. POSD-F is also developed in D1 and D2, as in the preceding cervical (Figure 3).

The PRPLs are only present in D3 and D4 (Figure 3), in which the parapophyses are positioned at the neural arches. The PRPL in D3 is complete, and is incomplete in D4 due to the preservation.

The SPDLs are present in D1 to D3, though most of them are broken. The SPDL projects posterodorsally from the diapophysis to contact the anterior margin of the metapophysis.

The SPRLs are present in D1 to D3, though some of them are broken. The SPRLs in D1 are divided into two laminae: lateral SPRL and medial SPRL (Figures 2 and 6). The lateral SPRL projects posterolaterally and dorsally from the posterolateral margin of the prezygapophysis to contact the anterior margin of the metapophysis, while the medial SPRL projects dorsomedially and posteriorly from the medial margin of the prezygapophysis to contact its partner, forming an inverted 'V' lamina at the anterior margin of the bifid point, as in CeU (Figure 6). This inverted V-shaped lamina is not seen in D2 and D3, in which only lateral SPRL is present. The TPRL is formed between the medial margins of the prezygapophysis, and the TPOL is formed between the medial margins of the postzygapophysis (Figures 2, 6 and 7).

The SPOLs are developed in D1 and D2 (Figure 3). They are oriented almost vertically from the metapophysis to contact the postzygapophysis, unlike in the preceding cervical in which the SPOLs are oriented posteroventrally. The length of the SPOLs of D1 and D2 are much shorter than those of CeU and CeP. There are lateral SPOL and medial SPOL present in D2 (Figures 2, 3 and 7), the lateral SPOL projects ventrally from the distal end of the metapophysis to contact the lateral margin of the postzygapophysis, while the medial SPOL projects from the medial margin of the postzygapophysis to contact the posterior margin of the metapophysis. As the postzygapophysis in CeP to D2 gradually migrates to the ventral aspect of the corresponding metapophysis backward, the angles between the SPOL and the PODL increased from acute angle in CeP to obtuse angle in D2 (Figure 9).

### 3.6.2.7  Dorsal ribs

The dorsal ribs are only preserved in D1, D3 and D4. The rib of D1 is incompletely preserved, with its distal end broken during the field work (Figures 2 and 4). The broken distal end is elliptical in shape, with a diameter of 1.5 cm. Unlike its preceding cervical rib, the distal shaft of this dorsal rib points laterally, and somewhat posteriorly. The dorsal rib in D3 only preserved its proximal end (Figure 8). The articulated left dorsal rib in D4 is relatively well preserved, just missing some proximal part and its distal end (Figures 2 and 4). Its preserved length is 43 cm. The capitulum is articulated with the parapophysis, while the tubercle is broken. The midshaft is comma-shaped in cross section, and becomes flattened distally. The broken distal end is 3 cm and 0.7 cm in diameter, indicating that this rib is gracile and relatively short, differing from *Opisthocoelicaudia*, in which the rib of D4 has a length of 153 cm, with the diameters of the midshaft being 10.5 cm and 3.5 cm, respectively. It is not known whether the rib of D4 possesses the pneumatic foramina in the proximal end due to the preservation.

## 4 Phylogenetic analysis

We ran phylogenetic analysis of a matrix modified from the Poropat, et al. (2023) matrix with *Jiangxititan* and the sympatric *Gannansaurus* added in. Eighteen characters were ordered following Poropat, et al. (2023) but no taxon was excluded *a priori*. The matrix was analysed with equally weighted parsimony using TNT v. 1. 5 (Goloboff, et al. , 2008; Goloboff and Catalano, 2016). It was first analysed using a "New technology search" with default settings except changing "Random additional sequences" from 1 to 1000 and applying the Ratchet and Drift during tree search. Then the resultant most parsimonious trees were subjected to an additional round of tree bisection and reconnection (TBR) branch swapping, which finally resulted 27, 720 most parsimonious trees each with a tree length of 2738 steps, a CI of 0.214, and a RI of 0.588 (we set the maximum number of trees in memory to 150, 000). We calculated Bremer support and bootstrap values for the recovered clades, which are in general very low. The strict consensus of the 27, 720 most parsimonious trees places *Jiangxititan* deeply within the Titanosauriformes but the sympatric *Gannansaurus* in a much earlier-diverging lineage forming a large basal polytomy near the base of the Titanosauriformes (Figure 10). More specifically, *Jiangxititan* has been recovered as a lognkosaur but *Gannansaurus* as a titanosauriform outside the late-diverging clade comprising the Diamantinasauria and Lithostrotia.

## 5 Discussions

*Jiangxititan* displays some features suggesting a titanosaurian affinity. The presence of acute posterior margins of pleurocoels in anterior dorsal centra and plank-like cross-sectional shape of anterior dorsal rib indicate that *Jiangxititan* is a macronarian (Mannion, et al. , 2013). Within Macronaria, *Jiangxititan* is more similar to Somphospondyli in displaying features such as presence of somphospondylous vertebral pneumaticity and posteriormost cervical vertebrae with low infrazygapophyseal region (region between centrum and prezygapophyses shorter than centrum height) (D'Emic, 2012). Furthermore, *Jiangxititan* possesses a titanosaurian feature: the presence of an elongate parapophysis in posterior cervical vertebrae

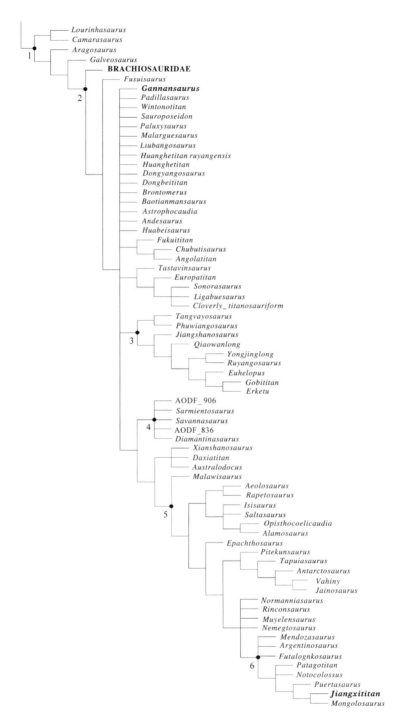

Nodes numbers indicate the clades retrieved：1−Macronaria；2−Titanosauriformes；3−Euhelopodidae；4−Diamantinasauria；5−Lithostrotia；6−Lognkosauria.

Figure 10　Phylogenetic analysis of *Jiangxititan ganzhouensis* (NHMG 034062)

［The data matrix follows Poropat, et al. (2023), with the addition of *Jiangxititan* and *Gannansaurus* (see Table 2). Brachiosauridae has been collapsed into a single lineage］

(D'Emic, 2012). Finally, a feature that the posterior cervical neural arch to centrum dorsoventral height ratio less than 0. 5 only presents in *Jiangxititan* and the titanosaurians *Malawisaurus*, *Rapetosaurus*, *Saltasaurus*, and *Alamosaurus* (Mannion, et al. , 2013). Thus, we refer *Jiangxititan* to Titanosauria, which is supported by our phylogenetic analysis.

At present, as many as 15 titanosauriforms are known from the Late Cretaceous of China (Xu, et al. , 2022), including *Huabeisaurus*, *Zhuchengtitan*, *Gannansaurus*, *Sonidosaurus*, *Borealosaurus*, *Baotianmansaurus*, *Dongyangosaurus*, *Jiangshanosaurus*, *Qingxiusaurus*, *Qinlingosaurus*, *Xianshanosaurus*, *Yunmenglong*, *Ruyangosaurus*, *Huanghetitan ruyangensis*, and *Jiutaisaurus* (Xue, et al. , 1996; Pang and Cheng, 2000; Tang, et al. , 2001; You, et al. , 2004; Wu, et al. , 2006; Xu, et al. , 2006; Lü, et al. , 2007, 2008, 2009a, 2009b, 2013a, 2013b; Mo, et al. , 2008, 2017; Zhang, et al. , 2009; Mannion, et al. , 2019b). In addition, some fragmentary fossils recovered from the Upper Cretaceous of China have been identified as titanosauriform dinosaurs (Han, et al. , 2017, 2019; Mo, et al. , 2018). Other titanosauriforms from the Late Cretaceous of Asia include *Opisthocoelicaudia*, *Nemegtosaurus*, *Abdarainurus*, *Quaesitosaurus* (Nowinski, 1971; Borsuk-Bialynicka, 1977; Kurzanov and Bannikov, 1983; Averianov and Lopatin, 2020). Among these Late Cretaceous titanosauriforms, only *Opisthocoelicaudia*, *Ruyangosaurus*, *Yunmenglong*, *Baotianmansaurus*, *Dongyangosaurus* and *Huabeisaurus* are represented by fossils preserving overlapping elements with *Jiangxititan*.

*Jiangxititan* is similar to the titanosaur *Opisthocoelicaudia* in several features present in posterior cervical and anterior dorsal vertebrae, such as spongy bone in centra and neural arches (neural spines, prezygapophyses, postzygapophyses, etc. ), centra compressed dorsoventrally, neural arches low, neural spines deeply bifurcated. However, *Jiangxititan* is markedly different from *Opisthocoelicaudia* by the following features: the ratio of mediolateral width to dorsoventral height of posterior articular surfaces of anteriormost dorsal centra (D1-D3) is greater than 1. 90 in *Jiangxititan*, while it is 1. 48 in *Opisthocoelicaudia*; the neural spines are higher and the bifurcations are more developed in *Jiangxititan* than those in *Opisthocoelicaudia*.

A further comparison with *Ruyangosaurus*, *Yunmenglong*, *Baotianmansaurus*,

*Dongyangosaurus* and *Huabeisaurus* which preserved overlapping elements with *Jiangxititan* suggests that *Jiangxititan* is a distinct taxon. For example, *Jiangxititan* differs from *Huabeisaurus*, *Ruyangosaurus*, *Yunmenglong*, and *Baotianmansaurus* in the following features: (1) posterior cervical and anterior dorsal centra strongly compressed dorsoventrally; (2) pleurocoels of the posterior cervical vertebrae complex and divided by bony septa; (3) neural spine height of the posterior cervical and anterior dorsal vertebrae greater than centrum height; (4) both the EPRL and SPDL present in posterior cervical vertebra; (5) inverted 'V' lamina present at the anterior margin of the bifid point in posteriormost cervical and anteriormost dorsal neural spines; (6) postzygapophyses in the posterior cervical vertebrae fan-shaped; (7) both the lateral and medial spinopostzygapophyseal laminae present in the anterior dorsal vertebrae; (8) anterior dorsal rib short and gracile.

*Jiangxititan* represents the second sauropod from the Upper Cretaceous Nanxiong Formation of Jiangxi Province. The first reported sauropod *Gannansaurus* is similar to *Euhelopus* in many features and thus was suggested to be closely related to the latter (Lü, et al., 2013b). *Jiangxititan* displays features indicating a later diverging position than *Gannansaurus*, and more specifically, *Jiangxititan* has been recovered as a lognkosaur but *Gannansaurus* as a titanosauriform outside the late diverging clade comprising the Diamantinasauria and Lithostrotia, as indicated by our phylogenetic analysis. Consequently, although *Jiangxititan* does not have overlapping elements with *Gannansaurus*, we are confident that *Jiangxititan* is a distinct species from *Gannansaurus*.

*Jiangxititan* is distinguished from all other known sauropods by possessing the very high, deeply bifurcated and widely separated neural spines present in the posterior cervical and anterior dorsal vertebrae. Although similar conditions are present in the anterior dorsal vertebrae of *Opisthocoelicaudia*, *Camarasaurus*, *Diplodocus*, *Apatosaurus*, and *Dicraeosaurus* (Figure 11), the deep bifurcation is less developed in *Jiangxititan* than in *Dicraeosaurus*, but more developed than in *Opisthocoelicaudia*, *Camarasaurus*, *Diplodocus*, and *Apatosaurus* (Hatcher, 1901; Osborn and Mook, 1921; Gilmore, 1936; Borsuk-Bialynicka, 1977). In addition, the bifurcated neural spines directed laterally in *Jiangxititan*, very different from *Opisthocoelicaudia*, *Camarasaurus*, *Diplodocus*, *Apatosaurus*, and *Dicraeosaurus*, in

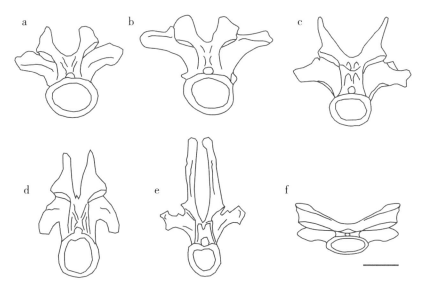

a–*Opisthocoelicaudia*; b–*Camarasaurus*; c–*Apatosaurus*; d–*Diplodocus*; e–*Dicraeosaurus*; f–*Jiangxititan* (NHMG 034062). Scale bar equals 20 cm.

Figure 11   Comparison of the anterior dorsal vertebrae in posterior view
(modified from Upchurch, et al., 2004)

which the anterior dorsal neural spines directed dorsally, rather than laterally.

## 6   Conclusions

*Jiangxititan ganzhouensis* is erected based on a partial skeleton from the Upper Cretaceous Nanxiong Formation of Jiangxi Province, southern China. It displays some features suggesting a titanosaurian affinity. *Jiangxititan* is unique among the Asian titanosauriforms by possessing the deeply bifurcated posterior cervical and anterior dorsal neural spines, and the dorsoventrally compressed posterior cervical and anterior dorsal centra. The discovery of *Jiangxititan* increased the diversity of the titanosaurians in the Late Cretaceous of Asia.

# References

[1] AVERIANOV A O, LOPATIN A V. An unusual new sauropod dinosaur from the Late

Cretaceous of Mongolia[J]. J Syst Paleontol, 2020, 18 (12): 1009–1032. doi: 10. 1080/14772019. 2020. 1716402.

[2] BI SD, AMIOT R, DE FABREGUES CP, et al. An oviraptorid preserved atop an embryo-bearing egg clutch sheds light on the reproductive biology of non-avialan theropod dinosaurs[J]. Sci Bulletin, 2021, 66 (9): 947–954. doi: 10. 1016/j. scib. 2020. 12. 018.

[3] BONAPARTE JF. The early radiation and phylogenetic relationships of the jurassic sauropod dinosaurs, based on vertebral anatomy. In: Padian K, editor. The beginning of the age of dinosaurs[M]. Cambridge: Cambridge University Press; 1986, pp. 247–258.

[4] BONAPARTE JF, CORIA RA. Un nuevo y gigantesco sauropodo titanosaurio de la Formacio'n Rio Limay (Albiano-Cenomaniano) de la provincia delNeuque'n, Argentina[J]. Ameghiniana. 1993, 30: 271–282.

[5] BONAPARTE JF, GONZÁLEZ RIGA BJ, APESTEGUÍA S. *Ligabuesaurus leanzai* gen. et sp. nov. (Dinosauria, Sauropoda), a new titanosaur from the Lohan Cura Formation (aptian, lower Cretaceous) of Neuquén, Patagonia, Argentina[J]. Cretaceous Res. 2006, 27 (3): 364–376. doi: 10. 1016/j. cretres. 2005. 07. 004.

[6] BORSUK-BIALYNICKA M. A new camarasaurid sauropod, *Opisthocoelicaudia skarzynski* gen. n. sp. n. From the Upper Cretaceous of Mongolia[J]. Palaeontol Pol. 1977, 37: 1–64.

[7] Bureau of Geology and Mineral Resources of Guangdong Province. Regional Geology of Guangdong Province. Beijing: Geological Publishing House, 1988.

[8] Bureau of Geology and Mineral Resources of Jiangxi Province. Regional Geology of Jiangxi Province. Beijing: Geological Publishing House, 1984.

[9] CHENG Y N, JI Q, WU X C, SHAN H Y. Oviraptorosaurian eggs (Dinosauria)with embryonic skeletons discovered for the first time in China[J/OL]. Acta Geol Sin-engl. 2008, 82 (6): 1089–1094. doi: 10. 1111/j. 1755–6724. 2008. tb00708. x.

[10] D'EMIC MD. The early evolution of titanosauriform sauropod dinosaurs[J/OL]. Zool J Linn Soc. 2012, 166 (3): 624–671. doi: 10. 1111/j. 1096–3642. 2012. 00853. x.

[11] FANG K Y, LIU Q H, WANG Q, et al. Discovery of stalicoolithidae in Shanggao County, Jiangxi Province, China[J]. Vert PalAs. 2022, 60: 69–79.

[12] GILMORE C W. Osteology of *Apatosaurus* with special reference to specimens in the

Carnegie Museum[J/OL]. Mem Carnegie Mus. 1936, 11 (4): 175–300. doi: 10. 5962/p. 234849.

[13] GOLOBOFF P A, CATALANO S A. TNT version 1. 5, including a full implementation of phylogenetic morphometrics[J/OL]. Cladistics. 2016, 32 (3): 221–238. doi: 10. 1111/cla. 12160.

[14] GOLOBOFF P A, FARRIS J S, NIXON K C. TNT, a free program for phylogenetic analysis[J/OL]. Cladistics. 2008, 24 (5): 774–786. doi: 10. 1111/j. 1096–0031. 2008. 00217. x.

[15] GONZÀLEZ RIGA B J, MANNION P D, POROPAT S F, et al. Osteology of the Late Cretaceous Argentinean sauropod dinosaur *Mendozasaurus neguyelap*: Implications for basal titanosaur relationships[J/OL]. Zool J Linn Soc. 2018, 184 (1): 136–181. doi: 10. 1093/ zoolinnean/zlx103.

[16] GORSCAK E, O'CONNOR PM, STEVENS NJ, et al. The basal titanosaurian *Rukwatitan bisepultus* (Dinosauria, Sauropoda) from the Middle Cretaceous Galula Formation, Rukwa Rift Basin, southwestern Tanzania[J/OL]. J Vertebr Paleontol. 2014, 34 (5): 1133–1154. doi: 10. 1080/02724634. 2014. 845568.

[17] GRIFFIN C T, STOCKER M R, COLLEARY C, et al. Assessing ontogenetic maturity in extinct saurian reptiles[J/OL]. Biol Rev. 2021, 96 (2): 470–525. doi: 10. 1111/brv. 12666.

[18] HAN F L, XING H, TONG Q M, et al. Preliminary study of a diverse dinosaur assemblage from the Upper Cretaceous of Zhuzhou, Hunan Province[J]. Acta Palaeontol Sin. 2017, 56: 1–9.

[19] HAN F L, XU X, SULLIVAN C, et al. New titanosauriform (Dinosauria: sauropoda) specimens from the Upper Cretaceous Daijiaping Formation of southern China[J]. Peer J. 2019, 7: e8237. doi: 10. 7717/peerj. 8237.

[20] HATCHER J B. *Diplodocus* (Marsh): Its osteology, taxonomy, and probable habits, with a restoration of the skeleton[J/OL]. Mem Carnegie Mus. 1901, 1 (1): 1–63. doi: 10. 5962/p. 234818.

[21] JANENSCH W. Die Wirbelsaule der Gattung Dicraeosaurus[J]. Palaeontographica. 1929, 2 (Suppl. 7): 37–133.

[22] JI Q. Study on dinosaur eggs in China: Yesterday and Today[J]. Acta Geos Sin. 2009, 30: 285–290.

[23] JIN X S, MAO F Y, DU T M, et al. A new multituberculate from the latest Cretaceous of central China and its implications for multituberculate tooth homologies and occlusion[J/OL]. J Mamm Evol. 2022, 30 (1): 1–20. doi: 10. 1007/s10914–022–09636–2.

[24] JIN X S, VARRICCHIO D J, POUST A W, et al. An oviraptorosaur adult-egg association from the Cretaceous of Jiangxi Province, China[J/OL]. J Vertebr Paleontol. 2019, 39 (6): 6. doi: 10. 1080/02724634. 2019. 1739060.

[25] KURZANOV S M, BANNIKOV A F. A new sauropod from the Upper Cretaceous of Mongolia[J/OL]. Paleontologicheskyy Zhurnal. 1983: 91–97.

[26] LI L G, LI D Q, YOU H L, et al. A new titanosaurian sauropod from the Hekou Group (Lower Cretaceous) of the Lanzhou-Minhe Basin, Gansu Province, China[J/OL]. PloS One. 2014, 9 (1): e85979. doi: 10. 1371/journal. pone. 0085979.

[27] LI C, WU X C, RUFOLO S J. A new crocodyloid (Eusuchia: crocodylia) from the Upper Cretaceous of China[J/OL]. Cretaceous Res. 2019, 94: 25–39. doi: 10. 1016/j. cretres. 2018. 09. 015.

[28] LÜ J C, AZUMA Y, CHEN R J, et al. A new titanosauriform sauropod from the early Late Cretaceous of Dongyang, Zhejiang Province[J/OL]. Acta Geol Sin-engl. 2008, 82 (2): 225–235. doi: 10. 1111/j. 1755–6724. 2008. tb00572. x.

[29] LÜ J C, CHEN R J, BRUSATTE S L, et al. A Late Cretaceous diversification of Asian oviraptorid dinosaurs: Evidence from a new species preserved in an unusual posture[J/OL]. Sci Rep. 2016, 6 (1): 35780. doi: 10. 1038/srep35780.

[30] LÜ JC, LI GQ, KUNDRÁT M, et al. High diversity of the Ganzhou oviraptorid fauna increased by a new "cassowary-like" crested species[J/OL]. Sci Rep. 2017, 7 (1): 6393. doi: 10. 1038/s41598–017–05016–6.

[31] LÜ J C, PU H Y, KOBAYASHI Y, et al. A new oviraptorid dinosaur (Dinosauria: Oviraptorosauria) from the Late Cretaceous of southern China and its paleobiogeographical implications[J/OL]. Sci Rep. 2015, 5 (1): 11490. doi: 10. 1038/srep11490.

[32] LÜ J C, XU L, JIANG X C, et al. A preliminary report on the new dinosaurian fauna from the

Cretaceous of the Ruyang Basin, Henan Province of central China[J]. J Parasitol Society of Korea. 2009a, 25: 43–56.

[33] LÜ J C, XU L, JIA S H, et al. A new gigantic sauropod dinosaur from the Cretaceous of Ruyang, Henan, China[J]. Geol Bull China. 2009b, 28: 1–10.

[34] LÜ J C, XU L, ZHANG X L, et al. A new gigantic sauropod dinosaur with the deepest known body cavity from the Cretaceous of Asia[J/OL]. Acta Geol Sin-engl. 2007, 81 (2): 167–176. doi: 10. 1111/j. 1755–6724. 2007. tb00941. x.

[35] LÜ J C, YI L P, BRUSATTE S L, et al. A new clade of Asian Late Cretaceous long-snouted tyrannosaurids[J/OL]. Nat Commun. 2014, 5 (1): 3788. doi: 10. 1038/ncomms4788.

[36] LÜ J C, YI L P, ZHONG H, et al. A new Somphospondylan sauropod (Dinosauria, Titanosauriforms) from the Late Cretaceous of Ganzhou, Jiangxi Province of southern China[J/OL]. Acta Geol Sin-engl. 2013b, 87 (3): 678–685. doi: 10. 1111/1755–6724. 12079.

[37] LÜ J C, YI L P, ZHONG H, et al. A new oviraptorosaur (Dinosauria: Oviraptorosauria) from the Late Cretaceous of southern China and its paleoecological implications[J/OL]. PloS One. 2013a, 8 (11): e80557. doi: 10. 1371/journal. pone. 0080557.

[38] MANNION P D, UPCHURCH P, BARNES R N, et al. Osteology of the Late Jurassic Portuguese sauropod dinosaur *lusotitan atalaiensis* (macronaria) and the evolutionary history of basal titanosauriforms[J/OL]. Zool J Linn Soc. 2013, 168 (1): 98–206. doi: 10. 1111/zoj. 12029.

[39] MANNION P D, UPCHURCH P, JIN X S, et al. New information on the Cretaceous sauropod dinosaurs of Zhejiang Province, China: Impact on Laurasian titanosauriform phylogeny and biogeography[J/OL]. R Soc Open Sci. 2019b, 6 (8): 191057. doi: 10. 1098/rsos. 191057.

[40] MANNION P D, UPCHURCH P, SCHWARZ D, et al. Taxonomic affinities of the putative titanosaurs from the Late Jurassic Tendaguru Formation of Tanzania: Phylogenetic and biogeographic implications for eusauropod dinosaur evolution[J/OL]. Zool J Linn Soc. 2019a, 185 (3): 784–909. doi: 10. 1093/zoolinnean/zly068.

[41] MARSH O C. Principal characters of American Jurassic dinosaurs[J/OL]. Pt. I. Am J Sci. 1818, s3–16 (95): 411–416. (Series 3), 16. doi: 10. 2475/ajs. s3–16. 95. 411.

[42] MO J Y, HUANG C L, ZHAO Z R, et al. A new titanosaur (Dinosauria: sauropoda) from the

Late Cretaceous of Guangxi, China[J]. Vert PalAs. 2008, 46: 147–156.

[43] MO J Y, TAN Q W, HU Y G, et al. New material of juvenile sauropod from the Upper Cretaceous of Xichuan Basin, Hubei Province[J]. Acta Palaeontol Sin. 2018, 57: 504–512.

[44] MO J Y, WANG K B, CHEN S Q, et al. A new titanosaurian sauropod from the Late Cretaceous strata of Shandong Province[J]. Geol Bull China. 2017, 36: 1501–1505.

[45] MO J Y, XU X. Large theropod teeth from the Upper Cretaceous of Jiangxi, southern China[J]. Vert PalAs. 2015, 53: 63–72.

[46] MO J Y, XU X, EVANS S E. The evolution of the lepidosaurian lower temporal bar: New perspectives from the Late Cretaceous of South China[J/OL]. Proc R Soc B. 2010, 277 (1679): 331–336. doi: 10. 1098/rspb. 2009. 0030.

[47] MO J Y, XU X, EVANS S E. A large predatory lizard (Platynota, Squamata) from the Late Cretaceous of South China[J/OL]. J Syst Palaeont. 2012, 10 (2): 333–339. doi: 10. 1080/14772019. 2011. 588254.

[48] NOWINSKI A. *Nemegtosaurus mongoliensis* n. gen., n. sp., (Sauropoda)from the Uppermost Cretaceous of Mongolia[J]. Palaeontologica Polonica. 1971, 25: 57–81.

[49] OSBORN H F, MOOK C C. *Camarasaurus*, *Amphicoelias* and other sauropods of cope[J]. Memoirs of the American museum of natural history, new series. 1921, 3: 247–387.

[50] OWEN R. Report on British fossil reptiles, part II[J]. Report of the British association for the advancement of science. 1842, 11: 60–204.

[51] PANG Q Q, CHENG Z W. A new family of sauropod dinosaur from the Upper Cretaceous of Tianzhen, Shanxi Province, China[J/OL]. Acta Geol Sin-engl. 2000, 74 (2): 117–125. doi: 10. 1111/j. 1755–6724. 2000. tb00438. x.

[52] POROPAT S F, MANNION P D, RIGBY S L, et al. A nearly complete skull of the sauropod dinosaur *Diamantinasaurus matildae* from the Upper Cretaceous Winton Formation of Australia and implications for the early evolution of titanosaurs[J/OL]. R Soc Open Sci. 2023, 10: 221618. doi: 10. 1098/rsos. 221618.

[53] SATO T, CHENG Y N, WU X C, et al. A pair of shelled eggs inside a female dinosaur[J/OL]. Sci. 2005, 308 (5720): 375. doi: 10. 1126/science. 1110578.

[54] SHAO Z F, FAN S H, JIA S H, et al. Intact theropod dinosaur eggs with embryonic remains

from the Late Cretaceous of southern China[J]. Geol Bull China. 2014, 33: 941–948.

[55] TANG F, KANG X M, JIN X S, et al. A new sauropod dinosaur of Cretaceous from Jiangshan, Zhejiang Province[J]. Vert PalAs. 2001, 39: 272–281.

[56] TONG H Y, MO J Y. *Jiangxichelys*, a new nanhsiungchelyid turtle from the Late Cretaceous of Ganzhou, Jiangxi Province, China[J/OL]. Geol Mag. 2010, 147 (6): 1–6. doi: 10. 1017/ S0016756810000671.

[57] UPCHURCH P. The phylogenetic relationships of sauropod dinosaurs[J/OL]. Zool J Linn Soc. 1998, 124 (1): 43–103. doi: 10. 1111/j. 1096–3642. 1998. tb00569. x.

[58] UPCHURCH P, BARRETT P M, DOSON P. Sauropoda. In: Weishampel D, Dodson P Osmólska H, editors. The dinosauria. 2nd. Berkeley: University of California Press. 2004, pp. 259–322. doi: 10. 1525/california/ 9780520242098. 003. 0015.

[59] WANG X L, BANDEIRA KLN, QIU R, et al. The first dinosaurs from the Early Cretaceous Hami Pterosaur fauna, China[J/OL]. Sci Rep. 2021, 11 (2021): 14962. doi: 10. 1038/ s41598– 021–94273–7.

[60] WANG S, SUN C, SULLIVAN C, et al. A new oviraptorid (Dinosauria: Theropoda) from the Upper Cretaceous of southern China[J/OL]. Zootaxa. 2013, 3640 (2): 242–257. doi: 10. 11646/zootaxa. 3640. 2. 7.

[61] WANG X R, YOU H L, MENG Q J, et al. *Dongbeititan dongi*, the first sauropod dinosaur from the Lower Cretaceous Jehol Group of western Liaoning Province, China[J/OL]. Acta Geol Sin-engl. 2007, 81 (6): 911–916. doi: 10. 1111/j. 1755–6724. 2007. tb01013. x.

[62] WANG S, ZHANG S K, SULLIVAN C, et al. Elongatoolithid eggs containing oviraptorid (Theropoda, Oviraptorosauria) embryos from the Upper Cretaceous of southern China[J/OL]. BMC Evol Biol. 2016, 16 (1): 67. doi: 10. 1186/ s12862–016–0633–0.

[63] WEDEL M J, TAYLOR M P. Neural spine bifurcation in sauropod dinosaurs from the Morrison Formation: Ontogenetic and phylogenetic implications[J]. PalArch's J Vertebr Palaeontol. 2013, 10: 1–34.

[64] WEI X F, PU H Y, XU L, et al. A new oviraptorid dinosaur (Theropoda: Oviraptorosauria) from the Late Cretaceous of Jiangxi Province, southern China[J/OL]. Acta Geol Sin-engl. 2013, 87 (4): 899–904. doi: 10. 1111/ 1755–6724. 12098.

[65] WILSON J A. A nomenclature for vertebral laminae in sauropods and other saurischian dinosaurs[J/OL]. J Vertebr Paleontol. 1999, 19 (4): 639–653. doi: 10. 1080/ 02724634. 1999. 10011178.

[66] WILSON J A, D'EMIC M D, IKEJIRI T, et al. A nomenclature for vertebral fossae in sauropods and other saurischian dinosaurs[J/OL]. PloS One. 2011, 6 (2): e17114. doi: 10. 1371/journal. pone. 0017114.

[67] WILSON J A, SERENO P C. Early evolution and higher-level phylogeny of sauropod dinosaurs[J/OL]. Memoir Of The Soc Of Vertebr Paleontol. 1998, 5: 1–79. doi: 10. 2307/3889325.

[68] WILSON J A, UPCHURCH P. Redescription and reassessment of the phylogenetic affinities of *Euhelopus zdanskyi* (Dinosauria: sauropoda) from the Early Cretaceous of China[J/OL]. J Syst Palaeontol. 2009, 7 (2): 199–239. doi: 10. 1017/ S1477201908002691.

[69] WU W H, DONG Z M, SUN Y W, et al. A new sauropod dinosaur from the Cretaceous of Jiutai, Jilin, China[J]. Glob Geol. 2006, 25: 6–8.

[70] XING L D, NIU K C, WANG D H, et al. A partial articulated hadrosaurid skeleton from the Maastrichtian (Upper Cretaceous) of the Ganzhou area, Jiangxi Province, China[J/OL]. Hist Biol. 2021, 33 (10): 2256–2259. doi: 10. 1080/ 08912963. 2020. 1782397.

[71] XING L D, NIU K C, YANG T R, et al. Hadrosauroid eggs and embryos from the Upper Cretaceous (Maastrichtian) of Jiangxi Province, China[J/OL]. BMC Ecol Evo. 2022, 22 (1): 60. doi: 10. 1186/s12862–022–02012–x.

[72] XUE X X, ZHANG Y X, BI Y, et al. The development and environmental changes of the intermontane basins in the eastern part of Qinling Mountains. Beijing: Geological Publishing House. 1996, pp. 1–181.

[73] XU X, HAN F L. A new oviraptorid dinosaur (Theropoda: Oviraptorosauria) from the Upper Cretaceous of China[J]. Vert PalAsiat. 2010, 48: 11–18.

[74] XU X, YOU H L, MO J Y. Saurischian Dinosaurs. Beijing: Science Press, 2022.

[75] XU X, ZHANG X H, TAN Q W, et al. A new titanosaurian sauropod from Late Cretaceous of Nei Mongol, China[J/OL]. Acta Geol Sin-engl. 2006, 80 (1): 20–26. doi: 10. 1111/j. 1755–6724. 2006. tb00790. x.

[76] YOU H L, JI Q, LAMANNA M C, et al. A titanosaurian sauropod dinosaur with opisthocoelous caudal vertebrae from the early Late Cretaceous of Liaoning Province, China[J/OL]. Acta Geol Sinica. 2004, 78 (4): 907–911. doi: 10. 1111/j. 1755–6724. 2004. tb00212. x.

[77] ZHANG X L, LÜ J C, XU L, et al. A new sauropod dinosaur from the Late Cretaceous gaogou Formation of Nanyang, Henan Province[J/OL]. Acta Geol Sin-engl. 2009, 83 (2): 212–221. doi: 10. 1111/j. 1755–6724. 2009. 00032. x.

[78] ZHAO Z K, WANG Q, ZHANG S K. Dinosaur eggs. Beijing: Science Press, 2015.

原载*Historical Biology*。DOI: 10. 1080/08912963. 2023. 2259413。

# Preliminary exploration of the ecological habits of *Odorrana lipucnsis*

Chen Weicai[1,2], Li Peng[1], Mo Yunming[3], Liao Xiaowen[3]

1. Key Laboratory of Environment Change and Resources Use in Beibu Gulf Ministry of Education,
Nanning Normal University, China

2. Guangxi Key Laboratory of Earth Surface Processes and Intelligent Simulation, Nanning Normal
University, China

3. Natural History Museum of Guangxi, China

【 Abstract 】*Odorrana lipuensis* occurs in an entirely dark karst cave in Lipu County, Guangxi Zhuang Autonomous Region, China. This paper discusses the ecological habits of the type locality of *O. lipuensis*, including the cave environment, daily activity rhythm, annual activity pattern, food, and predators. The results show that the life cycle of *O. lipuensis* is completed entirely in dark caves; cave temperature fluctuates around 19 ℃ ; there is no hibernation phenomenon, and it is active throughout the year. The daily activity rhythm does not differ between day and night, and breeding seasons range from March to June. Given the limited distribution range and small population size of *O. lipuensis*, it is recommended for inclusion in the national second-class protection animal list.

【 Keywords 】Karst caves; Dark environnement; Conservation; Cave fauna; Life cycle

Funds: This work was supported by Guangxi Natural Science Foundation, China (2020GXNSFDA238022).

# 1  Introduction

*Odorrana lipuensis* lives in dark karst caves and is currently only distributed in one karst cave in Maling Town, Lipu County, Guangxi Zhuang Autonomous Region, China[1] (Figure 1), which is the type locality. Little is known about the distribution and ecological habits of *O. lipuensis* since its publication. Field surveys were conducted around the type locality between 2013 and 2022, but no new distribution points were found in China. However, Pham, et al.[2] identified a second distribution point of *O. lipuensis* in Ha Lang District, Cao Bang Province, Vietnam, located near the Vietnam-China border. In the type locality, a population of approximately 20 individuals was found living in completely dark karst caves, and their ecological habits are not well understood. To improve our understanding of this species and enhance conservation efforts, we conducted preliminary research on its ecological habits from 2013 to 2022, and the results are presented below.

# 2  Materials and Methods

Study area and surveys: The type locality of *O. lipuensis* is Lipu County, Guangxi, China (110° 26′ E, 24° 38′ N; altitude: 182 m a. s. l. ) and it inhabits dark karst caves. From Spring 2013 to September 2022, we conducted surveys of the caves where *O. lipuensis* resides. These surveys involved visual encounter methods to determine the presence and abundance of tadpoles, juveniles, and adult *O. lipuensis*, as well as searching for egg clutches on the rock walls, crevices, and ceilings of the caves. The organisms encountered during the survey were recorded, and the tadpole stage was determined using the Gosner method[3].

Monitoring cave temperature and humidity: The Tp–2200 temperature and humidity recorder was used to record data every two hours, starting from 18:51 on October 15, 2016, and ending at 2:51 on November 13, 2017, covering one natural year. The VICTOR (model: VC230A) was used to record water temperature.

Monitoring activity rhythm: The activity rhythm of the *O. lipuensis* was studied using the Bestguarder (SG–990V) infrared cameras, which were set to take pictures every 30 seconds continuously for 24 hours. The number of times the *O. lipuensis* appeared in front of the camera within each halfhour period was counted.

Analyzing food composition and natural enemies: The stomach contents of the *O. lipuensis* were dissected and observed to determine its food sources. Potential food sources and natural enemies found in the cave were investigated and recorded.

## 3　Results

In March, we observed the amplexus behavior of *O. lipuensis* and collected tadpoles at the 39th stage towards the end of March and the beginning of April. Subsequently, in June, tadpoles at the 43rd stage were observed (Figure 1). Our surveys did not yield any eggs, nor did we find any *O. lipuensis* outside the caves. However, we did observe the presence of *Duttaphrynus melanostictus*, *Fejervarya multistriata*, *Hylarana guentheri*, *Microhyla butleri*, *Microhyla fissipes*, and *Rhacophorus mutus* outside the caves, but no anuran was found within the caves.

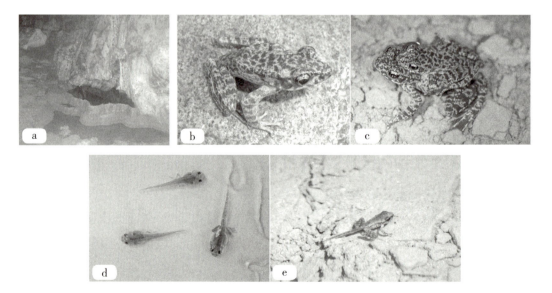

a−habitat; b−adult male; c−amplexus; d−tadpoles at the 39th stage; e−tadpole at the 43rd stage.

Figure 1　*O. lipuensis* in different stages

### 3.1 Annual Temperature and Humidity Patterns

Over the course of a natural year, 4721 temperature points were recorded in the cave, with an average temperature of $19.01 \pm 0.46\,℃$ (ranging from $18.25\,℃$ to $19.75\,℃$). The cave temperature remained stable throughout the year, and no changes in humidity were recorded due to a malfunctioning humidity sensor. The mechanical hygrometer indicated a humidity level of around 75% (GEMlead, model: TH101B). The water temperature was measured at $19.4\,℃$ (Figure 2).

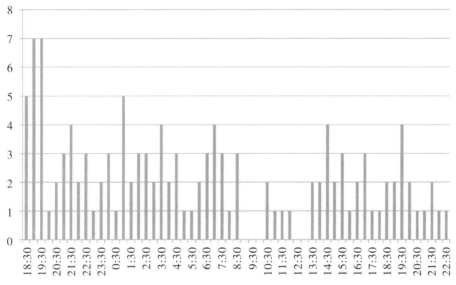

Figure 2　Circadian activity rhythm

### 3.2 Daily Activity Rhythm

From January 14, 2016 at $18:37$ to January 15, 2016 at $22:49$, the infrared camera captured a total of 3383 photos, among which 125 photos of *O. lipuensis* were identified, indicating an occurrence rate of 3.7%. Figure 2 shows that *O. lipuensis* was active throughout the day with no discernible diurnal rhythm.

### 3.3 Food Composition and Natural Enemies

The stomach contents of two adult frogs were examined, but no identifiable food species were found under the microscope. However, *Sinopoda* sp., *Triphosa* sp., *Diestrammena* sp., and *Glyphiulus* sp. (Figure 3) were observed in the cave, with the highest encounter rate being *Diestrammena* sp. These animals could all potentially serve as food sources for *O. lipuensis*. During the field survey, no direct predators of *O. lipuensis* were observed, but *Myotis chinensis* and mammal footprints were present in the cave (Figure 3), suggesting that they could be potential natural enemies.

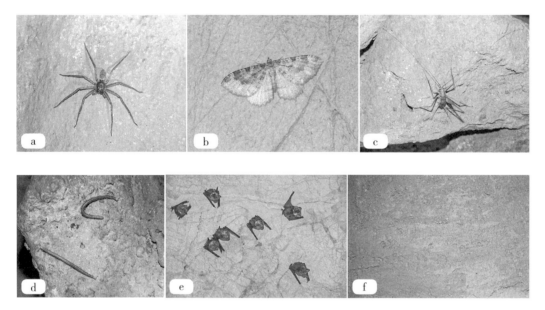

a—*Sinopoda* sp.; b—*Triphosa* sp.; c—*Diestrammena* sp.; d—*Glyphiulus* sp.; e—*Myotis chinensis*; f—Footprints of animals.

Figure 3　Prey and predator of *O. lipuensis*

## 4　Discussion

*Odorrana lipuensis* is exclusively found in a dark karst cave at its type locality and completes its entire life cycle there. The cave has no light and a narrow entrance that can only accommodate one person. It is located 80 meters away from the underground river outlet and has a stable temperature that fluctuates between 19℃. A water pool of approximately 2 square meters is inside the cave, close to the wall, and has many crevices. The water temperature remains at around 19℃ throughout the year, with water seeping out of the crevices during the rainy season. *O. lipuensis* is active all year round, with no hibernation period and no obvious diurnal or nocturnal activity rhythm. The breeding period of *O. lipuensis* lasts from about March to June. Observations were made on the amplexus behavior of *O. lipuensis* in March, and tadpoles at the 39th stage were collected at the end of March and beginning of April. Tadpoles at the 43rd stage were seen in June, as shown in Figure 1[3]. Additionally, dissection of two female *O. lipuensis* in March revealed yellow eggs in their abdomen. While *Odorrana liboensis* and *Odorrana wuchuanensis* also inhabit karst caves[4-6], their breeding seasons differ. According to Luo, et al.[6], the living environment and habits of *O. liboensis* are very similar to those of *O. lipuensis*, such as no light, stable water temperature and they are sister groups in terms of phylogeny. However, the breeding season of *O. liboensis* is speculated to occur from late June to mid-August. Meanwhile, *O. wuchuanensis* has yellowish eggs in their abdomen in July and amplexus behavior is observed in August, leading to an estimated breeding period of July to August[5, 7]. This is later than the breeding period of *O. lipuensis* and *O. liboensis*. According to Zhao, et al.[8], the distribution of *Odorrana* is influenced by the average temperature in July, the annual average temperature, and annual rainfall. However, since the frogs live and complete their life cycle in caves where the environment is stable, external environmental factors do not affect their distribution. Further research is needed to investigate the difference in breeding seasons between *O. lipuensis* and *O. liboensis*.

Pham, et al.[2] found that *O. lipuensis* in Vietnam lives in secondary karst forests, where they were found on branches near the cave entrance, about 0.2-0.5 meters above the ground. However, the life cycle of *O. lipuensis* is completed entirely in the dark cave environment, as evidenced by observations of morphology and habits at various stages inside the cave. The differences in living environments between the type locality and the Vietnam habitat of *O. lipuensis* require further study.

Caves have a relatively closed environment, resulting in significantly lower species diversity compared to outside the caves. The analysis of the stomach contents of two *O. lipuensis* individuals showed almost no visible digested food items. Only a few species of organisms such as *Sinopoda* sp., *Triphosa* sp., *Diestrammena* sp., and *Glyphiulus* sp. (Figure 3) were observed in the cave with relatively low population numbers. Compared to non-cave species such as *Odorrana graminea* and *Odorrana schmackeri*, *O. lipuensis* is relatively smaller and thinner, which could be attributed to long-term food shortages. Human activities and not just bats and small mammals, also severely impact the survival of *O. lipuensis*. Evidence of man-made theft of stalactites and the use of bat guano as fertilizer was found in the cave. Moreover, locals often catch *O. lipuensis* for medicinal purposes, believing it can cure children's fever, which is an erroneous belief that challenges their conservation. From 2013 to 2019, the *O. lipuensis* population in the type locality remained stable at around 20 individuals. However, during our September 2022 revisit, we discovered that the population had declined to less than 10 individuals, and the cave environment had been significantly damaged due to heavy soil disturbance. Outside the cave, we observed logging and charcoal burning. Due to *O. lipuensis*'s unique habitat and extremely small population, Guangxi has listed it as a key protected wildlife species [9]. We recommend the inclusion of *O. lipuensis* in the second level of national key protected wildlife species to facilitate its protection.

In addition to *O. lipuensis*, *O. liboensis*, and *O. wuchuanensis*, only a few species of frogs inhabit caves. These include *Eleutherodactylus cooki*[10], *E. cundalli* [11], *Cycloramphus eleutherodactylus* [12], and *Rana iberica* [13]. However, these species do not display troglomorphic characteristics such as degenerate eyes and depigmentation. Some species are occasionally found in caves for breeding or to avoid predators [13], while others exclusively reside in caves and complete their life cycle there. The adaptation mechanisms of these species to the dark karst cave environment require further research.

# References

[1] MO Y M, CHEN W C, WU H Y, et al. A new species of *Odorrana* inhabiting complete darkness in a karst cave in Guangxi, China[J]. Asian Herpetological Research, 2015, 1: 11–17.

[2] PHAM C T, NGUYEN T Q, BERNARDES M, et al. First records of *Bufo gargarizans* Cantor, 1842 and *O. lipuensis* Mo, Chen, Wu, Zhang et Zhou, 2015 (Anura: Bufonidae, ranidae) from Vietnam[J]. Russian journal of herpetology, 2016, 23 (2): 103–107.

[3] GOSNER K L. A simplified table for staging anuran embryos and larvae with notes on

identification[J]. Herpetologica, 1960, 16 (3): 183–190.

[4] WU L, XU R H, DONG Q, et al. A new species of *Rana* and records of amphibians from Guizhou Province[J]. ACTA Zoological Sinica, 1983, 29 (01): 66–70.

[5] XU J, LIU J X. *Odorrana wuchuanensis*[J]. Forest & Humankind, 2009 (01): 46–53.

[6] LUO T, WANG S W, XIAO N, et al. A new species of Odorous Frog Genus *Odorrana* (Anura, Ranidae) from southern Guizhou Province, China[J]. Asian Herpetological Research, 2021, 12 (4): 381–398.

[7] LIU J X, ZHANG Z Y, ZHANG Z P, et al. Preliminary report on the habitat and current situation of the critically endangered cavity-dwelling frog, *Odorrana wuchuanensis*[J]. Bulletin of Biology, 2009, 44 (05): 14–16.

[8] ZHAO Y Z, GUO Y, ZHAO H B. Study of environmental factors on geographical distribution of *Odorrana* in Guizhou[J]. Agricultural technology services, 2013, 30 (7): 763–765.

[9] (2022) List of key protected wild animals in Guangxi. Forestry Bureau of Guangxi Zhuang Autonomous Region.

[10] ROGOWITZ L G, CANDELARIA C L, DENIZARD L E, et al. Seasonal reproduction of neotropical, the cave coquí (*Eleutherodactylus cooki*)[J]. Copeia, 2001: 542–547.

[11] DIESEL R, BÀ˙URLE G, VOGEL P. Cave breeding and froglet transport: a novel pattern of anuran brood care in the Jamaican frog, *Eleutherodactylus cundalli*[J]. Copeia, 1995: 354–360.

[12] LIMA AMX, ARAÚJO C O, VERDADE V K. *Cycloramphus eleutherodactylus* (Alto button frog): Calling among rocks and caves[J]. Herpetological Bulletin, 2012, 120: 39–42.

[13] ROSA G M, PENADO A. *Rana iberica* (Boulenger, 1879) goes underground: Subterranean habitat usage and new insights on natural history[J]. Subterranean Biology, 2013, 11: 15–29.

原载*International Journal of Zoology and Animal Biology* 2023年第6卷第2期第1-5页。